The Australian Short Story
before Lawson

The Australian
Short Story
before Lawson

edited by

Cecil Hadgraft

Melbourne
Oxford University Press
Oxford Auckland New York

OXFORD UNIVERSITY PRESS
Oxford New York Toronto
Delhi Bombay Calcutta Madras Karachi
Singapore Hong Kong Tokyo
Nairobi Dar es Salaam Cape Town
Melbourne Auckland
and associates in
Beirut Berlin Ibadan Nicosia

National Library of Australia
Cataloguing-in-Publication data:

The Australian short story before Lawson.
Bibliography.
ISBN 0 19 554582 6.
ISBN 0 19 554729 2 (pbk).

1. Short stories, Australian. I. Hadgraft, Cecil.

A823'.0108

Edited by Sarah Brenan
Typeset by Syarikat Seng Teik Sdn Bhd
Printed by Kyodo Shing-Loong Printing, Singapore
Published by Oxford University Press, 7 Bowen Crescent, Melbourne
OXFORD is a trademark of Oxford University Press

Contents

PREFACE

Though the production of critical and historical writing on Australian literature has become a minor industry, some gaps still remain. No single publication, for instance, traces the history of the Australian short story before Henry Lawson. Janet Hine's pioneering but unpublished thesis, An Evaluation of the Australian Short Story Before 1880 (1945), an apparent exception, is true to its title in dealing with matters of theory rather than history. There is likewise no anthology. Some general collections contain examples, but the great mass of material after 1900 necessarily limits the amount to be chosen from the earlier period.

The Introduction to this volume is an attempt to sketch the changes in the short story from about 1830 to Lawson's first volume in 1894. It is followed by a selection which, however biased and imperfect, may give some indication of the quality and types of the stories of these sixty years. My overriding concern, naturally, was to pick the best of the period; but using this criterion alone would have led to a certain narrowness because of the domination of two or three writers. So I have also looked for stories that were perhaps not as good but which illustrated contemporary concerns and literary style. If one or two choices may appear unwarranted, judged by their intrinsic merits, they may serve, however, as examples of a species or trend.

I have left intact the original spelling and punctuation of the stories, but obvious misprints have been corrected.

It is a pleasure to express gratitude to the librarians in the various State Libraries: Perth, Adelaide and Melbourne, with special thanks to those in the Mitchell (Sydney) and the Fryer (University of Queensland).

The Utah Foundation provided funds without which this volume might not have appeared or at any rate would have been much delayed. I am extremely grateful to the members of its committee.

Cecil Hadgraft

INTRODUCTION

The short story, as the tale of an incident, is doubtless as old as history. But the short story as a recognized literary form is a matter of the nineteenth century. It is the creation of the Russians, the French and the Americans: until the appearance of Kipling the English made no notable contribution. Nor did Australia before Henry Lawson. Potential authors in early Australia had raw material and to spare: the convict system; the Aborigines; bushrangers; and the country itself, forbidding, bizarre, fascinating. But with an audience small and scattered, and in the absence of good English models, it is scarcely surprising that Australia did not excel in the field of short fiction. Nevertheless, in the history of our literature the early short stories are not negligible, as this anthology may demonstrate.

In the outline history that follows I have adopted a two-pronged approach: I have used chronological divisions (1830–60, 1860–80, 1880–93) for convenience, and within each section there is first an account of the major writers of that period and their stories, and second an outline of the genres or themes that emerged or flourished. It is a somewhat arbitrary approach, but it may help to set the context for the stories.

1830–60

An early piece of fiction set in Australia appeared in *Tales of the Colonies* (1830) by John Howison, 'of the Honourable East India Company's Service'. Most of the stories are set in Ireland and the West Indies, but 'One False Step' is set in Australia: 'Nearly one hundred convicts had just been landed at Sydney, from an English ship . . .' It is really a short novel rather than a short story, written in a high-falutin' style that fits its theatrical setting, at one remove from reality. It contains some of the themes that were to be recurrent through the rest of the century—well-born young Englishman falling into debauchery, forgery, resistance to harsh treatment, bushranging, escapes, seizure of a ship, repentant end:

'No, no, mother,' replied he faintly, and almost inarticulately: 'your hopes are vain—*One step in the path of crime seldom can be retrieved.*'

There is no reason to believe that Howison ever set foot in Australia, but the story has some resemblance to English tales of adventure and criminality—exciting and fast-moving, yet with a lesson to be conveyed—and to later Australian examples of the same kind. Strait-laced readers could be excused for reading such thrilling fiction because it concluded with moral affirmations. The general principle appeared to be that of the boy found swearing at the family parrot, who excused himself with the reply that he was only telling the bird the words it shouldn't say.

Better known than Howison is David Burn, the first to write plays in Australia, who in 1842 issued *Our First Lieutenant and Fugitive Pieces in Prose*. It contains five sketches and stories, set variously in Ireland, Brazil, England and the Pacific.

In the longest piece, 'The Three Sisters of Devon', Burns' characteristics are found in full flower. It is a story told by Frederick Wilford, who falls in love with Isidora, a beautiful heiress guarded by her uncle and cousin, both eager to lay hands on her money. Their vessel is captured by pirates, whose captain, Don Patricio Morpheo, turns out to be an Irishman named Paddy Murphy, speaking with a dark brogue. What is more, he is a Freemason, like the captain of the *Three Sisters*. This piece of luck sets them free to continue to Rio, where Wilford luckily encounters a friend of his schooldays, Inglis, who is to help defeat the wicked uncle and cousin. There follows a duel, a fight with rebels, the death of Inglis, the cunningly planned escape of the lovers, and at last their marriage in England.

Things happen in this narrative not because they derive from the character of a participant or as the result of previous actions—they simply happen. If they did not, the reader would not miss them. One is tempted to think of it as a picaresque novel condensed. But condensation on a smaller scale it is not in Burn to provide: he writes by circumlocution and indirection. Eyelashes and eyebrows, for example, are concealed in this thicket: 'the heaven of her large, dark, lustrous, yet melting eye, that was shaded by a deep rich

fringe of ebon dye, overarched with a silky pencilling of corresponding hue.'

The euphemism is punctuated by literary clichés: 'vale of tears',
'a passion . . . of boundless intensity', 'remorseless talons', and the
rest. Love, an elevated sentiment, finds expression through an elaborated syntax: 'Tell me not I am so miserable as to err in conceiving
that it finds responsive echo in the breast of one whose love is the
sole bright jewel of my hopes?' Villains behave in orthodox fashion:
'he leered upon me with the malignant fury of a baffled demon'.

For the next half-century many writers of the short story used
these mechanisms, but Burn is more sophisticated than most. His
excesses are his absurdities; the excesses in other writers are too
often their norm.

From Burn in 1842 to the appearance of John Lang's *Botany Bay*
in 1859 there were about fifteen volumes of tales with Australian
settings and themes, most of them also published in Australia. Mrs
Vidal's volume, *Tales for the Bush*, appeared in 1845, and ran
through four editions in seven years. It contains extreme examples
of the hortatory tale, but her stories are divided into quite short
chapters, so that the reader has frequent welcome breaks. Most
concern incidents in the lives of girls or women, and were doubtless intended for servants or those of the 'lower classes' who could
read. Their mistresses presumably did not require Mrs Vidal's
admonitions to cultivate Sunday observance, modesty and hu-
mility, respect for one's betters, cleanness and neatness, and most
of the other social and religious virtues. In return for such
conformity one gained peace of mind on earth and eternal bliss
hereafter. The amount of sickness and sorrow in her stories is very
great indeed, and occasionally a reader may have wondered if virtue
were really worth the trouble. In 'The Convict Laundress'
(included in this anthology), for example, Grace, though innocent,
is convicted of theft and transported, and at last dies in a lunatic
asylum. Her 'fault' lay in putting her trust in this world instead of
in the Almighty. Her consolation would need to be drawn from
another story, 'Little Anne and Her Nurse', where a mistress
addresses her maid: 'Think of God, and that He orders all. It is He
who afflicts you, and for some wise and merciful purpose'. Vidal,
it is unsurprising to learn, was the wife of a parson, and acquaintances spoke of her as a charitable and even saintly woman. It is a
pity that her tales, sermons in fictional form, have so little impact.

In 1850 or thereabouts appeared *The Black Troopers*, by an anonymous author, possibly (to judge by a few hints in the stories) an
Englishman. Nobody would expect much of a volume that is, in
the words of the Religious Tract Society (the publisher), 'suited for

readers of both sexes, and well adapted for circulation in Sunday School libraries'. Nevertheless, one of the four stories (three set in England), the title story, has a claim to be noticed. It is long for a short story (about 25 000 words), but the second half of it can be excerpted as a separate tale and appears in this anthology under the title 'A Dispersal'. It deals with the pursuit of an Aboriginal criminal by troopers of his own race led by a white lieutenant. There are not many of its kind in the fiction of last century. There are accounts, both in fiction and memoirs, of a small tribe of Aborigines being hunted down and shot by white settlers, but there are few dealing with the pursuit of an individual. It can stand comparison with some parts of Thomas Keneally's novel, *The Chant of Jimmie Blacksmith* (1972).

The narrator is a doctor, presumably English, who admires courage and resource, and who has some understanding of resentment engendered by ill-treatment and revenge actuated by brutality.

Three other writers may be mentioned before looking at our first native-born teller of tales. One is Mrs Charles Clacy, who provides in her *Lights and Shadows of Australian Bush Life* (1854) rather more diversity than most other short-story writers of her time. The characters are shown either as moving from England to Australia or as having arrived not so long ago. They are fairly solid middle-class people, sometimes a little 'U', and they migrate for various reasons—the family estate is in difficulties, a woman is deserted, a girl is jilted, opportunities are too limited in England. The new land seems to them very odd, with black swans, white eagles, trees shedding bark instead of leaves, bright flowers without perfume and bright birds without song (a legend that started some time in the 1820s), but it does allow honest toil to be rewarded. There is more incident and excitement than is normal in other moral tales, with bush fires, herding and branding, a shipwreck, an attack by Aborigines, and encounters with bushrangers. All this might sound promising, but the performance is rather dull, and Mrs Clacy enlists coincidence rather too often. Her style can be on occasion so formal as to be unnatural, and at other times it can verge on the infantile; she is often at pains to explain or expatiate when any normally intelligent reader has no difficulty at all in seeing the implications or intentions. The general effect she produces is that of a well-mannered and well-intentioned promoter of emigration to the colonies.

Something of a contrast is Henry Giles Turner, whose two long stories, 'The Confessions of a Loafer' and 'The Captive of Gippsland', were collected in *Tales of the Colony* in 1857.

Written by a man of some versatility—banker, editor, critic, historian—these two tales are nevertheless mediocre. Their date is relevant, for information about Australia as a remote and strange land was still the staple of much fiction written for English readers. And, again, the goldfields were still attracting immigrants. This applies particularly to the first story, which is a first-person account of a young man with a disinclination to work, and indeed with few noticeable virtues, who leaves England to try his fortune in Victoria. Until the end, when he reforms rather uncharacteristically, he experiences a series of misfortunes, not all of his own contrivance—bad luck on the diggings, an arrest for murder (and an acquittal), loss by robbery of his few possessions. Finally he falls in with a school friend (also from England) and joins him in running a trading vessel.

It is an odd story. The anti-hero does not like anybody; even his benefactors he mistrusts. But for its ending, this story is a catalogue of disasters, and it is difficult to see why Turner wrote it, except possibly to counteract the optimistic propaganda of the 'guidebook novels' of the 1840s and 1850s (see below). It is probably the only one of its kind.

Equally disastrous are the events in the sketches by Richard Rowe, who spent five years in Australia (1853–58), felt that he was doomed to be a failure here, and returned to England. *Peter Possum's Portfolio* (1858) was collected on the eve of his departure. Three pieces in it are confessions of his poverty and drunkenness. The first, 'Arthur Owen', written in the first person like the other two, details the sufferings of a dwarf hunchback, especially at the hand of masters and his fellow-pupils at school. It need not be taken for truth, but it has a heartfelt indignation that Rowe preserved for injustice through his life. 'A Trip up the Hunter' is remarkable for its violent imagery and grotesque humour: 'The funnels, with their cauliflower heads of rising steam, look like gigantic pots of foaming beer'. 'The Confessions of an Australian Brandy Drinker' details a drinking bout that ended up in prison, from which he was bailed out by his patron Stenhouse. No writer before Lawson drew more bitter pictures of the Australian landscape:

the same charred, prostrate trees . . . the same black, jagged stumps, like foul, decaying teeth . . . the same not grass, but graminaceous scurf, as if the earth had got the ringworm . . . the same bark-roofed slab-huts, not so respectable as English pigsties.

Rowe, loyal to friends and benefactors, was probably his own worst enemy. He contrasts with Lawson in the flavour of his self-pity, which is literary and cynical, seldom self-indulgent. He can tell an incident, but hardly compose a story. It is, one may think, the penalty paid by the autobiographer.

With John Lang we meet the first of the writers who deal with events in the history of the colony. His thirteen short stories, which had previously appeared in English periodicals, were published in one volume, *Botany Bay*, in 1859. Most of them were based on real incidents and on persons known fairly widely during the period of transportation that ended in 1840. (Lang left the colony in the early 1840s and spent the rest of his life in India and England.) 'The Ghost upon the Rail', for instance, is the first full account of Frederick Fisher, ticket-of-leave man, and of his murder, and his re-appearance as a ghost. Practically all later versions and speculations are based on Lang's story. 'Barrington' retails an incident in the life of that famous pickpocket; 'Sir Henry Hayes' tells how the inimitable Irish 'Special' kept his house free from snakes; and 'Kate Crawford' is based partly on the life of Margaret Catchpole and partly on that of Mary Haydock, both transported for theft and both prospering in Australia. Other stories centre on less famous— or notorious—figures. A couple introduce the Aborigines, deprecating some of their habits while paying tribute to their tracking and hunting skills.

Lang made no attempt to hide his debt. In his Preface he writes:

It behoves me to inform the English reader that, though the entire contents of this volume are founded upon truth, the names, dates and localities have been so altered that to all intents and purposes they form merely a work of fiction.

He is, clearly, not claiming ingenuity or imagination (though he has a measure of both), nor the authority of an historian. Nevertheless a reader of these stories does gain insights into the life of the period. Lang does not, it is true, write much about its most notable feature, the convict system and its brutalities, though convicts appear frequently. What he does is to give illuminating glimpses of customs and regulations and oddities during the convict period. We learn why Barrington begs to be excused from shaking hands with the wife of an officer, of the price that a piano (one of five in the colony) may fetch at an auction, of master and man walking (but not together). These details, which even an elaborate social history does not normally afford, convey the atmosphere of Sydney and parts of New South Wales in a certain period. There is not much individual violence in the stories, no chain-gangs or floggings, though firearms appear and bushrangers are not uncommon, while action and trickery are the essence of a few plots. Perhaps this is because of Lang's favourite device: of the thirteen stories eleven are first-person narratives, and six of these are ostensibly told to the writer by an old lady long resident in the colony.

Perhaps Lang needed to build his fiction on actual persons and events, but he had the capacity to shape his material: nobody could call Lang dull. Though the interest is generally (though not always) material—in the sense that it derives from things, from happenings, and not much from character or nuance—it still gives Lang more claim upon our attention than has perhaps been generally granted.

He differs in three ways from some of the short-story writers that followed him. His descriptions of landscape and of flora and fauna seem more or less essential parts of the story; he does not, for instance, indulge in elaborate depictions of natural backgrounds that serve little purpose other than to provide opportunities for floridity. Again, he spares us the moralizing that was to become so frequent (especially in the women writers). And last, Lang's style, workmanlike, clear, direct, has worn pretty well. The rather official composition of the Preface is seldom evident in the stories. With the exception of Marcus Clarke and perhaps James Skipp Borlase, his are the most vigorous short stories produced before 1890.

Many nineteenth-century Australian short stories do not fall into categories or types. Nevertheless one can distinguish certain genres. Among those that began in the years 1830–60 and continued to flourish are stories about Aborigines, moral tales and historical tales, and it is worth looking at these separately.

The moral tale
Perhaps the greatest handicap for the Australian story writer—unlike the poet or the novelist—was the lack of good English models. But although direct influence is hard to trace, one English attitude was only too available—the habit of preaching through fiction. A society with a convict basis must surely be corrupt and in need of reformation: perhaps exhortation or, more indirectly, tales with moral lessons (the gilded pill) might serve to correct the bias. That was one attitude. Another was the conviction that all men are fallible creatures and need guidance. Occasionally the driving force towards reformation was simply personal, a conviction that the writer was the instrument of enlightenment. Whatever the motive, tales with a moral were frequent last century in Australia. Here, as in England, stories and novels told of good

resisting evil and, with few exceptions, of the ultimate discomfiture of the latter. But quite often a reader could feel the structure of events and the moral conclusion were too artificial for acceptance. A writer might try to overcome that reaction by increasing the excitement, by multiplying the incidents; the result was popularity for such fiction in both countries. In England the Society for Promoting Christian Knowledge and the Religious Tract Society both used the method.

Critics approved: as late as 1868 they could write of J. R. Houlding's *Christopher Cockle's Colonial Experiences* (1867), for example, using terms such as 'amusing and instructive', 'a healthy and moral tone', 'vivid pictures of Christian life', 'calculated to effect much good', 'a deep and good purpose'. The question of literary value separate from moral value was seldom raised.

Some eight writers or so were addicted to moralistic fiction, half of them women. Mrs Vidal, already mentioned, is a standard example. Sometimes it is a matter for regret that her laudable purpose makes the stories less effective as stories: she has an eye for detail, she knows the bush, she can give us the feel of an area or time; but the reader is constantly harassed by the feeling that Vidal may have him in mind as a brand to be plucked from the burning.

Mrs Clacy, nearly ten years later, is less overt in her reforming methods and more varied and entertaining in her themes. Whatever misfortunes or deficiences are experienced by the characters in England, the new land will make up for them all. The lesson is something not insisted on but latent or implicit; the pervasive decent morality suggests that Clacy would arrange, or could have arranged, the world more equitably if she had been given the chance.

Another exponent of the moral tale is J. R. Houlding in *Christopher Cockle's Colonial Experiences* (1867), where he urges honesty in business dealings, and as an instructor gives advice about training the young and helping others to be good. But in other tales he still leaves the reader some scope to make up his or her own mind. The worst thing about Houlding—and it does not seem to be a result of his attitudes or beliefs—is his dull and old-fashioned style. Consequently the moral tale in his hands often fails to entertain, and as a further consequence it fails to edify.

The moral tale continued to reappear at intervals to the end of the century, and even beyond. J. M. Conroy, in *False, and Other Tales* (1872), wrote fiction full of implicit and even enunciated moralizing, but it is not, so to speak, aimed at the reader.

G. Bunster in 'Pipkin's Conversion'[1] showed the influence of Dickens, an influence strongly felt throughout the period. Pipkin, rich and well-fed and selfish, is led by a ghostly figure (Christ instead of Christmas?) to view scenes of misery, and in consequence becomes a reformed man. Ellie Tranmar and Evelyn Blackett in 1888 produced *The Chinese Interpreter*, containing four short stories, two by each woman, that express considerable trust in the mysterious workings of Providence:

And when the revolving years shall have ceased to roll and all things come to an end, and the unerring Judge shall have put everything into perfect order and pattern, we shall know the meaning. (Blackett, 'A Tangled Skein')

A reversion to purposeful moral teaching, with certain sins and failings clearly indicated, is found in the stories of Ellen Augusta Chads, a second Mrs Vidal, but more varied and more entertaining in her own unbelievable way. *The Snowdrop's Message* (1888) contains ten stories, and except for one or two these all give good counsel to the reader. We are shown the evils of jealousy, the returning of good for ill, fate that punishes evil-doers, the way circumstances may mould selfishness into altruism, destiny's concern for courageous innocence. Yet Chads has not the artless insistence on reforming the reader that others have: her distinctive trait is the persevering faith in Providence manifested by her characters, and this despite the large amount of suffering and the frequent deaths and disasters. It is unkind but tempting to say that her approved characters are always good and mostly unbearable.

Perhaps the nadir of this type of fiction is reached in the three stories in *Christmas Bells* (1882) by Matilda Congreve, who wrote under the pseudonym of Maud(e) Jean(ne) Franc. In real life the wife of a Baptist minister (and for a time a headmistress), she is not as reformative as others: the authorial intrusion, indeed, appears only in her advocacy of sobriety—or, rather, her detestation of 'the demon drink'. But even here she does not directly draw or point a moral; she simply describes the misery and grief of a wife and two children while they await the return of the husband who has gone off, determined not to return until he has conquered his weakness. As with the other two stories, this happy incident occurs on Christmas Eve.

Her persistent indulgence is sentimentality. For example, the young wife of the struggling young clerk has 'the dimples, and the blush, and the sweet childish lips'; the baby resides in 'a little basket

1 in Whitworth (ed.), *The Australian Christmas Box* (1879?).

basinet . . . a little velvet rose-leaf of a mortal, half hidden by the pink and white curtains'. Dispensing grace or at any rate rewards, Franc makes her characters suffer a little, and then with the help of coincidence leaves them happy. Like others writing in the same fashion, she sold well.

The last writer of this type of story who need concern us is Andrew Robertson, writing in the early 1890s. His stories in *The Kidnapped Squatter, and Other Australian Tales* (1891) are in the expected vein, but separating more definitely than most others the sheep from the goats, and apportioning rewards and punishments in the orthodox manner. The action moves readily enough, the incidents providing more adventure than the general run of moral tales; sometimes indeed they are frankly sensational. Robertson does not stress the lesson: he simply shows us or tells us that good is rewarded and evil is punished. If we are adolescent, we may believe him.

It can be seen that these moralistic tales persisted long after the convict system had ended, so that a ready excuse for the existence of later examples is not obvious. It is not a hypocritical exhortation to obey and be good, to be content in that sphere of life to which it has pleased God to call us and in which, despite our efforts, He is keeping us. It is not a wilful blindness to abuses nor an accompanying and specious attempt to stifle discontent. That cannot be said even of an extreme example like Vidal. These writers have a certain frank, if insistent, kindliness about them, an unsophisticated trust, a belief that this is the way to contentment. Such writers really believed they could help: they had an innocent naïveté.

Stories about Aborigines

Another type of short story that early manifested itself was that dealing with black-white relations—attacks on settlers, massacres of Aboriginal tribes, and so on; in fiction as in life trust between the races was rare, antagonism frequent. 'The Black Troopers' (discussed above) is the first significant piece of our shorter fiction with an Aboriginal background. Many other tales were to follow. It would indeed have been rather surprising if such material had been neglected: of the obviously promising subjects—reversed seasons, odd flora and fauna, the convict system, the black inhabitants—the last would surely present itself as the most obviously fruitful in incident.

Treatment of the Aborigines in fiction, as in life, would depend on white attitude and reaction. This was partly wonder, occasionally fear, but mostly contempt. The treatment that resulted from these attitudes became harsher when any overt black hostility (no matter how justified) became manifest.

The attitude of the English government was mostly mild: the Aborigines should be conciliated, they should be treated with understanding; they were in theory lieges of the Crown. The reality in Australia was quite different. As late as 1856 *The Emigrant's Guide to Australia*, by John Capper, FRAS, warns intending home-steaders of 'tribes of dangerous though cowardly natives'. These may be usefully hired on occasion, and some serve as mounted police, but in their 'aboriginal state, the natives appear to be as degraded as any race with which we are acquainted'. Perhaps no harsher condemnation is found than that by A. J. Boyd, an acerbic commentator on much of the outback. As late as 1882, in his *Old Colonials*, he attacks the conception of the Aborigine as an example of the Noble Savage. He is, says Boyd,

when stripped of poetical imagery, nothing but a sneaking, filthy, thievish, murdering vagabond . . . Laziness is a mild term to apply to the utter and complete want of energy which characterizes the Australian savages . . . Of all beastly places on this earth commend me to a blackfellow's camp. The miserable gunyahs of bark or boughs are surrounded with filth of every description, and so vile does the stench become at last that the very occupiers are compelled to remove, burning down the gunyahs on their departure.

Probably by reason of such attitudes there is (apart from 'The Black Troopers') no narrative where the central figure is an Aborigine in his native habitat. He is generally seen in action—in attack or flight.

One of the numerous varieties of white-black encounter is the capturing or keeping of white woman or child. Then there are the frequent attacks by Aborigines. White reprisals, where a tribe may be wiped out, are recounted, if not with relish, at least with satis-faction. Or an Aboriginal child may come into white custody, to be trained and respond later with devotion, or else later decamp. Some mixture of these and other themes is found in Mrs Clacy's 'Mikka' (1854), the story, in part, of a piccaninny.

An example of a white taken by blacks appears in the anonymous 'The Squatter's Story'(186–), where the son of a settler is captured after an attack, but is later recovered. A reason is offered for Aboriginal hostility in this instance, the killing of an Aboriginal by a shepherd. In Borlase's 'The Lubra's Revenge' (1868) a lubra steals a white child as an expression of the tribe's resentment for the killing of one of its members. Brooke, chief character in Borlase's stories, in one of his adventures as trooper rescues the child. Henry Winstanley in 'Yarrena' (1884)[2] introduces romance in the narrator's tale of his rescue from the blacks of a white girl whom he later marries. H. G. Turner's 'The Captive of Gippsland' (1857) starts with the wreck of a vessel in 1844. Only the mate and a young woman escape to shore, where they are captured by a tribe of Aborigines. One of these helps the mate to make his way to a white settlement, where they gather a band of rescuers. The rest of the tale is full of unlikely adventures—pursuit of the tribe, attacks on the tribe, ambushes, and the death of all the whites (including the mate) except one. The girl is not seen again.

Fiction that deals with this theme—a white woman captured or preserved by Aborigines—generally permits her rescue or escape, as in Angus McLean's novel, *Lindigo, the White Woman* (1866), and in the most famous, Patrick White's *A Fringe of Leaves* (1976). Less frequently is the woman lost to sight. Mary Howitt's short story, 'The Lost White Woman' (1857),[3] has an unusual twist. The narrator tells of the generally strained or hostile relations between whites and blacks, of the danger he found himself in, and how a white woman, 'clothed in skins, and a mantle of her own magnificent black hair falling past her waist', led him to safety. She, her husband and another convict had escaped from Tasmania in a boat, but only she had reached the Victorian coast. She had been succoured by the Aborigines and was now the wife of Bungil Woornin. The narrator urges her to flee with him to the white settlement, but she refuses, whether through love for her black husband or gratitude to the tribe is not made clear. This may be the only story where the white woman willingly remains with the Aboriginal tribe. The origin of such tales was probably either the real-life adventures of Mrs Fraser, widely known in the 1830s and 1840s, or rumours that were prevalent in certain districts.

While writers occasionally indicate that the Aborigines may have some reason for an attack, R. P. Whitworth in his *Under the Dray* (1872) seems to consider that in a group they are treacherous and will attack without observable provocation.

Attacks on whites, indeed, are the most frequently treated incidents. Horace Earle in 'Ned White' (1861) has an old shepherd telling how troublesome the blacks were and how in an attack he saved the life of an owner of a run. The consequences for the attackers are often dire. N. W. Swan in 'Two Days at Michaelmas' (1875) portrays the reaction of a man whose wife has been killed:

2 in *Authors on the Wallaby—Bush Yarns.*
3 in *Journal of Australasia* (1857).

he devotes his life to a personal feud against all blacks, Spencer Browne in 'The Sub-Inspector's Story' (1890) treats the same theme. The young settler, after the death of his wife at the hands of the Aborigines, sells his station, joins the Native Police, and kills Aborigines whenever the occasion presents itself. The language of the period, which all too clearly expresses the attitude, is seen in the terse summary of a 'dispersal': 'In four days they were on the niggers, and the Lord have mercy on the black devils' souls, for these six desperate men had none on their bodies.'

Rather more measured is the retribution on Melvil in Francis Adams' 'The Red Snake' (1892). Feared by the Aborigines, he punishes individuals (often by death) as he thinks fit. Warned that they are about to attack him, he wipes out the small band in a trap. In revenge others kill a lubra who has borne his son, and the son also. Much more violent and indiscriminate is the slaughter in Adams' other story published in the same year, 'Long Forster' (1892). In this story (which is included in this anthology), the contrast is marked—perhaps a little too contrived—between his ferocity and his tenderness with children and his tears as he grieves for his dead friend.

Most stories of such attacks, however, eschew such subtleties, and deal more facilely with ways of resisting or escaping from attacks. In Hume Nisbet's 'Left in Charge' (1889?)[4] a little girl in the Riverina, left in drought time, sends a dog for help when Aborigines attack. But floods providentially intervene. The man in E. S. Rawson's 'In the Back Blocks' (1888),[5] though his friend is killed, simply escapes with no particular complications. J. A. Barry has two stories of escape, one of them, 'On the Grand Stand' (1893), providing a precipitous rock which the narrator scales in time.

There does not appear to be a story of legal redress for any 'dispersal', though W. H. Suttor in one of his historical reconstructions, 'Vengeance for Ippitha' (1887), recounts how William Burton, Attorney-General of New South Wales, in 1838 prosecuted seven whites for a massacre of Aborigines and had them executed. Not often do we find the Aboriginal case presented, though C. H. Chambers in 'The Little Gold Nugget' (1884)[6] tells how an honest and faithful native, while ensuring the safety of a nugget entrusted to him, is mistaken for a thief and shot. To press beyond acknowledgement of virtue, or justice by law, was rare—for

4 in Martin (ed.), *Over the Sea.*
5 in Martin (ed.), *Oak-Bough and Wattle-Blossom.*
6 in *Authors on the Wallaby—Bush Yarns.*

instance to show or imply that black might have equal cause with white for individual feud or revenge. Ernest Favenc, however, has two such stories, both in his 1893 collection, *The Last of Six*. In 'The Missing Super' a native, flogged with a whip, bides his time for a year, and takes his revenge. 'Malchook's Doom' (reprinted in this volume) is a shocking tale of atrocity.

The reality in most stories of attacks by natives is grim, but it is often concealed by the telling and the manifest identification of the writers with the white settlers. Many tales read like adventures, cowboy and Indian romances produced for adolescents.

The historical tale

A third genre which had just begun to emerge by 1860 was the story based on historical fact. The examples by John Lang, already dealt with, were actuality transmogrified, particularized and, as it were, humanized. It is different with Marcus Clarke, who dug into the records and worked, it would seem, rather like any research student. The results conform to this assessment. His tales in *Old Tales of a Young Country* (1871), if they may be called tales, are a trifle longer than Lang's, they have almost no dialogue, and they deal with a sequence of events rather than with an individual happening. To read them is rather like reading parts of a detailed history or a sequence of articles in a large historical dictionary. Their virtue derives not from their truth—one would hardly rely on them for that—but from the telling: Clarke can use the language better than most historians. And his comments on what he is relating have their relevance even today.

The stories are a marked contrast to his great novel, that litany of horrors, where the convict system is starkly delineated. Of the fifteen stories nine concern events or conditions that are products of the System: if it had not existed, these could not have been written. One may expect, then, that the horrors will be laid bare. But they are not. The tales concern the lives of characters like Barrington (pickpocket), Buckley (escaped convict), Jorgensen (a Danish adventurer transported for debt) and Mitchel (a political prisoner), none of whom was particularly ill-used; bushrangers like Howe; convicts who seized vessels; and an account of Governor Darling's treatment of Sudds and Thompson, two soldiers who had committed a theft so that they might become convicts with hopes of later freedom and prosperity. The other account is that of Macquarie Harbour, to the brutality of which Clarke devotes a page of generalized comment.

He was, then, not much concerned in these short historical tales to attack the System. He was simply writing history, now and then in his strictures (as on Mitchel's attitude to parole) affording the non-expert reader new light on events and characters.

Much the same attitude and aim were professed by W. H. Suttor, a New South Wales politician, in the Preface to his *Australian Stories Retold* (1887). He affirmed that there was nothing imaginative in the seven stories, which had been culled 'from the Press records of the day, and from the word of mouth of old colonial friends who have some recollection of the events narrated'. Occasionally Suttor can be prolix and elaborate, but normally he is very terse. Indeed, he can appear like Clarke after verbal fasting. A good example, to be contrasted with Lang's account, is his story of Fisher's ghost. It is much shorter than Lang's and reads like a report from an investigator.

A concern with the System is registered only in a story about the unjust flogging of a ticket-of-leave man, inducing him to decamp and become a bushranger, and in a gruesome story of cannibalism among a small band of escapees in Van Diemen's Land. There is a touch of the schoolmaster in Suttor—more than a hint of instruction, and even a moral tag as conclusion to one account.

Thomas Walker's *Felonry of New South Wales* (1891) lays no claims to historical accuracy or imaginative reconstruction; but the sub-title, *Realistic Stories of the Early Days of the Convict Settlement of Botany Bay*, seems to indicate Walker's assessment and intention. Two of the tales are detective stories; the rest are about convicts, most of them escapees who have become bushrangers. One of the convicts is a woman, transported for burning the sheds of a harsh landlord, thereafter subjected to a succession of temptations and trials, then escaping, reunited with her lover, and at last being killed. There are few short stories of women convicts meeting with such a fate.

Walker's most fearsome tale is that of Lynch the Murderer, convict, absconder, bushranger. The story is an even narrative of shocking atrocities. Lynch gives a girl, aged fourteen, ten minutes to pray; he then violates her, and murders her. At frequent intervals in his career he asks for Divine help. But Walker's control over horror is limited. He goes on his impassive way, with no attempt to isolate or highlight an incident, with an amorphous impartiality. Walker implies that the cruelties of the System make convicts into bushrangers, who then perform further worse cruelties in their turn.

But all these practitioners are dabblers in the abuses of the System compared with William Astley (Price Warung). His method has been well termed 'ironic melodrama', and it is seen in his first collection, *Tales of the Convict System* (1892). The irony appears crudely in the authorial intrusions, but more effectively in the

contrast of setting and event (a massacre of convicts in a church),
or intention and result (as in 'How Muster-Master Stoneman
Earned His Breakfast', one of the stories chosen for this collection).
As for the melodrama, it is unremitting: Warung writes at the top
of his voice.

No other writer of short stories has concentrated his attention
so much on the evils of the convict system, which Warung maintained 'has knotted itself into fibres of our national being'. This he
felt he had an obligation to expatiate upon. His assertion has been
accepted at its face value by some critics.

It is noteworthy that of these writers of historical tales, only
Lang could have seen a chain gang or (however unlikely) a
flogging—the others were born too late. (The System ended in
1840 in New South Wales and about fifteen years later in
Tasmania). Though Clarke in 1870 saw ironed convicts taking
'dog-sleep in the little forecastle' or at meals in the prison, and the
miserable relics in the asylum, and crippled, self-maimed emancip-
ists in the streets of Hobart, he witnessed no chain gangs nor any
active brutality. These writers are dealing with events they have
only read about or heard about. And the more distant the writers
were from the events, the more vivid became their depictions. The
fictions of Lang's *Botany Bay* are more interesting than Clarke's
nearly true accounts in *Old Tales of a Young Country*. And Warung,
the furthest in time from the period he was dealing with, the most
selective and partial in his choices, the least truthful (what with his
dialogue and details), has produced the most vivid and readable
(however horrifying) stories of them all. With Warung, fiction is
always stranger and more engrossing than truth; art, in its sphere,
is made to blaze and twitch and scream more piercingly than life.

1860–80

In the thirty years before Lang's collection was issued in 1859 there
were about eighteen such volumes of stories published. In the next
twelve years, up to the publication of Marcus Clarke's first volume
of stories in 1871, there were also eighteen collections, a rate two
and a half times greater. It seems natural enough: the free population (and probably the literacy rate) had increased and was
increasing, and an indigenous tradition of fiction writing was
slowly building up. But there are few figures in these twelve years
whom a critic would care to spend much time on. Those before
Lang have an historical interest, as literary pioneers. A critic feels

constrained to give them an attention that their talents may otherwise hardly warrant.

In the years from Lang to Clarke, three writers have enough
idiosyncrasy or individuality to need noting. One is Horace Earle,
whose short stories had affiliations with a certain kind of fiction,
the 'guidebook novels', a sort of hybrid that flourished in the years
1840–60. Their purpose was twofold: to provide information and
at the same time to entertain. Since they were written for English
readers, they described some aspects of Australia—the flora and
fauna, for example—that were different from those in England, as
well as the life an immigrant could expect.

In 1861 Earle issued his *Ups and Downs*, a volume containing a
short novel of about 50 000 words, and eleven short stories. His
Preface, rather surprisingly, declares that 'With few exceptions, life
in Australia, in the year 1861, is much the same as in England'. He
was probably thinking of city life. Accordingly he deals with the
early 1850s. It is significant that, with the exception of two stories,
all are set in the bush. And in one story is a list, quoted by both
earlier and later writers—that in Australia there flourish trees that
shed bark but not leaves, cherries with the stone outside, beautiful
birds with no song, and so on. Other stories each offer their
modicum of information in a form easily digestible—life on the
diggings, attacks by the Aborigines, the work of a shepherd, a
bushfire, the licence system on the gold fields, attacks by bushrangers. All this is rather less skilfully done than in the guidebook
novels; for the latter often assimilate their information into the
narrative, so that the reader may be instructed as he races along.
But Earle is rather more didactic, in each story pausing to inform
the reader that he is about to purvey his dose of instruction. This
is so reiterative that it almost has a comic effect. The stories themselves do not offer a great deal of help, since they are not so much
stories with an attempt at plot as incidents that read as though they
had been plucked from the common stock as excuses for the daily
lesson.

The second writer is James Skipp Borlase, whose short stories
in *Daring Deeds* (1868) are all of adventure and detection, with
many told in the first person by James Brooke, detective and
mounted trooper. Since like Earle's they were written for English
readers, Borlase considers it necessary to explain things in the new
land. We have therefore descriptions of Melbourne streets in 1852,
Sydney Harbour, Victorian diggings, a 'brickfielder', a gaming
house in Sydney, and almost any other scene or setting that might
not be familiar. He is rather like an alert tourist, fascinated by

novelty. The danger is that such diversions may hold up the story.

Borlase is a straightforward and perhaps superficial writer: structure is confined to his mysteries and crimes; he has little interest in character; he recounts adventures with a sort of schoolboy gusto; and indeed we feel that he directed his efforts to adolescents and adults needing to fill in the time. Brooke creeps up to a bushranger on guard, for instance, and then bounds upon him with drawn sword: 'my sword hissed through the air, and so true was the stroke that the man's head was severed from his body, and rolled for more than a yard along the ground'. As a detective Brooke is more vigorous even than John Lang's George Flower, and correspondingly less cerebral than Poe's Dupin.

Borlase is of his time in his respect for wealth and birth; Brooke gives, for instance, a brief sketch of each of the eight men in his troop, revealing that six at least of them were 'gentlemen' in his terms. Borlase's narrative style for the most part is looser and easier than that of many others then writing; he reserves formality, oddly enough, for dialogue and even reverie or soliloquy, so that these parts can read rather like excerpts from a speech by a literate politician on some official occasion. His chief quality, which must bulk large for most people, is his sheer readability.

The third writer is J. R. Houlding ('Old Boomerang'), already noted as one of a durable line of moralists. With him the tone is tempered. The stories in his *Australian Tales and Sketches from Real Life* (1868), however, are more indirect in their preaching than those of other moralists, and the reader occasionally is left to draw his own inferences. And Houlding is more concerned with prudent practicalities—insure against fire, be careful of 'kites' (worthless bills or promissory notes), don't frighten children into obedience, choose a suitable time for religious exhortation—than with virtue. Nearly all his tales are a little too long, mainly because he takes too much time to get started. Nor does brevity result from his often clumsy formal style. But, unlike most of the other moralists, Houlding makes attempts at humour and occasionally succeeds. The names he gives his characters—Mrs Lemonpip, Moans, Dollop, and so on, showing the influence of Dickens—may be crude, and he cannot draw humorous characters; but situations and their effects on the participants can raise a laugh. His best effort is his description of the difficulties a drunk has in his attempt to row a boat. It is a sort of piled-up, non-stop sequence, without much subtlety, but resulting in a kaleidoscopic scenario resembling the old Mack Sennett films. Like the victim, the reader finds developing in himself a bursting exasperation with the perversity of the inanimate.

Houlding wrote other fiction, much of it addressed to the young. Something of this tone seeps into these presumably adult pieces, and the reader can feel he is being addressed from above. Many of the tales would have made good Sunday school pamphlets.

The most important writer of short stories in the period 1860–80—indeed the most important prose writer of the whole period to the appearance of Lawson—was of course Marcus Clarke. He issued seven volumes of shorter fiction, though some contained only a few stories. Various collections were published after his death.

During his seventeen years in Australia Clarke produced a great amount of literary work of the most diverse kinds—novels, plays, polemics, newspaper reports, reviews, history, and even poetry. He wrote sketches—of the bush, of bush townships, of characters ranging from drunks to squatters—symposiums, and speculative projections into the future. In short narratives he attempted the broken romance, the *femme fatale* with her nemesis, farce, detection, and mystical experiences (dream- and drug-induced). A few themes were stock: the child lost in the bush, the humble adorer sacrificing himself for the adored (in this instance a dumb dwarf—presumably to stress the gap between him and the beloved), and the self-abnegating love of woman for handsome wastrel.

Now if a man can write *For the Term of His Natural Life*, a novel that nearly all critics and readers acknowledge to be something of a flawed masterpiece, then it seems likely enough that he might produce some very good short stories. But the plain fact is that Clarke's stories do not rank with those of the masters. Perhaps the only one that strikes a reader as completely satisfactory (in its trivial kind) is 'King Billy's Troubles', a skit on bureaucratic red tape, which was published in Clarke's *Australian Tales* (1896). It tells of the vain attempts of the narrator to extract from the powers that be a pair of breeches for an old Aborigine. It is farcical, in parts hilarious, and every item of absurdity and frustration has a fleeting relevance for any modern citizen in his dealings with government.

This is not to deny that the stories can be effective: it is simply to deny that they are great. Clarke has some good comic-ironic touches, and he can hit off a character: Sporboy in 'The Romance of Lively Creek' (one of the stories collected here) is the best of these—confident, alcoholic, with a gift for quotation, misquotation, and vivid anecdote, an ominous master of black humour, prototype of that grim comedian W. C. Fields.

Why, then, are Clarke's short stories not completely satisfying? Enough laughter has been justifiably expended on his sentimentality, especially in 'Pretty Dick' (also published in *Australian Tales*), to require no further comment. All that need be said is that such indulgence was widespread last century. It was long-lived, and was found in unexpected places. (Even a fashionable sophisticate like Oscar Wilde could yield to temptation: in *A Woman of No Importance* (1894) Lord Illingworth threatens to employ as secretary Gerald (aged twenty-one), the illegitimate son of Mrs Arbuthnot and himself. Mrs Arbuthnot pleads with him: 'Leave me the little vineyard of my life; leave me the walled-in garden and the well of water; the ewe-lamb God sent me, in pity or in wrath, oh! leave me that.' To use a witticism of Wilde's against him—one must have a heart of stone to refrain from laughter. Allied to this, the occasional moralistic endings strike a reader as not entirely heartfelt: Clarke, as we know from some of his articles, was not benevolently disposed to kindly Providence, being atheist or at least agnostic. But, again, it was customary to use such tag endings.

His sketches, generally included in collections of his shorter fiction, have an exaggeration that fits the comic but not the ostensibly serious. His famous descriptions in 'Australian Scenery' are a case in point, the tone of Weird Melancholy being sustained throughout—some may think strained throughout. When we come upon this sentence—'from out the bottomless depths of some lagoon the Bunyip rises, and in form like a monstrous sea-calf, drags his loathsome length from out the ooze'—then we may feel a certain adult reluctance to respond to a demand so blatantly enunciated. In another example, 'Holiday Peak', filled with mystic sights and sounds, Clarke dredges mythology for figures with appropriate associations—Mithra, Isis, Osiris, Tammuz, Hypon—and the accompanying practices ('the painted and naked priest reared high the thirsty knife and flung himself—blood-red in the fire-glow—upon the panting victim') and then moves to visions of authors and fictional characters, ending in the land of might-have-been and should-have-been. It is a little difficult to take quite seriously.

Structure in a story is Clarke's technical virtue. In 'The Romance of Lively Creek' the events are seen through the eyes of a disengaged narrator, and the end is nicely poised: the reader, like the narrator, may be undecided as to what happened. It has a certain theatrical plausibility. And other stories, published in *Australian Tales*, such as 'Poor Jo', 'Gentleman George's Bride', and 'A Romance of Bullocktown', though the themes are well-worn, are not the awkward contrivances of contemporary hacks.

But competence is hardly enough, and even plausibility is sometimes lacking. 'The Future Australian Race' is a case in point. The sketch is based, at least in part, on a belief in the evidence of

physiognomy—as you look, so you are. It was part of the super-
stition of his age, related to phrenology (having one's 'bumps' read)
and other fads.

One thing that Clarke lacked in both stories and sketches was
any deep engagement with his material. This was inevitable: in his
year and a half or so in the bush near Glenorchy he was, by reading
and intellect, a Gulliver among the Lilliputians, and he can hardly
have been unconscious of the fact. He was not of the community,
and this appears in his sketches of country towns. He can write
'the ground was as bare as a billiard table', where the comparison
evokes his background. It is as a visitor or outsider that he writes
'The first impression of Grumbler's Gully is, I confess, not a
cheering one . . . The hideously excellent cemetery of Grumbler's
Gully always seemed to me to realise the life of the colony . . .'
and 'in this free colony, where everybody is so tremendously equal,
the tyranny of cash is carried to a greater extent than in any other
country on the face of the earth'. The tone is not really unkind nor
always condescending, but it is very different indeed from
Lawson's. Essentially urban, bohemian, Clarke could have but an
intellectual insight into and sympathy with bush life.

A different lack of engagement with his material may account
for the lack of depth in his stories proper. He was brilliant and
precocious—'suffered at sixteen to ape the vices of sixty'—exiled,
running through his money, failing in jobs (not because he could
not master them but because they bored him), then finding what
fitted his talents, the opportunity to write and get paid for doing
so. So he wrote on almost anything and everything, but not on any
one thing for long. (Though the novels exhibit his perseverance:
indeed what is astonishing about *His Natural Life* is not so much
that Clarke could write it as that he did finish it.) A devoted
apprenticeship to a particular craft, that of the short story (*vide*
Maupassant), it was not in his nature to endure. A reader is left
with the impression that Clarke did not take his shorter fictions
very seriously, that he produced them readily enough with a bright
professionalism, as he could any other short pieces. And almost
always in a style that has verve, is seldom pedestrian, is vivid and
actual, the style of a cultivated narrator talking to another person
of understanding.

It is interesting to note that something of this was felt by
contemporary readers. In 'The Critic' (1873) the reviewer is willing
to accept accounts of Bullock Town and Grumbler's Gully, and
even 'Pretty Dick' may pass; but the pathos has 'a false ring . . .
It is made to order, so to speak'. Clarke is considered to possess
and exhibit humour, wit and pertness. Though this last may seem

to us a rather odd attribution, it is possible to feel what the reviewer was labouring to define: there can be, in some passages, a decline from a sophistication to a certain cheaper assurance—as if the writer were confident he could get away with almost anything. In 'The Island of Gold' (1886),[7] also entitled 'El Dorado', unashamedly a sensational story, the adventurers fit their roles ('Allan Forbes laughed his own dangerous laugh, and followed it with his usual sneer'), and utter the appropriate threats ('Stand back, assassin, coward, liar'). It rings a little hollow, and beside a story by, say, Conrad it appears rather gimcrack.

One is tempted to say it is unfortunate that Clarke could do so well with such material. The glitter of style, the touch of originality in incident or point of view, the affectation of seriousness—all these refurbish situation and subject of not much importance and give them a factitious significance. It is like watching an exhibition by a polished performer going through feats of no consequence (but made to seem difficult by very skill) and yet confident of being greeted at the end with a burst of clapping.

As a man he was kindly and charitable—as well as impatient and cynical. But as a short-story writer he does not give us that quality of insight and spread of sympathy that illuminate great short stories. His are essentially about happenings, the exciting or entertaining or mysterious details of life and fancy. Even when charity and pity are expressed, the story stays where it was. It is ended, with few implications wider than itself.

It may seem harsh or perverse to say this. After all, Clarke remains our best writer of short fiction before Lawson, while his near-masterpiece demands its separate tribute. Perhaps that is the explanation: the critic cannot help drawing the comparison and marking the contrast. Had Clarke not produced *His Natural Life*, his short stories might awaken a greater admiration in us. He compels us, as it were, to judge him by that high standard.

If we look for his finest stories, we find a delightful and satirical farce, 'King Billy's Troubles'; a mystery laced with humour, 'The Romance of Lively Creek'; a domestic drama, which suggests something of the brutality and yet wry understanding of a country township, 'A Romance of Bullocktown'; and probably his best story, with its originality and supernatural overtones, 'Human Repetends' (which is reprinted here). The variety is as notable as the skill. It is this that is lacking in other writers after him who produced a few stories that possibly stand comparison with these.

7 in *Sensational Tales.*

Clarke is a pivotal figure. There are a few good stories before him; after him the general level is higher, though only occasionally rising to his level. And certain strands converge in him and then spread from him—stories of Aborigines (though he wrote only one we remember); detective or mystery stories; historical tales, where he provides insights and information; tales of the supernatural, where he does not give us ghosts but suggests the presence of some mysterious realm where laws apply that are not our own; and last, one of the most famous—or notorious—examples of a child lost in the bush, 'Pretty Dick'.

In the middle decades of the century three new genres or story situations emerged: tales of mystery and detection became popular, as did stories about children lost in the bush and stories dealing with the supernatural.

Tales of mystery and detection

The use of historical incident might, but more probably might not, assist in giving coherence to a story, for life is generally not as comely as art. Better would be a mysterious incident which demands an explanation, a problem asking for a solution. Edgar Allan Poe was the earliest to use this approach, and his Dupin long held the field as the superlative detective, the master of pure reason. Poe wrote these tales in the early 1840s, and it was almost ten years before the first detective appeared in our shorter fiction, in *The Black Troopers* (1850?), and even then tracking down the perpetrator of a robbery, set in England, depends more on coincidence than intelligence.

Another few years saw John Lang presenting George Flower, the first Australian detective, at work in the convict era. This was not a short story but an episodic novel, *The Forger's Wife*, which preceded by five years Wilkie Collins' famous *The Woman in White* (1860), generally considered the first detective novel in English. But in his short stories, perhaps because they were mostly based on historical events, Lang dealt only once with detection in 'Giles! As I Live!' This complicated tale, involving fraud and mistaken identity, contains no professional sleuth, but an intelligent settler who patiently, over several years, unravels the skein.

The next fictional detective is James Skipp Borlase's James Brooke. If Flower is less cerebral than Poe's Dupin, Brooke is less cerebral than Flower; but he has a sort of hearty shrewdness and is not easily duped. His most astonishing deduction is made from a bruised golden hair from an eyebrow.

The third writer of short stories concerned with mystery and detection was Marcus Clarke, who wrote these in the 1870s. 'The Romance of Lively Creek' is the most overtly concerned with detection. Its ending on a note of suspense, of unresolved mystery, is a device Clarke employs in other stories, for instance in 'The Man with the Oblong Box' (1878) where the ambiguously sinister host, we are told, will meet his end later. If we ask why, we are referred to the police files. It is a truncated tale, and rather unsatisfactory. There are others by him that leave us puzzled, and in them a supernatural ingredient serves as both theme and reason for the ending.

In 1871 appeared *The Detective's Album*, written by W.W. (Waif Wander? Mrs Fortune?), the most fertile producer of short mystery stories in our literature last century. There are seven stories in the volume, and some of them are told in the first person by W.W.'s detective, Mark Sinclair.

The stories are nearly all complicated, especially one entitled 'To Be Left Till Called For'. A parcel containing a dead child is left at an hotel by a woman who maintains that the bundle was full of skirts she had made. The landlord's absent wife says the barmaid has had a baby. The detective, helped by luck and a dream, discovers that the woman with the parcel and the barmaid are enemies (the barmaid lost her lover to the woman). So the barmaid casts suspicion on her. The landlord kills his wife and he and the barmaid bury the corpse. If this sounds puzzling, then it truthfully represents the original. Indeed the stories are not so much skilfully woven nets of intrigue as capriciously involved sequences. In each of them there are two or three people under suspicion, one falsely accusing another. Practice in the craft does not appear to have improved the skill of the author, for the last story has a plot no more plausible than the first. Oddly enough the length, greater than is needed, does not help to clarify the confusions. W.W. was wedded to the type, for she(?) later wrote a series of about two dozen for the *Australian Journal*, running from September 1887 to August 1889.

The other authors of mystery tales before the 1880s are not of much consequence. Grosvenor Bunster, for example, stresses the melodramatic in 'Blood for Blood' (1872),[8] his story of attempted assassination: 'I felt a fierce lust for his blood; and as it gushed forth

---

8   in Stephen & Bunster (eds), *Our Christmas Budget*.

from his throat, and covered my face, hands, and clothing, I laughed aloud in exultation'.

Richmond Thatcher in 'Something to his Advantage' (1875) uses coincidence in the story of a masquerader's claim to an estate in England. It seems to owe much to the notorious Tichborne case. In 'The Lady of Ivan Station' (1876),[9] the anonymous author combines love and jealousy and violence in a complicated and improbable story that nevertheless hangs together. In another tale, comedy results from the work of a ghostly compositor on a newspaper who reveals a murder, thus increasing the paper's circulation. This is one of the more successful stories by the industrious Garnet Walch ('The Phantom Compositor', 1879).[10] These are the most notable—if that is the right word—of the tales of the lesser authors in this period, the others being run-of-the-mill concoctions.

From 1887 tales of mystery, intrigue and detection become more numerous. Campbell McKellar's volume, *The Premier's Secret and Other Tales*, appeared in 1887 with its grim story of murder in a shearing shed and the subsequent effects on one of the participants. It is not a detective story in the usual sense, for the tale is told to the narrator by the chief agent in the crime.

We may wonder if there were some reason for this spate. Conan Doyle had just created Sherlock Holmes in 1887: this figure had a European as well as an English reputation, and translations and imitations flourished. What more likely than a spread to Australia? On the other hand, the increase in detective stories may be due simply to the fact that more short stories of all kinds were being written. For example, from 1887 to the appearance of Lawson's first volume in 1894, a period of seven years, there were published about forty collections or anthologies of short stories by Australian writers, a figure much greater than for any previous period of the same length.

Though the Australian writers may have been encouraged by the popularity of Doyle, they did not imitate very closely; Sherlock Holmes is in the line of descent from Poe's Dupin, pondering, analysing, logically assessing possibilities. This is not the usual method in the Australian tales. The first-person narrator or the detective or the author relies for solutions on accident or coincidence, or the story is told as over and done with, as a slice of things that arranged themselves. Only occasionally do we find the detective solving a problem by thought alone.

Later exponents of the mystery story make use of various

9 in Geary (ed.), *Mrs Sloper's Bundle*.
10 in Martin (ed.), *An Easter Omelette*.

devices. The crudest is coincidence, which Mrs Blitz employs in
'The Wurtamurtah Estate Prize' (1888)—a lucky lottery ticket, a
lucky meeting, a happy marriage resulting. But intrigue or plotting
is, fortunately for the reader, most frequent. The buying and selling
of shares in the diggings and the merited misfortune of the bad
character appear in J. C. F. Johnson's 'Towball's Christmas Gifts'
(1888); Reginald Clayton in 'His Chinese Cook' (1890),[11] a
thoroughly racist story, is well into what looks like a murder
mystery when he reveals it as the trickery of some Chinese on a
station; Haddon Chambers, smoothly competent in a magazine
style, tells of the intrigues in a detective agency and other intrigues
by women concerned with the partners in a comic tale, 'The
Private Enquiry' (1891). Perhaps more modern in conception, and
more effective in structure, are the stories that have surprise
endings, or at any rate endings that keep the reader in some
suspense. E. S. Rawson in 'Jim's Ghost' (1889)[12] gives us a deserted
camp, a tale by an old stockman of a naked man seen across a
lagoon, and the mystery of his flight; in 'Done' (1891)[13] the
author (writing as 149) introduces a nice domestic touch when a
wealthy squatter gives his reason for not prosecuting some
gamblers who have defrauded him; Haddon Chambers, competent
as ever, has the murderer solve the crime, but leaves him unbe-
lieved in 'An Underground Murder' (1891), and in 'Murdered' uses
a scientific myth of the age (the retina of the eye retaining the image
of the last thing seen before death) to solve another murder;
Thomas Walker, perhaps constrained by his sources—it is ostensibly an historical story—tells in 'Murder Will Out' (1891) how the
third of the suspects, not the first two, is guilty; and to introduce
a comic note, Ernest Favenc in his best-known tale—'The Parson's
Black-Boy' (1893)—leads the reader, through the clues given but
oblique, to a disconcerting disclosure.

A later writer, Francis Adams, is probably the best of those
concerned with mystery, puzzles, intrigue—better than Clarke,
indeed, in that respect. There are aspects of the supernatural—to
be dealt with later—that he uses in a few stories, but apart from
that he is adept in the use of the open ending. In 'Dr Fletcher's Love
Story' (1892) we have partly a mystery, partly a study of a child,
precocious and odd. A reader asks himself, as the story progresses
and at the end, various questions about the guilt of two people.
And he is left in doubt when the narrative is over. Another study of

11 in Martin (ed.), *Under the Gum Tree*.
12 in Mennell (ed.), *In Australian Wilds*.
13 in *Volcanic Gold*.

female reactions is 'Lily Davenant' (1892), the story of a flirt, a tease, who both attracts and repels—or is it, attracts and rejects? And here we wonder about the perfect objectivity of the narrator. Can he really bear, or afford, to tell what happened just as it really did? In 'Miss Jackson' (reprinted in this anthology) neither narrator nor reader can be sure of the woman's guilt though they may have suspicions. It is of interest to notice that these stories, adult and sophisticated, all deal with nuances of feminine emotion and reaction.

'Lost child' stories

Unlike mystery-detective stories, fictional accounts of children lost in the bush focused on a peculiarly Australian concern. The danger must have been a perpetual and recurrent fear in many areas, and even townsfolk could have direct and indirect acquaintance with it. Newspaper accounts, sometimes reading almost like short stories, were written, while the stort-story tellers found the theme fruitful enough.

To avoid repetition they developed variations of detail. Sometimes the child or the children were found, and here the Aboriginal tracker could be introduced. Or the child could be found in varying ways. In 'A Perilous Tale' (1881) Per Se (Percy Sinnett) tells how a child falls over a small cliff but is saved by tangled vines. A woman finds her, climbs down, but cannot climb up. After that, it would be a heartless author who would refuse them rescue. Or the child could be found by somebody who wanted to keep it, or who simply looked after it until the searchers arrived. Or the child itself could come upon a forsaken hut and remain for days. If, say, three or more children were lost, the eldest of the group would display qualities of responsible leadership and preserve the others. A child breaking from the group could be lost. An ingenious writer could have it both ways. In one tale, 'Recovered' (1872) by J. M. Conroy, the bright pupil, Charley, is lost in the bush. His father, a drunkard, is shocked enough to forswear alcohol. He is confirmed in his reformation when Charley at last is found, having been incapacitated by a broken leg. Occasionally the narrator would take the opportunity to expatiate upon the danger of disobedience in the child; or a moral could be extracted as a general observation—we are all wanderers from the truth, a truism enunciated in 'Lost in the Scrub' (1862).[14]

Quite often, because more pathetic and presumably affecting most poignantly the sensibilities of the reader, the child dies or is

14 in *The Children's Magazine*.

found dead. Rosa Praed tells in 'The Sea–Birds' Message' (1889?)[15] of a little boy and girl lost in a variation of the bush setting: they float off on a small island of reeds into a lake, which is very peaceful, and may be a symbol of something. A child lost and dying appears in three very famous examples, those by Kingsley ('How the Child Was Lost' in chapter XXX of *Geoffrey Hamlyn*), Clarke ('Pretty Dick') and Furphy (in *Such Is Life*). It is a cliché of criticism now to point out that only Furphy's story can be counted successful, probably because the story is told by one of the searchers. Emotions of children are, it seems, almost beyond capture: young, we have no words for our feelings; old, we have the words but not those feelings.

The child is generally presented as innocent, appealing, and shedding grace around it. Clarke's 'Pretty Dick' served as a model for at least one close copy, J. C. F. Johnson's Bonny Nellie (in the story of the same name, published in 1872), a beautiful little girl, also aged seven, influencing coarser souls in much the same way, described in much the same words: 'the most depraved and hardened 'old hand' on the place . . . would hush the rude oath or song, and drop the cards, if Nellie peeped in at the door.' But Johnson, more tender-hearted than Clarke, cannot bring himself to kill her: she is tracked by an Aborigine, helped by a dog, and is found alive.

The effects of the loss on the adult survivors provide other variations, as in J. F. Hogan's 'Little Louey' (1886). The child, a pupil at a country school, dies in the bush. Her teacher, though transferred later to a city school, returns periodically to visit her grave. Much the same is Lawson's variation, children lost but never found, in 'The Babies in the Bush', where he deals with the effects on father and mother, the father away in Sydney on a spree at the time of the loss, the mother now believing that the children are still alive, taken by the fairies. It allows scope for dealing with the relations between husband and wife, and evades some of the constant dangers of over-indulgence in pathos to which his predecessors were so prone.

The supernatural

Since Australia in the nineteenth century was concerned with industrial, pastoral, and material growth, and since the second half of the century was in addition the age of Darwin and Huxley, it might be expected that the supernatural would not find a natural home here. In truth our only lasting contributions to mystic lore

15 in Martin (ed.) *Over the Sea.*

have been the bunyip and Fisher's Ghost. Both have become known outside the country. Lang's famous pseudo-historical account, 'The Ghost Upon the Rail' (1859), the story that made the legend, is an example not of belief but of use—he tells what a man said he saw. And this led to the solving of the crime—so Lang said in his turn.

But if they invented little, the Australian writers had stock to draw on if they wanted to. About the middle of the century the cult started in the USA with spirits, seances, and presiding mediums; and the developments were too rewarding to be neglected— palmistry, astral bodies, teleportation, magnetic fluids, ectoplasm. The mysterious East provided—or had attributed to it—adepts and reincarnated souls. There are few such creations in the Australian stories; for the most part, indeed, their favourite intruders from the occult world were plain old-fashioned ghosts.

Some writers treated ghosts in comic terms. 'Tasma' (Jessie Couvreur), verbose as usual in her earlier tales, gives us 'The Rubria Ghost' (1878),[16] telling how the young lover, for a reason never made convincing to the reader, plays ghost on a station until the elderly husband of his beloved dies (not because of the ghost), and then marries the young widow. It is too long for its trivial content. Disguise is the device in H. W. H. Stephen's 'Metempsychosis' (1884).[17] To persuade a man to consent to his sister's marriage, a family plus doctor plus servants engage in beneficient deception, with the result that the brother, a believer in reincarnation and the transmigration of souls, is persuaded to change his mind. Rather more farcical, 'Donovan's Sperrit' (1888), by J. C. F. Johnson, tells in an Irish accent how Dinny Malone was helped to a treasure by a ghost which then, mistrusting Malone's fecklessness, continued to supervise the finder's financial affairs.

Others used ghosts more seriously, or even reverently. Even James Skipp Borlase, whose detective, James Brooke, one might think would automatically suspect a ghost as a criminal accomplice, succumbs in 'Mystery and Murder' (included in this collection). A benevolent ghost appears in P. J. Holdsworth's 'A Tale of New Year's Eve' (1875), and saves a friend at the point of death; the haunted house looms in 'Brushwood Grange' (1876), in which ghostly footsteps are heard and sounds as of something being dragged (an old man had been murdered there ten years earlier).[18] Less direct and more vaguely mysterious is G. A. Walstab's 'The

16 in Hopkins (ed.), *The Australian Ladies' Annual*.
17 in *Authors on the Wallaby—Bush Yarns*.
18 in Thatcher (ed.), *Something to His Advantage*.

Return Ticket' (1879?),[19] telling of a friend's suicide after he had
given ambiguous warnings of the danger threatening a child. The
devil, evasively and ambiguously helpful, warns the narrator of
'The Devil and the Swagman', by Frank Morley (1884).[20] Despite
this, the narrator suffers in a bushfire and sees his mate burned to
death. To make up for his misfortunes he learns later that he is heir
to an inheritance.

Neither comic nor serious use of ghosts resulted in very effective
stories. The supernatural is best used by the writers when it is more
vague, less manifest in spectre or warning. Here Marcus Clarke
produced some of his better-known work. In his 1886 collection,
Sensational Tales, for example, is a story called 'The Mind-Reader's
Curse'. Anthony Venn is given the power to read minds, but the
gift is a mixed blessing, for he becomes aware of the problems,
dangers, and griefs that can ensue. In despair, he is awakened by
Dr Zauberracher, who has put him into a trance by mesmerizing
him. The next story, 'The Dual Existence', is told by Professor
Peppenhausser, another savant from Germany, that repository of
darkly romantic erudition. Warned by the example of his grandfather, Karl Pläafer fears to gamble. A man, successful at the tables,
is murdered. The story ends after some complicated manoeuvres,
and we are left wondering if Karl has a double, or is two persons,
or if some more mysterious influence has been at work. The third
is Clarke's most satisfying effort in this genre—'Human Repetends', also published as 'The Mysterious Coincidence'. It is an
ingeniously contrived story, consistent in its details, the equal of
anything of the same kind in Poe.

Also rather like an allegory by Poe is Donald Cameron's 'The
Valley of Shadow' (1882),[21] a picture of Gippsland after the gold
rushes. The title has its quality of suggestiveness, so has the slightly
portentous style, while the four Crones add their ominous presence. Though it tries a little too hard to do what lies a little beyond
its powers, it does have its effect. In 'A Strange Experience' (1888)
A. F. B. Hull introduces mesmerism and the interchange of souls:
a deputy-sheriff momentarily feels the pain of death when he is
present at a hanging.

One of Francis Adams' stories, 'Flowers for the Dead' (1892),
might or might not be concerned with the supernatural. The
narrator comes to a brilliantly lit hut and follows a girl who has
been gathering flowers—perhaps in her sleep. She lays these beside
a corpse on a bed, croons a nursery song, and then enters the next

19 in *We 5*.
20 in *Authors on the Wallaby—Bush Yarns*.
21 in *Australian Stories*.

room and goes to sleep on a bed holding two children. It is eerie enough as Adams tells it, but it still remains ambiguous in tone and in intent. Quite unambiguous in tone is 'The Hut by the Tanks' (1892)—it is frankly supernatural. The sceptical narrator enters an empty hut. But the curlews are crying, and he feels there is something terrible in the next room. He looks in, to see that a man—the murderer, it is apparent—has dug up the body of the woman he stabbed and is crying over it. The narrator sees this for a frozen moment, and then all lights go out. There is nothing there. Adams' intent is not so clear: there is, strictly speaking, no story. We have a sudden shocking vision, but it leads nowhere. Nor has it been led up to: it just happens, a spontaneous generation. In the use of the supernatural it is not enough simply to display the supernatural. It is here that Clarke reveals his capacity for invention and structure, and here that Adams is lacking. Favenc has some of this capacity in 'Spirit-Led' (1893) which, despite some divergences and a rather convoluted sequence, leads to its startling, but at least partly plausible ending.

Of all these stories, and of others hardly worth discussing, it may be said that, except for one of Clarke's, which has its power of almost logical form, they are too literal: a ghost remains a ghost, a supernatural scene is hardly more than a vision to be frightened or startled by. There is not much of the suggestion that can induce us to muse and to wonder for a moment whether there may be a world beyond mundane experience.

1880–93

The production of short stories continued to increase after 1880. The quality also rose, in general, even if there was no individual writer to equal Marcus Clarke. For one thing, there is improvement—to a modern reader at least—in the manner of writing. Apart from Lang, nearly all the earlier writers now seem very old-fashioned in their formality and lack of directness. For authors and readers at the time they presumably provided certain effects; for us today they generally do not.

One intended result of both the inflation and the periphrasis was humour, a notoriously fickle and changing product. Examples that depend upon polysyllables and indirection are numerous even near the end of the century:

making our physical sensations a highway for our rational intelligence, we are indubitably appraised of the fact that supper is under way, by receiving, through the medium of our olfactory organs, a very commendable second edition of a kidney pie. ('Poverty Point'[22])

This is Bernard Espinasse in 1887. Even a reasonably competent writer like Edward Dyson, three years later, can inflate a normal statement—'They wore their clothes unwashed until these fell to pieces'—into

They acknowledged but one limit to the time an article might be retained in wear without washing, and that was regulated by the durability of the garment in question. ('The Washerwoman of Jacker's Flat'[23])

Only occasionally, perhaps in Houlding, certainly in Clarke, do we find comic theme and normal prose together.

One example of much failure and possible success is C. H. Barlee. He intends to be humorous, calling his volume *Humorous Tales and Sketches of Colonial Life* (1893). A few are serious, a few are successfully funny, for example, 'Jones v Jenkyns', a burlesque, a skit on the bushranging themes that had been frequent enough before Barlee, and on politicians and on spiritualism. The tone is deliberately high-spirited, a contrived absurdity that shows no sign of exhaustion from page to page. In a way, Barlee wears the reader down—one feels that such unremitting effort should have some reward.

Though inflated language was used frequently for comic effect, its more frequent appearance was in dramatic scenes. There is no reason to doubt that it was seriously meant: when the situation was tense, when a threat loomed, when defiance was to be exhibited, then this language was thought to be not merely adequate or permissible, but obligatory. It was frequently used in dialogue ('Come nearer, fiend and triple slayer'), or as an expression of inner conflict ('I cannot hate her infernal beauty, although it has been my destruction,'), or, rising to heroic and exclamatory heights ('Fool!' sneered the woman, 'I defy you! At your peril molest me!').[24]

The formality of style resisted temptations to become natural speech. The hero reproaches one of his helpers who has a problem of his own:

'You cannot expect me to understand your feelings, if you can compare your chagrin at not being able to catch a man to whom you owe a thrashing with my misery at this prolonged suspense, which, with all its attendant horrors, is fast becoming worse than a painful certainty.'[25]

22 in Walch (ed.), *The Victorian Jubilee Book* (1887).
23 in *A Golden Shanty* (1890).
24 in *The Australian Souvenir* (1851).
25 H. G. Turner, *Tales of the Colony* (1857).

This grammatical and formal rhetoric issues from a man distraught with anxiety over the fate of a woman he loves.

When it is not dialogue, but narrative, then we can find 'Why stands she there in her scanty attire, on this black night?', or, a trifle more prophetically dire, 'Drink was resorted to by her to drown reflection, and madly she sped in the race to ruin'.[26]

Now and then the elevated becomes the sensational and resembles the language of the cheap thrillers that delighted the English working-class readers about the middle of last century. Here the wealthy are castigated:

. . . these perfumed daughters of fashion and wealth, in their silks and velvets, could not think of permitting their dainty, aristocratic thoughts to show vulgar compassion for a ragged little street vagrant . . .

This is the product of Tony the Pieman in his *Night Scenes of Melbourne* (1877). He writes of a criminal:

There was a desperate yet craven look in his besotted eyes, which bespoke the character of one ever willing to perform a deed of darkness . . . blood-thirsty yet chicken-hearted . . .

Evoking a different response, he describes a woman disrobing:

her golden tresses falling in profuse luxuriance upon the alabastor [sic] beauty of her full, voluptuous bust, a smile of cruel triumph played upon her lascivious mouth.

The picture of a man corresponding to the *femme fatale* appears in Frank Donohue's *A Sheaf of Stories* (1888). He is a heartless young Englishman who abandons an Australian girl; he returns to England to claim an inheritance, and

handsome and debonnair [sic], has gone back blithely and with a light heart to the scene of his riotous youth, to gladden the salons of the noble and the boudoirs of the fair with his handsome Saxon face and his faultless physique . . . See him there, among the half-nude beauties of the ball-room . . .

There are other differences between the language of then and now. It is tempting to smile at the colloquial terms of the educated a century or more ago, with their 'awfully', 'absolutely', 'piffle', 'rot', 'blessed'—but for contemporaries these were natural widely used expressions. Australian fiction—novels or short stories—last century resounded with 'old man', 'old fellow'. The term 'mate' as address was less frequent: it occurred in the third person, not so much in the second, though there is a lot of the latter in Horace Earle. Oddly enough, it has become very frequent in

26 J. R. Houlding, in *Australian Tales and Sketches from Real Life* (1868).

address this century, apparently corresponding to 'Mac'—or 'man' in certain areas—in the USA.

What one can say is that much of the language often appears comic to us today, quaintly outmoded, inadequate to the situation—or, perhaps worse, perfectly adequate to outmoded situation. Sometimes periphrasis, so often used to produce humour, became cliché; 'the flowing bowl', for instance, could be used with no ostensibly comic intent. In general, a sort of creaking formality prevailed.

Naturally enough, writers were unlikely to be conscious of anything humorous or objectionable in their own prose or that of their contemporaries. The nearest approach to conscious parody is in C. H. Barlee's 'Jones v Jenkyns' (1893):

In the Grecian upper lip, the Hibernian nose, and the haughty but carefully arranged curl of scorn upon his noble brow, the phrenologist would have seen in the dim distance the wealth and distinction which were to follow.

Yet even here Barlee may be mocking not the diction of previous writers but the pretensions of the son of a fisherman.

But if most accepted the stylistic conventions of their time, occasionally a writer did, in hope or exasperation, declare he would abjure clichéd themes or subjects. He did not always keep his word. J. M. Conroy in *False, and Other Tales* (1872), a collection of bush stories, looks at tales of the gold diggings:

The diggings are going to be mentioned. But let it be hastily understood that no revolvers or red shirts will be in the story. Neither will thigh-boots. Heaven knows there is enough thigh-boot literature in Australia already . . . No shots will be fired even in self-defence; but that is because there will be no attack. There will be no 'Joes' . . .

He is true to this intention in one story, but in others he succumbs to other temptations, and gives us the child lost in the bush, rescues, reconciliations and the rest. Even when the unexpected appears, Conroy reveals himself as a failed master of surprise, which in his hands dissolves into the trivial or banal or anti-climactic.

C. H. Barlee, noted above for his skit on themes and style found in some fiction, seems to glance at themes and titles in 'The Out-and-Outer', which he attributes to 'the author of . . . "Fowl Play", "The Three Convicts", "His Unnatural Life" . . .' It is the story of a murderer, at last captured and condemned: 'He was to die by the hands of the commonest executioner that could be found'.

The orthodox Australian background comes in for comment by E. W. Hornung in 'Strong-Minded Miss Methuen' (1892). The young woman from England finds the sandy monotony of the diocese does not live up to what she has read and heard of the Australian landscape: 'gullies, gum-trees, caves, ranges, kangaroos, opossums, claims, creeks, snakes in the grass, and chivalrous robbers on the highroad'.

Though a move to more modern prose and less stereotyped themes is marked in the last two decades of the nineteenth century, relics of the past persist. The urge to moral enlightenment, for instance, continues in *The Snowdrop's Message* (1888) by Ellen Augusta Chads (dedicated to the Right Rev. The Lord Bishop of Melbourne), but it is less overt than in the tales of Mrs Vidal, and also less comprehensive. Though Chads warns against other failings, she concentrates on two—drinking and gambling. Some of her characters wear the badge of the Temperance League, as though in mute support of their creator.

Coincidence is frequent enough—a bushranger shoots a lone rider from ambush, for example, finds to his horror that he has shot his brother, and at the moment of recognition is struck dead by a bolt of lightning. The numerous deaths occur not because the plot demands them, but perhaps they serve to emphasize that life is mostly a vale of tears, where men and women suffer disaster as tests of faith and as opportunities to endure what Providence sees fit to impose. A woman saves a child from drowning, for example, catches a chill, develops rheumatic fever, and becomes an incurable invalid. Chads, it is clear, demands much of her characters, and the good ones respond nobly and audibly: most of them quote Scripture with exquisite appositeness.

Morality, however, may be inculcated less directly. In Andrew Robertson's *The Kidnapped Squatter* (1891) each of the four stories contains examples of the author's belief that virtue is rewarded and wickedness is punished. The author shows little control over what plot there is and few graces of style in the plain, often staccato, sequence of sentences. Events happen, but they are not often linked; characters act, but motivation is not explored.

The world is seemingly divided into two areas, one inhabited by the deserving, the other by the vicious. The former may suffer for a time, but the clouds disperse at last, the sun shines, and they receive their meed of material and spiritual bliss. It is a well-ordered world, this fictional dichotomy, and Providence might well learn from Robertson. Only occasionally do doubts arise: a decent poor family, growing daily poorer, suffers its final blow when the bedridden father dies. Starvation looms, and the mother feels that God has forgotten her. Her daughter, more trusting, urges her: 'Tell God, mother, that we are hungry'. The mother on her knees conveys this information, and in prompt response the miserly landlord deposits a basket of food inside their door. This supernal benevolence may seem to some readers a trifle ostentatious.

The stories lay no stress on vindictiveness or revenge in the punishment of evil-doers. Only in 'A Bush Adventure' is there a suggestion of this. The narrator (in 1854, the year of the Eureka Stockade) comes upon two men in the bush. They tie him up and take his money. Then they think he is one of the agitators for whom a reward is offered, and decide to take him to the police. He leads them on and confirms their suspicions. But once at the police station, he has no difficulty in proving he is an innocent citizen and that they are thieves. It is rather like what the American lawyers term 'entrapment'.

Young people, reading these healthy if occasionally unreal stories, could easily draw their own conclusions: crime does not pay; be good and work hard, and then Providence will reward you. It is, so to speak, an attractive business deal.

Some of the themes that writers utilized throughout the century derived from the differences between Australia and England. There was one subject, however, that was constant, independent of time and place—love: even in adventure stories it often had a minor place. A writer required originality on the one hand, or intensity on the other, to transform this commonplace. No writer before the 1880s, except Clarke, had much of either virtue. There are, however, a few later writers who have some claims to one or both.

As with some other women writers, the physical background, bush or city, of the short stories of Mrs A. Blitz in *Digger Dick's Darling* (1888) plays little part in the narrative: she deals with relationships within four walls, and women are the chief characters. Most, men and women, have recently arrived from England and find themselves enmeshed either in complicated series of events or emotional entanglements. Snobbery and the search for security or affluence play major parts, and here Blitz, though certainly snobbish in her own attitudes, at least recognizes that others are snobbish also and that their acts of kindness are often conditioned by the status of the recipients.

Her chief concern is with young love, where she can be as sickly as Dickens, but more prone to inflated formality. Like many others, she can inflict on her characters speech that today appears quite stagey and unreal. Her plots, now and then complex and absurd, are dependent for their resolution on coincidence. She likes her young people, mostly decent and honest, to be happy. Consequently, after a sequence of misfortunes or mistakes or threats, the sky clears and they receive their merited reward. She follows the old adage for a time, but cannot bear to do so for long: the course of true love, in Blitz's world, always runs smooth at last.

Of the writers on love Blitz is among the less important. The others in this period are more subtle in treatment, more adult in tone, and deal with other themes as well. As it happens, they all are better known for their novels than their short stories. An example is 'Tasma' (Jessie Couvreur). By one or two critics she has been regarded as the best of the writers of short stories before Lawson. One may doubt the verdict, and wonder if it has been influenced by the fame of her novel, *Uncle Piper of Piper's Hill* (1889). She did not write many stories; in her selection of them, *A Sydney Sovereign* (1890), for instance, there are only five. Not one of them equals the best of Clarke or Adams.

Her main fault is diffuseness. Not every story has a long explanatory or descriptive introduction, it is true, but even when she starts immediately upon a story she makes up for her restraint by pieces of elaboration on dress, or motive, or some other aspect. Her earlier story, 'Malus Oculus', published in *The Vagabond Annual* (1877), set in France and dealing with mesmerism, a fad at the time, which a reader might approach with an expectation of thrills to come, has a long slow start that provides little encouragement. Her second, 'The Rubria Ghost', in *The Australian Ladies' Annual* (1878), a rather pointless and unlikely tale of a young lover posing as a ghost near a station in Victoria, is wordy and ends unaccountably with moralizing.

Ten years later she still has not shed the habit entirely. 'Monsieur Caloche' appeared in *In Australian Wilds* (1889) and has had its share of praise, one critic terming it 'a little masterpiece'. But even here one may be a trifle impatient of the long detailed analysis of Sir Matthew Bogg, a wealthy, bullying businessman. It has its obvious function: displayed thus, he is to have a traumatic shock later which is dependent on the fact that, if not humane, he is human. The contrast, then, is presumably heightened by the elaborated initial picture, but it is all a little forced and mannered. One more example may be cited. In her best-known story, 'How a Claim Was Nearly Jumped in Gum-Tree Gully', a mate of the husband, finding he is in love with the wife, decides to go off. It has its own simple direct appeal, but is prefaced by a long section that sets the scene in language very different from Lawson's, in a place 'where only the magpie had hitherto tuned his voice on his own grotesquely melodious key, and pretentious native companions had not been afraid to stand in a ludicrous row.'

These aberrations of expression are found, luckily not in very

significant spots, in other of her stories. 'Barren Love' is an
example. The cynic, moved despite himself by the grief of a young
girl who bids farewell to her lover as the ship leaves England for
Australia, pities and loves unknown to her, has her looked after by
captain and steward, and gives her his money and saves her when
the ship catches fire and room can be found in the lifeboats only
for the women. Beauty has been preserved, but why did the Beast
not approach her before? He was in a dilemma: if he remained
anonymous, he suffered; if he came forward he ran the risk of shat-
tering his ideal, for a ready response from the girl would reveal her
as fickle. Tasma puts it: 'Were such a passion immediately trans-
ferable, at what value must the new recipient place it in the sum
of human emotions?' Such stiffness and formality of phrasing
almost present us with a legalistic subject of debate.

Her endings, on the other hand, unlike most of her beginnings,
are effective. In 'Monsieur Caloche', after a perhaps tedious first
half, the movement hastens near the end, and Sir Matthew Bogg
to his horror finds that the dead young man whom he has struck
with his whip is a girl. 'An Old-Time Episode in Tasmania' (which
is included in this anthology) ends with a revelation not likely to
be foreseen. Again, in a tale aptly entitled 'A Philanthropist's
Experiment', the kindly Boundy, 'maintaining that every entity
had what he called its "nook" in creation', on a trip to Europe
rescues a thin and starving woman and her child from a platform
in Paris and takes them to Burrumberie, a decayed mining township in Victoria, where he deposits them in the bosom of a
butcher's family. A few months later, on one of his periodic calls
at the butcher's, he is told that the woman has gone off with a
French swagman, leaving the child behind. The 'nook' of the
confirmed Parisian is obviously not Burrumberie.

This wry humour occurs in most of her stories, 'Monsieur
Caloche' being the notable exception. To call this cynicism would
be extreme, but there is a perceptible tartness. Even in 'Monsieur
Caloche' the ending has its ambiguity, Bogg, repentant at having
been in part the cause of the death of the girl—scarred with
smallpox and fleeing from her country—

left the bulk of his money to the purpose of constructing and maintaining
a magnificent wing to a smallpox hospital in the south of France. It was
stipulated that it should be called the 'Henriette' wing, and is, I believe
greatly admired by visitors from all parts of the world.

The second half of the concluding sentence may give us pause. Is
it simply bathos, a piece of unconscious ineptitude? Or does
Tasma, with her frequent insights into human vagaries, deliberately

glance sideways at the possible dividend that may accrue to a charitable act?

In 'A Sydney Sovereign', a thoroughly honourable man, falling in love with a vital young girl, feels constrained to marry the colourless woman who has remained faithful and hopeful for twelve years. In Tasma's words, 'Lucy's fidelity would prove too strong for him in the end'. One may pay dearly for decency. 'Barren Love', with different motivation involved, has something of the same irony. Philanthropy, in 'A Philanthropist's Experiment', is shown to lack worldly wisdom, and suffers accordingly. Even 'How a Claim Was Nearly Jumped' contains its dubieties about mateship. There are hints, for example, that the wife might not have been quite unresponsive to approaches from the husband's mate.

An acquaintance with her early life may lead us to think that there is much of Tasma in her fiction, all of which deals with different aspects of different kinds of love. In her novels men do not appear or manage very creditably. In her short stories, written earlier, they are finer creatures. But they are no more fortunate. In both novels and stories, then, men suffer or are defeated: in Tasma's fiction, at any rate, women (and Tasma?) get their own back.

Technique is more important than nuance in the seven stories in R. Spencer Browne's collection, *Romances of Gold Field and Bush* (1890), five of which deal with emotional relationships between men and women. The other two are more violent—'The Sub-Inspector's Story', where we have wholesale revenge taken on Aborigines for an attack on a station; and 'The Story of Wills' Leap' (reprinted here), where suicide solves some problems for the parties concerned.

The love stories are more subtle than these, if no less unusual. Sometimes the novelty resides in the narrative device—the narrator for instance receiving a bundle of letters from a man to the girl he could not marry because he was poor. Sometimes a situation, though trite, is handled fairly well: a girl marries a wealthy man to save her father from disgrace but later is enabled to marry the man she loved. Another ends less happily with the death of a woman to whom a man is hastening, having discovered he is really single, since his presumed wife, a 'danseuse' (a type presumably suspect), was already married when he married her. Equally unhappy is the story of a seducer who stabs his victim with the knife of her true love, who is consequently hanged.

Probably the best of Spencer Browne's love stories, with the most human and plausible theme, concerns two honourable but rather touchy persons, a prospering squatter who continually puts off proposing to the daughter of an even more prosperous squatter, and the girl herself. At length drought ruins the procrastinator; a proposal now is obviously out of the question. So the impasse continues despite the fact that he saves the girl from Aborigines and is wounded in the process. At last her father intervenes and puts sense into the pair. The cross-purposes and the resentments are competently handled, and even the providential interposition of the Aborigines does not unduly detract from the effect.

Another novelist occasionally turning to shorter fiction is Rosa Praed, in 1888 called by A. P. Martin 'the first of Australian novelists'. By 1893 she had written fifteen novels and was recognized in England as a literary figure. But short stories were a side-issue. Presumably they were less likely to be profitable or to attract much notice. Whatever the reason, she had not written many. Perhaps it was as well, for of her half-dozen or so published by then, only one today seems really adult.

In 'The Sea-Birds' Message' (1889?)[27] a little boy is punished by his cruel step-mother. His sister tries in vain to protect him. So they both run away, are lost, and die. It starts like a story for children and ends like a parable. 'A Disturbed Christmas in the Bush' (1890)[28] is an adventure, with a raid by Aborigines, the cause being a dusky beauty. 'Old Shilling's Bush Wedding' (1890)[29] portrays the comic mishaps of an elderly suitor who marries a robust young woman, who is Danish or Norwegian. Then Praed turned to myth and the supernatural in 'The Bunyip' (1891).[30] What was the strange cry from the lagoon heard in the camp? Was it certainly from a snake-bite that the little girl had died? There are oddities left unexplained, but they are disconnected and contrived.

The only tale that gives an indication of Praed's competence and her insights into human relationships, however limited in depth or subtlety, is 'Miss Pallavant': this story (reprinted here) is set in England and has no concern with Australian life—her fourteen years abroad had produced their effect. The description of Miss Pallavant—

She was certainly a striking-looking woman—tall, dark, slow in movement, and extremely graceful. She had soft, deep, violet eyes, jet black hair, a clear, pale complexion, and a fascinating, mysterious smile. She had a look of high fashion, and the air of expecting admiration as her due, though her supreme indifference to it was also remarkable—

27 in Martin (ed.), *Over the Sea.*
28 in Martin (ed.), *Under the Gum Tree.*
29 ibid.
30 in Martin (ed.), *Coo-ee.*

despite its generalized adjectives, contrasts to its advantage with the strained excesses of other writers

If there is little time, one must learn quickly. This is what E. W. Hornung did in the two to three years (1884–86) that he spent in Australia. After he returned to England he produced eight novels dealing wholly or partly with Australia, as well as a volume of seven stories, *Under Two Skies* (1892), of which four are Australian. The fiction he wrote later, dealing with Raffles, a criminal in fashionable circles, is that for which he was best known.

His four Australian tales are all set in the outback, on stations or in bush townships. The best is 'The Luckiest Man in the Colony', a wry semi-ironical story of a father's self-sacrifice. The other three may be called love stories because love is the central theme. But they have convolutions that make them rather different from the usual run. 'Jim of the Whim', for instance, builds gradually to an ending that is not quite a surprise ending for the reader but is for the unlucky man. 'Strong-Minded Miss Methuen' is more direct, the character of the girl evolving, its effect on others coming in bursts, and the relationship of father and daughter mounting to a denunciation. Something of the surprise ending is found in 'Sergeant Seth', where either of two decisions would be possible, not only in the mind of the novelist but also in the heart of the returning and repentant lover.

In each of these three stories a flaw in one of the characters is the cause of what follows. Two of them end unhappily, the third with only the possibility of happiness. A woman opens a letter not addressed to her, acts on the contents, which are misleading, and destroys the possibility of a happy marriage with the man who loves her. A young man, a reformed drunk, looks forward to rehabilitation with a woman, and finds his trust unexpectedly misplaced; so he returns to his former life and dies not long after. A man, who abandons a loving girl in Australia in order to claim his inheritance in England, becomes engaged to his former English love, but repents, is urged by her to act decently, and returns to Australia to find the girl he abandoned has turned, in despair, to his friend. In two of these tales, then, the women are guilty, in the other tale the man is. And there are overtones of irony in all three: the guilty ones act either for their own benefit, which they do not think of as selfish, or for what they think are good reasons. All seek happiness, and do so by individual acts. The results are outcomes they have not envisaged or consequences the opposite of what they intend. These designed turns of fortune where coincidence, once a favourite device, hardly enters, stand to Hornung's credit.

The last of the these writers on love spreads his net widely, is

more complex in his attitudes, and is the most significant of short
story writers up to 1893 apart from Clarke. In general terms,
Francis Adams is either simply better than or pleasingly different
from most short-story writers who preceded him. In only a few
particulars does he appear as inept, and even then a reader feels that
his is a failure of art and theirs is a failure of ignorance. His openings, for instance, often seem too long: but then we can find that
the description of the meeting with the narrator or the account of
the narrator himself may help to enrich the story. Again, the
prolixity, the occasional side-issues of reminiscence, often dis-
tracting, sometimes could be construed as having some importance,
however minor.

The other weakness, at least to modern ears and eyes, lies in
some applications of his style. In general he writes a better prose
than most of his predecessors, but the control can become literary,
in a pejorative sense; an old rather illiterate narrator, for example,
may talk in polysyllables. And the dialogue still mouths and
grimaces. Even the educated, we may feel, do not normally speak
like a poetic character in an affected play:

She is the sort of feminine type one meets in the drawing-rooms of old
superb civilisations, one of the ladies of Imperial Rome, or medieval Florence or Venice, at the court of Henri Quatre . . . The music to which such
a woman walks is that of a Galuppi or a Chopin . . . ('Miss Jackson')[31]

And then, to atone, Adams can reproach us for too carping a
reaction by being allusively acute; a vignette, for example, gathers
to unexpected point:

the little crowd gathered round Paddy and listened with that solemn silence
peculiar to a country crowd which listens to the earnest exposition of
opinion with which it does not disagree. ('The Last of the Bushrangers')[32]

For the rest, he is much in advance of the other writers. In modes
of narration he is almost experimental: he uses both first person and
third person in telling a story, and sometimes both in the one story;
or the narrative is in letter form to a friend; or he divides a story
into parts—morning, noon, night, corresponding, he suggests, to
birth, life, death—which is not very startling, but which does stress
the stages in a young man's life. Oddly enough, it does not seem
too heavily symbolic. Or, more technically innovative, he starts a
story at the point where the course of events is about to end; one
participant quite naturally retraces for his listener the events up to
that point; and then the suspended ending, gradually becoming

31 in *Australian Life* (1892).
32 ibid.

evident to the reader as to the listener, occurs with an air of inevitability. It is true that sometimes previous writers do attempt experiments, but none has the variety that Adams exhibits.

Most of the stories in his *Australian Life* (1892) are set in Queensland, and deal with three subjects—violence, the supernatural, love. Neither of the two dealing with the supernatural is very effective, though one ('The Hut by the Tanks') has for some reason or other been the most frequently reprinted of his tales.

The stories of violence are brutal and powerful, each telling of one or more killings. One, dealing with two youthful bushrangers, has its ironical implications. The leader, confident in his superior intelligence, thinks his companion a liability who has been the cause of some failures. Almost on the spur of the moment he shoots him. Freed from the incompetent, he will, he feels sure, succeed in his plans. But the shot is heard by two riders passing some distance away. And this leads to his later capture, trial, and condemnation. Intelligence has not allowed for chance.

The other two tales deal with the relations between whites and blacks; and they provide a contrast between what a man seems to be and what a man does. In one, a huge simple man is kindly, but he kills thirteen blacks. In the other, a man in north Queensland is highly thought of by a friend:

He comes of very good family, I believe. He's an educated gentleman . . . a very decent fellow, take him all round, and kind-hearted too, and wouldn't hurt a fly unnecessarily . . . ('The Red Snake')

We are perhaps prepared for some excusable excesses when the friend goes on to say that 'a man needn't be quite a fiend because he'll shoot blacks when his blood's up'. It is an illuminating glance at current attitudes of the period, but it hardly prepares us for all that follows in the story—the calculated shooting of fourteen blacks. The attitude of Adams, whether favourable, neutral, ambivalent, or condemnatory, is not apparent.

It is variations on love, however, that concern Adams most. This is generally shown as an intense emotion, enthralling the victim. 'Lily Davenant' describes a coquette, a woman who both entrances and rejects, but the man even after a final parting wants to hear of her. More dismissive is the young woman in 'A Bush Girl', who finds a young Englishman affected and complacent especially after his remark: 'You thought I was too proud, I suppose—that I would never ask you to marry me?' But rejection can take harsher forms, and so too can the reactions. In Adams' stories men and women can die from unrequited love—or at least have their deaths hastened. Kate Robinson, in the story bearing her name, dies of

love—or is it typhus? So with Dick Ward—or it is consumption?
Sometimes rejection is avenged. Ward's death, related by his friend
to the woman who married for wealth, shocks and distresses her.
Or a man, now acceptable (after success) to the woman (now a
wealthy widow), berates her and rejects in his turn. More violent
are three ambiguous stories: 'Dr Fletcher's Love Story', where
either a very young girl of her own accord poisoned her older rival
or was iñduced to do so, or else an attractive and increasingly
sinister figure in the background did so; 'Miss Jackson', where the
woman may or may not have pushed overboard the man who may
or may not have seduced her, but who at any rate has grown tired
of her; and 'Aggy', where the violently embittered lover may
have returned years later and strangled the woman who rejected
him. They are not cheerful stories: not one ends happily. A reader
may wonder vaguely and vainly if that short disease, his life, cast
its embrowning shadow over Adams' fiction.

Not less unusual are the endings, noted for instance in the last
three stories above. Adams is a connoisseur, one is tempted to say,
of the inconclusive. The narrator tells with an air of uncertainty the
things he has observed; they have deeply impressed him, but the
connection between the events is not certain. The explanation of
a puzzle or the rational analysis of a mysterious vision is left to the
reader: not only is there no solution in the story, there is no attempt
at a solution. Not all the stories end like this, but there are enough
of them to mark Adams as a practitioner of the teasing or
provocative.

His best stories, probably the brutal ones, are more brutal, more
graphic, than those of Clarke, but they lack that veneer of brilliance.
The two, Clarke and Adams, each writing novels and journalistic
pieces and criticism as well, are the best writers of short stories
before Lawson.

It would be invidious to single out a particular collection of
stories as typical of the two decades before Lawson, for the
majority of them are banal enough, at least in themes they exploit.
But *An Austral Christmas* (1888) has some claims to representative-
ness, for it not only contains standard subjects, but also contains
no foreign ingredient. Its author, J. C. F. Johnson, chooses the
early 1850s as the period, the goldfields and bush townships as the
setting. Of the eleven pieces in the volume, eight are short stories
with such subjects as a comic ghost, self-sacrifice by a poorly-
esteemed fellow, a person whose tough resistant exterior covers the
kindness and softness beneath, farcical trickery, a child lost and
found in the bush, a deserving new chum having good fortune.

Despite a certain liveliness and some flavour and humour

provided by his use of dialect and colloquialism, Johnson is of his time with its failings. Occasionally he has, as it were, learned to be ineffective; the child Bonny Nellie, for example, too good not to be lost in the bush, is described almost in the words Clarke used of Pretty Dick. If the collection has any originality, it resides in the structure: men gather for a Christmas party on Carringa Station, and each is required to tell a story. Another collection of this kind is *Stories Told Around the Camp Fire* (188–) by G. C. Evans. The device of course is almost immemorial in literature, but it is not so common in nineteenth-century Australia. And some credit may be given to Johnson for occasionally differentiating the styles of the narrators.

A contemporary of Johnson's, J. A. Barry, was a professionally competent writer for whom almost any character, scene or incident could provide the basis of a readable yarn. He sold his stories readily to the *Australasian*, the *Queenslander* and other periodicals in Australia, and the *Pall Mall Gazette* in England. And when he gathered them into a volume, *Steve Brown's Bunyip* (1893), it went into three editions in the same year. He travelled and worked in widely separated places, so that he was kept busy. He says in his Note that the stories 'were written in the rare intervals of leisure afforded by a roving life over sea and land; and are, in many instances, records of personal adventure'.

Now it would not be too difficult to pillory Barry—if one made discreet and biased selections. His humour, for instance, can be vaudevillian, and the title story supports the assessment, being highly improbable and dealing with stock subjects. But then in justice a reader must cite 'The Duke of Silversheen' and admit that it is natural and ingenious and funny. In his other stories, too, we often find that the unacceptably trite has its compensatory counterpart. The tired theme of beautiful child lost in the bush, 'Dot's Claim', we can readily discard, but 'Keeping School at "Dead Finish"' is a true enough and effective enough picture of certain outback areas. One of his stories of revenge, 'A Cape Horn Christmas', is vaguely supernatural and highly melodramatic, but 'Sojur Jim' (which is included in this anthology) has a grimness that is adequately matched by its telling. His stories of the sea are not very likely, and can depend too much on coincidence, but his stories of the outback can give us glimpses and even insights that are unexpected. Here he is best in his treatment of small bush townships: 'The Officer in Charge' is a good sketch, while 'Books at Barracaboo' is probably the only story we have of the itinerant outback book vendor.

Barry, then, is full of faults and redemptions. When we have readable and racy prose, a story easy to follow and possessing a

facile appeal, then we may feel we are a trifle ungrateful in deni-
grating the author. But we come to feel that he is too much of his
age. He favours decent folk, even the working class, though he
clearly prefers the well-to-do such as the squatters; and he belongs,
or would wish to belong, to the 'old boy' class. When dealing with
Aboriginals, he is, like many others, fleetingly sympathetic but
generally mistrustful: the blacks may be expected to attack whenever they have a suitable opportunity; the whites, outnumbered,
can use their superior intelligence. There is something of the
schoolboy adventure spirit in his stories. He provides adequate
means of passing idle moments—which was precisely his intention.

Less competent is A. G. Hales, whose first book *The Wanderings
of a Simple Child* (1890), is made up of bits of autobiography, brief
character sketches of local identities, pictures of the area round
Silverton and Broken Hill in the 1880s, much of it reprinted from
the *Barrier Miner*. Some incidents are told baldly and with little
apparent art. Hales writes in a style that is influenced by and often
nearly parodies the more calculated prose of Bret Harte and Mark
Twain. Indeed his contemporaries were aware of this, and Hales
became known as 'the Bret Harte of the Barrier'. His attempts at
humour provide the most obvious targets: the literary vulgar ('I sit
me down to chronicle the deeds'), the stock phrases ('the editorial
sanctum'; 'a sporting scribe'), the portentously solemn ('not
desiring to exclusively enjoy the sweet charm of my own society
on the track'), pretended dignity ('smote some one else on the
frontispiece'), the mock epic ('Now it came to pass in those days'),
and so on.

Now, after such an outline, dismissal may seem appropriate.
And yet in a few stories there is a sort of casual impact that leaves
its traces: the reader is not absolutely certain that there is nothing
more intended. One shocking story, 'Chinese Ginnie' (reprinted
here), tells how forty Chinese prospectors were driven from a claim
with pick handles, and two of them were killed and 'had to be
planted later on in an old abandoned shaft'. The racial overtones
are similar to those in Lawson's poem, 'The Cambaroora Star'. In
a writer of a different calibre it could easily be an ironically
'patriotic' story. Nearer to irony is 'Bob the Finisher', half-comic,
half-serious—that's how death was regarded in that area, at that
time.

The comment by Jack Drayton that Hales' book was the first to
reflect Australian nomadic life is probably true. To that extent
Hales anticipated Lawson. And in an occasional paragraph we may
momentarily feel that we are reading Lawson; but it is only for a

moment, only by contrast with some of the pious inanities that preceded both.

More professional in style and effect is Ernest Favenc, the author of about a dozen volumes, half of them poetry and fiction. In his preface to Favenc's *The Last of Six: Tales of the Austral Tropics* (1893) Rolf Boldrewood claimed:

> In these 'Tales of the Austral Tropics' will be found the strange romances which write themselves, often in letters of blood, amid the half-unknown, mysterious regions of Tropical Australia. That they are not less true than terrible, I take it upon myself to affirm.

Boldrewood goes on to contrast the tales with most other writing 'professing to describe Australian life and character', so it seems that 'true' here means characteristic of the period or place, rather than historically factual: which is just as well for Boldrewood's credibility. When, for example, in 'A Haunt of the Jinkarras' we encounter hairy, smelly, chattering 'savages of the most degraded type' living underground, yet having control over fire and possessing three inches of tail, we can justifiably attribute their existence to Favenc's imagination.

More extravagantly, but more orthodoxly, this imagination is employed in his tales of fantasy and the supernatural—'Spirit-Led', where an epileptic is abruptly transformed into a skeleton which 'the outcast spirit was striving desperately to reanimate', or 'The Spell of the Mas-Hantoo', a treasure hunt for gold or diamonds guarded by a vast serpent, or 'The Track of the Dead', in which footprints of the dead lead the living. In some stories the emotional strain is so great that participants become temporarily or permanently insane.

Favenc's own wide experiences in the outback serve him well in stories of certain localities—the Gulf area and some desert and mountain terrains. Perhaps the most striking is 'A Lucky Meeting', when only familiarity with the conditions could have produced the picture, an almost technical portrayal.

His attitude to the Aborigines is reasonably impartial—a sympathy for their losses, a pity for their sufferings, an understanding of their revenge. In 'Pompey', the existence of a half-caste boy leads eventually to tragedy, when in a 'dispersal' father and son unknowingly kill each other.

Favenc's forte lies in his invention, his ability to construct plots and endings. Sometimes this results in comedy, as in 'The Parson's Blackboy', his best-known story; at other times in solutions of mystery, for instance in 'The Mystery of Baines' Dog'. But the stories have an air of being consciously built: one can faintly hear the wheels going round. It is this impression that weakens the effect of 'That Other Fellow', a story of a friend's abnegation in court-ship, bearing some resemblance to Tasma's 'How a Claim Was Nearly Jumped in Gum-Tree Gully', and having some of Lawson's insight without his deceptive ease.

The variety in these seventeen stories, some of which appeared in the *Bulletin*, is wide—adventure, revenge, fantasy, supernatural, detection, comedy, and mateship. All, however melodramatic or brutal, have the quality of readability, all have vigour and move-ment; even the poorest are better than most of their predecessors; but even the best are not the equal of many to come.

Of the sixty-five or so collections of short stories published between 1880 and 1893, even a student of our literature might be excused for not being familiar with more than about half a dozen. These would include the collections by Tasma, Adams, Warung, Favenc. But perhaps the best-known volume would be *A Golden Shanty* (1890), Archibald's selection from the columns of the *Bulletin* from 1880 to 1890. More than half of this volume is verse. The prose comprises seven tales and sketches, three of them by Edward Dyson, one by Lawson ('His Father's Mate'). The remaining three are pieces ostensibly humorous, drink playing a large part.

Lawson had contributed so far only two stories to the *Bulletin*, the other being 'The Story of Malachi', the dope as hero, an unim-pressive piece. As for 'His Father's Mate', most modern readers would call it an indulgence, partly because of its prose, mostly because of its piling up of unmerited misfortunes—the death of the boy, then that of the father, then the just-too-late arrival of the elder son. Lawson has squeezed out of that situation all the pathos it was likely to yield.

Dyson's three stories show him as essentially of his age, or even of a period ten or twenty years earlier. He is, for example, rabidly racist, like so many before him. The Chinese in 'A Golden Shanty' (which gives its name to the volume) are 'Chows', forming 'a colony of squalid, gibbering Chinese fossickers'. Their thefts and deceit are detected, and they are driven empty-handed away. 'Mr and Mrs Sin Fat' (which is reprinted here), shows the same bias. The third story, 'The Washerwoman of Jacker's Flat', set in a mining township, contains a number of stock characters—a large coarse brutal man, a dandy, a besotted drunk, his guileless vulner-able daughter, and a big masculine woman who does washing. And the story itself has the fairly worn ingredients of former tales—the girl betrayed giving birth to a boy; her later suicide; the adoption of the child by the washerwoman; the contributions of the township to help rear it; the rise to eminence of the orphan when he grows up, hinted at but not detailed.

It says a lot for Dyson's ingenuity and originality that the handicap of trite materials has not rendered these stories sterile. Despite characters that have been handled often enough and situations all too familiar, he manages to provide some arrangements that have a novel twist to them—old pieces, new patterns. Moreover he could draw on first-hand experiences in the city and on the diggings. And the vividness and liveliness that the *Bulletin* welcomed, even demanded—but did not invariably get—were qualities he could readily supply. Except for some orotund circumlocution that then passed for humour, his style is one that does not too loudly alert us to old-fashioned clumsiness on the one hand or hollow inflation on the other.

It is worth noting that the *Bulletin* was ten years old by the time it published this volume. The result of its efforts over that period to foster Australian fiction was, if this volume is the witness, three short stories, which are inferior to the best of Clarke and Adams. But Dyson's do have an atmosphere that is to be found only occasionally in any of the writers that preceded him—the indefinable smell or suggestion or feel of the places where they are set. Romanticism has not diluted realism, no vague wash of words bleaches out the details.

It is convenient enough to end with a writer who does not fit into any of the previous useful, if a little artificial, classifications. The brutalities inflicted on convicts under the System might be thought a promising, if distasteful, theme. But so far no short story writer had treated it except incidentally. Now at long last William Astley was to do it more than justice. By the end of 1891, under the pen-name of Price Warung, he had contributed to the *Bulletin* over fifty short stories, in three series, nearly all of which dealt with convictism. In 1892 was published his *Tales of the Convict System*, containing eleven tales from the first series.

Warung had collected and studied convict records, and had over a period of years talked with Dr Henry Graham, formerly an official in the System for about ten years. The stories, then, might be considered historical reconstructions, modified by the demands of the short story form. They are, claims the Preface to the volume, 'true in essence', not necessarily objective accounts of particular incidents. The Preface says: 'There is not one in which the motive has not been suggested by, or based upon, fact . . . the writer feels that he can honestly claim that he has sought to communicate

. . . the quality of historic truth.' His aim was the preservation of 'the appropriate local colour and the historic atmosphere, and not the mere presentment of dramatic episodes'.

Oddly enough, the result is almost completely the opposite. A reader is fascinated by the details, the occasional introduction of historical figures under their own names, the places, and the circumstances. A particular incident may not have occurred just as Warung relates it, but others we know of, quite similar, did occur. Despite the disclaimer, it is the 'mere presentment of dramatic episodes' that is the essence of the stories. It is the claim to the overall effect, 'the historic atmosphere', that leaves us sceptical.

All this, of course, is quite irrelevant if we consider the tales merely as tales, as fiction. But since Warung was at pains to stress the essential general truth of his presentation, there seems warrant enough to discuss the matter.

The black and brutal account that Warung gives us is true enough, if not quite true in particular incidents, as an account of things that *could* happen. The objection is that it is all so highly selective: Warung's settings and incidents come from the small areas of 'secondary offenders'—Macquarie Harbour, Port Arthur, Norfolk Island—which contained only a small proportion of the convicts. Of those assigned as servants or those freed under varying conditions he makes little mention. And there was, even then, another world in the colony outside felonry. So that a reader soon begins to feel that he is being confronted with a highly biased picture. Officials are corrupt: 'from the Representative of Royalty to the vilest prisoner-constable there was no degree of administration that, at times, failed to "cook" its reports' ('The Special Commission'). The (seemingly) reluctant qualification, 'at times', a sort of parenthetical concession, it is easy to glide over and forget. Individual officials fare no better at his hands: the not-so-noxious Barron Field, for example, is portrayed as a veritable Judge Jeffreys.

Parsons are sometimes good and merciful, sometimes venal and heartless; but for the most part employment under the System corrupts them. Chaplain Ford, at first, does not envision what he will feel 'in the future, when being completely embruted, he would come to regard it as a very curious circumstance indeed that Christ had omitted eulogistic reference to the System from the Sermon on the Mount'. The convicts themselves, instead of being reformed, are simply confirmed or submerged in criminality:

'The Probation Gang' was the latest invention of the English people, through their authorities, for the reform of transports, and more than any other device had it been successful in the multiplication of vice and in the contamination of younger and less guilty convicts.

While he shows convicts in general brutalized by the System, with a few better types vainly resisting the process, and a few conscious of innocence and the injustice of their sentence, Warung does not idealize them: Convict Glancy (sentenced to seven years for stealing a silk handkerchief)

will suffer the extreme penalty of the law for having, in an intemperate moment, objected to the mild discipline with which a genial and loving motherland had sought to correct his criminal tendencies. In other words, Convict Glancy, metaphorically goaded by the wordy insults and literally by the bayonet-tip of one of his motherland's reformatory agents—to wit, Road-gang Overseer James Jones—had scattered J. J.'s brains over a good six square yards of metalled roadway.

With what passes for subtlety he glances at a group: 'With these nine we have nothing to do here. They were very ordinary offenders, killers of warders, fellow-gangers, and so on.'

Free citizens, though less violent, are no less brutal. In an account of a mass execution, by hanging, of twelve convicts Warung depicts the onlookers' 'delirium of blood-thirst. The people of Hobart Town were about to enjoy a rare treat, and their lips were dry for it'.

This fearsome state of affairs, Warung insists again and again, was the product of England. Now the System had ended some fifty years earlier in New South Wales, and about thirty-five years earlier in Tasmania, so reform of abuses was not his problem. A reader develops an uneasy feeling that the corpus is an indictment of English society, that the stories were written to a considered aim: Warung is a prosecutor before the bar of history. If we ask why, then only surmises answer: some real or fancied misfortunes of his own family in England; the possible influence of Dr Graham; his own researches, which confirmed his democratic sympathies; a purely business arrangement, with Archibald (anti-English) of the *Bulletin* encouraging him, and the *Bulletin* welcoming his stories. Even those who are not confirmed cynics may give weight to this last. It is true that Warung after parting from the *Bulletin* went on to write other convict stories for others papers, but why not? He had gained a competence in a certain field.

It may be repeated that much of this is extra-literary, and that truth in detail or distortion in the whole does not make the stories better or worse. But some of the passages quoted can give us insights into Warung's talents and weaknesses. Writing at the same time as Lawson, and publishing his first volume just before

Lawson's, with his oddities he often reminds us of an earlier age. He is free for the most part from its more blatant absurdities, but he still has some of its trademarks. His irony, for instance, with its repetitions and stress, is heavy-handed. He has no hesitation in employing coincidence when he finds it convenient. He can be bombastic and melodramatic. At the other extreme he melts into sentimentality: the wife of a good parson plays the organ at the request of convicts when they are led out to be hanged on beautiful Norfolk island:

Smiled on daily by the softest and bluest of skies, its witchery never stole into their hearts till the organ proclaimed their kinship with the eternal world . . . When the instrument sang, it filled sin-stained breasts with unutterable aspirations . . . she played as she had never played before, and, as she ended, a peculiar sound that was neither a sob nor a sigh, but like unto both, arose from the grey and yellow ranks, as an echo to the dying chord.

'It seemed to me,' she said simply to her husband that night, 'like an angel's heart-break.'

More usually, the pictures he gives, whether of persons or places or happenings, are grim, brutal, repellant. As good an example as any from his first volume is the almost technical analysis of the art of flogging as practised by Scourger Muggins:

he could 'cross the cuts' with such nicety as to define small rectangles on the flesh with almost mathematical exactitude . . . and he could detach with each tail of whipcord a narrow strip of skin. Indeed . . . he could compass with his left hand that most brilliant of all flogging feats—the marking of the back with three rows of pendant strips of skin, with one drop of blood, no more, tipping each point of cuticle, like a glowing ruby on a piece of velvet.

This lovingly detailed picture may strike many readers as psycho-logically perverse, but it is rationally directed. Warung knew what he was doing—he penned the account to produce the revulsion: that was what the System could be, that was the sort of man it employed, that was what it could do to human beings. He wanted from his readers certain reactions to extremes of human behaviour, and he employed extreme means to ensure that. It is success of a particular kind. And it is in this respect that we may lodge objec-tions. His concern is with the material, the tangible, the physical; he does not concern himself with the inner life of his characters. In consequence we find no extension, no aura or spread of implication.

Warung then is unique, a polemicist in fiction. Nobody rivals him in his field; in fact there is nobody else in his field. The wry comment of course follows: Who could want to be his rival, to exhaust the dregs of that bitter cup with that fascinated deliberated assiduity? And does this feeling that Warung was writing as a prosecutor provide a sort of spurious absolution for our uneasy and guilty satisfaction in Warung's stories?

Retrospect and Prospect

The short-story writers discussed here covered most of the themes that Lawson and others were to deal with in the 1890s. The best-known novelists, on the other hand, concentrated on a few standard themes such as pastoral life, the convict system, and bushranging. They did not cover town life, for example, until the late 1880s, when Rosa Praed, Tasma, and Ada Cambridge used that setting and its products.

The short-story writers spread their nets widely. They produced of course genres like mystery and detection, the supernatural, the historical, the story with a moral, and one or two recurrent themes such as encounters with Aboriginals, the lost child; but these and the variations within them exhibited a great diversity. No particular situation or character, even of the most obvious and bizarre kind, served as a recurrent object of attention; there was, for instance, nothing like Varney the Vampire or Sweeney Todd, two grotesque gothic figures that fascinated cheap fiction writers in England from the late 1840s.

Within the diversity there is no obvious tradition or line of development in the history of the short stories. Even short stories based on the historical records have no noticeable connecting thread apart from their ostensible sources. This is seen in the examples like Lang, the imaginative dealer in incidents; Clarke, the literate historian of characters and periods; George Sutherland in *Tales of the Goldfields* (1880), biographer and historian; W. H. Suttor, rather more inventive than either of the last two despite his assertion that there was 'little or nothing imaginative in the volume'; W. T. Pyke in *Australian Heroes and Adventurers* (188–) and *True Tales of the Early Days* (1890), rather like an editor of documents and letters; Thomas Walker, belying the title of his volume *The Felonry of New South Wales* (1891), dealing with crimes of various kinds outside as well as within the System; Warung, affirming the documentary truth of his horrors.

One might think that the System with its brutalities would (as in the novels) have resulted in a genre. But it did not. There is practically nothing of it in Lang. Clarke, it has been claimed was determined in his stories 'to tell the whole truth about the horror which had been the early reality of life in colonial Australia', but one finds little more than brief generalities. (Even in 'Port Arthur 1870' he is satisfied with a few vivid comments, as in his visit to a cell containing an aged lunatic convict: '"We find that a man who does more than twelve months' solitary," said Mr Dale in a whisper, "becomes weak in his mind." '

Only Warung, consistently, obsessively, deals with this theme.

There are only a few themes in the stories before Lawson that were to be dealt with by him or were to persist. One that did, however, is 'mateship'. There was some fellowship among convicts, loyalty among those linked by resistance to brutal authority. Those who hate are kin. But there was also disloyalty, betrayal with hope of pardon or reward. And constables, overseers, and scourgers, venting thwarted and released hostility on their charges, were drawn generally from convict ranks. Even among the Irish convicts, bound by national sentiment and political aspirations as well as by a common hatred of the English, informers existed. News of the rising at Castle Hill in 1804, mostly led and shared by Irish convicts, had been previously leaked to the authorities, who refused to credit it. In the words of J. B. Hirst, in his *Convict Society and Its Enemies* (1983), 'convict treachery was generally regarded as the basic guarantee of the colony's safety.'

There was loyalty among 'bolters' and later bushrangers like the gold-rush bandits and the rebels against officialdom (such as the Kelly gang)—and also betrayal.

Mutual dependence, friendship perhaps, also appeared in the outback. To move into the vast emptiness was to encounter a constant and unforgiving foe—the land, with its distances and dangers. It was folly to depend only on oneself, so men went in pairs or small groups. This is when mateship developed into a more dependable if sometimes sexual relationship. Yet even here there were dark undercurrents. Mates did not have to be friends. Lawson's neglected comments later in 'Crime and the Bush' bear witness:

You might be mates with a man in the bush for months, and be under the impression that you are on the best of terms with him, or even fancy that he has a decided liking for you, and yet he might brood over some fancied slight or injury—something you have said or done, or haven't said or done—anything, in fact, that might suggest itself to an ignorant, morose, and vindictive nature—until his alleged mind is in such a diseased condition that he is capable of turning on you any moment of the day or night and doing you to death.

The gold rushes incubated a mateship of shared endeavour in groups of two or three or four diggers working a claim, victims of *auri sacra fames*, the cursed hunger for gold. There was of course not necessarily friendship between groups. Nor was there invariably trust within a group. Mrs Clacy in her *Lights and Shadows of Australian Bush Life* (1854) confirms this: 'perhaps the greatest drawback a steady man will experience at the diggings is the being cheated by his "mates"'.

Thirty years later A. J. Boyd in *Old Colonials* (1882) comments: "a most remarkable confidence and trust is reposed in the banking establishment by men who would not trust even their mates with their hard-earned gold.'

A communal bond developed from the shared hostility in the early years of the rushes—the widespread hostility to officialdom, to the troopers or 'joes' who descended on the diggings to examine licences and to arrest those who did not have them.

The growth of unions near the end of the century expressed both the hostility to employers and the desire for greater economic security. Those who broke ranks were a danger to the movement and were 'scabs', a bitter term that revealed fear as well as hate.

Some of these aspects are found in the short stories before Lawson, but there is little that interprets friendship or dependability among men as an Australian patent as 'mateship'. The concept owes much to him, and the finished product is his. Here, however, as elsewhere Lawson is ambivalent: a man as a writer and a man as a man can be two different things. The champion of mateship in his stories is described by Ray Lindsay writing to Jack Lindsay (*The Roaring Twenties*): '*Bulletin* old-timers who knew Lawson well have told me that he was a thoroughly unpleasant character with as much feeling of "mateship" as a crab walking frontwards'.

It is chiefly in the outback that Lawson sets his stories of mateship. Like some others, he saw the bushmen as the 'real', the typical Australians. In *The Australians* (1893) Francis Adams classically enunciates the dogma: 'The one powerful and unique national type yet produced in Australia is,' I have asserted, that of the Bushman'.

It is, however, not difficult to find earlier stories and sketches that provide wry qualifications. In *Echoes from Bushland* (1881) by Reginald Crawford (?) one of the stories, 'Our Minister', tells how it is a drunk who helps the parson save his family in a flood: the people of the township are deaf to his pleas. There are some satirical glances in another story, 'A Political Banquet', where politicians and country people are depicted with some humour and as much distaste. Garnet Walch in his *Annual* (1882) provides a sketch

of a country township—Sloptown (population 450). He visits it
during rain, which does not add to its attractiveness, and he is glad
to leave it.

There does not appear in the earlier stories much recognition of
what Lawson was to express, the muted heroism of those who
lived in loneliness and deprivation among such surroundings,
resistant, self-dependent. It is a matter of response. Some of the
writers knew the bush quite well and depicted conditions and
incidents with fidelity—to the externals. They had keen eyes. So
had Lawson. But there was something else: Lawson, with his
uncertainties, his resentments, his raw touchiness, was by
comparison a man without a skin. That sensitivity, together with
a knowledge and appreciation of the life lived by outback people,
was to make the difference. And the details of living, the feel of
surroundings, the cups or pannikins people drank from—these
seldom appeared in the stories before Lawson. And there should
be added Lawson's apparent naturalness. There are good stories
before him, but in them we are conscious of the words that
transmit the message, that evoke the scene. It was Conrad who
wrote that he sought to render this veil of words transparent. Often
in Lawson we can feel that we are in direct touch with an actuality—it has not transpired through a verbal medium.

A Dispersal

'I AM VEXED that you should be dragged out on such a miserable expedition as this', said Stevenson to me as we rode together; 'but you know my motives. I feel very sad when I think of the fate about to befall these unhappy wretches. I can venture to say this much to you. Were I to speak thus to nine out of ten squatters, they would stare at me in astonishment. It is enough for them that these blacks have killed white men. They must, therefore, be shot down if they run, or be hanged if they are taken alive. But I cannot help feeling that all those so-called murders were perpetrated by these ignorant savages in retaliation for innumerable atrocities practised by the overlanders and their men, who, until a year or two back, when this station was first formed, used to travel from the Sydney side with their sheep and cattle to take up this country. Had we white men only done our duty by these poor creatures, and used our superior power a little more mercifully when we seized and occupied their country, such atrocities as those we are now going to punish would never have occurred. It is enough to make one's blood run cold to hear some of my neighbours speak of these blacks. "How many did you shoot when you came over?" one will ask another. "Only eleven," he will reply. "How many did you?" "Fourteen altogether." And in town I have more than once met— gentlemen, I suppose I must call them—who openly asserted that they made it a point to *shoot all they came across*.'

'I have heard men say the same,' I replied, 'more than once, when in Melbourne. It is perfectly horrible.'

Walters riding up at this moment put a stop to the conversation, and presently we overtook the troop.

The blacks whom we were going to surprise were stationed six miles off, at the upper end of a long plain, and a hundred yards or so from the banks of a creek, which for some miles above their camp was closely bordered on one side by a swamp and on the other by mallee scrub. The miamis were pitched near the lower end of the swamp (which was on the right or station side of the water-course), and in such a position that the blacks could see all over the plain the approach of danger, and, taking to the reeds, could escape across the creek into the mallee, which there ended, abruptly extending back in a solid wall at right angles with the bank for half a mile. After passing the camp, the creek wound through the centre of a perfectly level open plain, which plain was bounded on one side by a dense wall of scrub, and on the other by a line of open timber; both the mallee and the timber running parallel to the general course of the creek, at a distance of ten or twelve hundred yards, except at a spot one mile down, where a point or promontory of scrub approached the bank much more closely. At that part of the creek there was an out-station hut.

It happened, however, that the lower portion of the swamp, which protected the rear of the blacks from the approach of horsemen, was almost entirely detached from the upper by a bay or indentation of the plain; and guided by young Harris, who also knew the ground well, and favoured by the hour, the darkness, and a high cold wind which had sprung up, accompanied with a drizzling rain, the troops succeeded in passing the blacks and reaching this spot unobserved. Descending into the bed of the stream, which was nearly dry, and ten feet below the surrounding plain, nine of the twelve, with Walters and myself, then silently crept down it, until we came opposite to the fires. A scout sent forward to reconnoitre reported that, entirely unsuspicious that their dreaded enemies were near them, the blacks and their dogs were all lying close, and sheltered from the cold wind and rain beneath their miamis, and apparently all asleep. Walters had planted three sentries in the interval between the two swamps, and across the creek at the edge of the scrub, which terminated just opposite that spot; the lower part of the swamp continuing some two hundred yards farther down the watercourse. If any of the blacks, therefore, escaped into this lower patch of reeds, they would be prevented from passing higher up the creek, or across the intervening two hundred yards of plain, into the mallee scrub.

My feelings were not very pleasant as I stood by my horse's head shivering, and watching over the edge of the bank the showers of sparks which the wind, now increased to a gale, caught up and scattered over the plain. I felt sorry for the miserable destiny of the poor creatures for whom we had prepared so unpleasant an awakening. But I cannot say my sentiments were at all shared by my companions. The rascals were all alive with energy, and waited impatiently for the moment when they were to be let loose on their unfortunate countrymen. Not that they had the slightest desire to avenge the deaths of the white men; they were not so weak; but because, under the guise of duty, they hoped to wreak their vengeance upon those whom they regarded as their hereditary enemies. I had heard their commander tell them to capture, not kill; and very much disgusted they were with the order. I fully appreciated Stevenson's reluctance to let loose such a set on his blacks.

The different colonial government, well aware of the savage and bloodthirsty character of these same native border police, had often meditated suppressing the force altogether. But they had hitherto found themselves unable to do so. White constables are useless on the borders. It is only the aboriginal, with his keen senses and power of tracking his enemy, who can be depended upon to protect the settlers in those districts where native outrages prevail, or to inflict chastisement upon the perpetrators of them.

With the first faint streak of dawn the cry of the mopoke rang through the foliage above our heads. It was the signal agreed upon, and emerging from the bed of the creek the troopers silently placed themselves in a semicircle between the reeds and the eight or ten miamis which constituted the camp; and, removing the pads which had deadened the sound of their advance, waited until the blacks should become aware of their presence. Like most savages who are given to surprise their enemies, the Australian aboriginal is yet careless in guarding against surprise. It was broad daylight before a shrill cry announced that they were at last aware of their danger. Springing up from their sleep, and taking in the whole situation at a glance, they fled in a body over the plain, the only way left open for them. Guided by Harris and Stevenson, who had remained behind the reeds, but who now rode out and across the course of the fugitives, the troopers galloped after, and soon succeeded in securing the murderers, of whom one only offered any resistance. This was. an active fellow, who had caught up a spear and waddy; the first he fixed as he ran, and hurled at one of the troopers, who dexterously diverted it with his sword; and when Walters, who had selected and followed him, called on him to surrender, his reply was a blow from the waddy, which took effect on the horse's head. Losing patience at last, the lieutenant was about to cut him down, when Stevenson shouted to him to hold on; and taking his stock-whip, which always hung on the saddle-bow, he brought it down on the fellow's hide with a report like a rifle shot. The black had made up his mind to be killed, but this whip was too much for his nerves, and at the second crack he gave in. But the man most wanted, Bobby Peel, was nowhere to be seen amongst the flying herd. From one to the other they galloped, until they quickly overhauled and headed back the whole tribe, which numbered some thirty or forty individuals of all ages; but in vain: he had somehow evaded them.

When the troopers passed through the camp, each man gave a sharp look at the miamis, to see that no blacks remained. These were merely sheets of bark, or boughs set up on end, so as to form a sloping wall between the fires and the wind, so that they could not conceal anybody. Owing to the haste, apparently, with which the blacks had sprung up, one of these miamis had got knocked down, and the boughs had fallen on the fire in front, where the leaves, damp with the rain which had fallen, were smouldering. Beneath these fallen boughs, and running the risk of being burned to death, lay hidden the black Walters so much wished to capture. He had had the presence of mind, on the alarm being given, to roll himself close to the fire, and, lying flat under his blanket, to knock away the prop which supported the bark and boughs of his miami; and as I rode up the camp from the creek, for I had remained behind the troop, having no desire to be other than a mere spectator, Bobby Peel, dressed once more in cotton shirt, jacket, and trousers, was just rolling himself from beneath them.

My first impulse was to detain him, but he gave me such an appealing, eloquent look, that I hesitated. I remembered what Stevenson had told me as to the infamous treatment endured by this man's tribe; how Peel's first experience of white men was being fired on when awaiting the approach of a party of overlanders who came near, making signs of friendship until within range, when they delivered a volley which killed his father and two brothers. Old Toby had often shown me the patch of reeds he and Peel, then a lad, took shelter in on that occasion. I had warned Stevenson I would not in any way aid in the capture, even if I saw them escaping. In the short time I had been on the run, I had mingled much with them, had taken long shooting and botanical excursions with two of these very murderers, and been of service to them professionally; for European disease was rife amongst their miamis, and that they were grateful to me I could easily see by the gleam of pleasure which lightened up their visages when 'doc, doc,' as they called me, appeared amongst them. Moreover, as I looked round, there seemed no possibility of escape for Peel. The mallee and swamp were guarded, and across the plain he could not move unseen. Was it for me to hasten the miserable creature's doom by a few minutes? I could not do it; and when the black, raising himself on his elbow, after a keen look at the troop, at that moment in full career after his countrymen, pushed the wet boughs farther on to the fire, so as to raise a dense smoke, which the high wind blowing carried along the ground, and ran unobserved under its shelter to the reeds, I did not interfere to prevent him.

A very short time, however, elapsed before Walters was on his track. Not finding him with the rest, and suspecting what had actually occurred, he galloped down to the camp, and his men soon found the footmarks of the fugitive in the wet grass. But upon following these through the swamp, the bird was flown. Peel had crept to the margin of the creek, and there seeing the sentry by the mallee, instantly suspected that the upper swamp also was guarded, for he knew well the number of the troop. His only resource, then, was to enter the bed of the creek and run down it until near enough to the point where the scrub approached its banks, to afford him a chance of reaching it before being overtaken. This was, as I said above, only a thousand yards or so away in a straight line, but by the creek bed, owing to its great winding, the distance was nearly doubled. To succeed, he required a far longer start than Walters' vigilance had left him, for not many minutes had elapsed from the time he had disappeared in the reeds, before the lieutenant had sent troopers down to guard the bed of the watercourse and the plain on both sides; after which he put three expert trackers on the trail. Then, riding to where Stevenson and I were patching up two or three wounded blacks,—for, in spite of all his injunctions and efforts, some of his men would use their weapons,—and hastily ordering the prisoners to be taken to the head station, whither Harris also went, to bring the spring cart for one of the wounded men who had bled very much, he invited me to join him in the hunt; for I had in the course of conversation the previous night expressed a wish to witness a specimen of the tracking powers of his men. I eagerly consented, not only because I was desirous of seeing exercised some of those keen faculties which the savage possesses in such perfection, but because I somehow felt a great interest in the fate of the miserable fugitive, and wished to be present to witness the result of the chase, whatever it might be, whether escape or capture. I could not help secretly hoping, as I noted the eager and ardent way in which his own countrymen set to work to hunt him down, that the poor wretch might escape. But there was, to all appearance, but small hope of that.

The creek down the bed of which the fugitive had fled was not an ana branch of the Murray, but one of the ordinary watercourses called by that name in Australia, which is, however, only properly applicable to an inlet of the sea. A raging torrent in winter, it was in summer a succession of 'water-holes' or pools, with spaces of dry ground between them. Some of these water-holes were from fifty to a hundred yards in length,—a few much larger, but in general they resembled small ponds,—the breadth being some forty or fifty feet. In depth many greatly exceeded this. The banks were fringed with the 'yarra' trees, which almost invariably, even when they are passing through plains otherwise treeless, margin the smaller watercourses of Australia, and which in this particular creek grew more closely than usual together at that level of the bank reached by the floods in winter-time. Unlike the generality of Australian timber, which shoots up to a considerable height before giving off any branches, these yarra trees in form more often resemble those of English growth (such as the oak); the trunk, gnarled and stunted, dividing at a few feet into large branches, the inner ones growing with an inclination downwards towards the water, into which at flood-time their ends often dip. From the blacks' camp to the out-station hut, a mile off, the course of the creek somewhat resembled the letter S.

We soon overtook the trackers, who had not much difficulty in following, as the fugitive had not had time to resort to any elaborate artifices. At one spot he had taken to the water, and some time passed before the place where he left it could be ascertained. The margin of that particular water-hole was rocky in some places. A slight drizzling rain had continued to fall, but beneath the trees the ground as yet was comparatively dry. The drippings from the fugitive's clothes would quickly betray his passage, but none such could be seen. It was concluded that he lay hidden in a patch of reeds which grew in a shallow part of the water at one end, and search was being made there by two of the blacks as we rode up. The third, however, more cunning than the rest, instead of joining them, ascended on to the plain, and commenced making casts round about in the neighbourhood. At first he also was unsuccessful, but in working his way round the water-hole he caught sight of a tuft of pretty thick bushes some thirty feet or so out. Instantly he ran up to them, as if pretty certain of there finding what he was looking for, and, stooping, he drew out a couple of dead, flattened, bushy boughs. Beneath these were the footmarks of the hunted man.

The bush in Australia is everywhere littered with dead trees and branches, the beds of the creeks in particular, where they are torn from the banks and deposited in heaps by floods. The leaves of one small bushy species adhere most tenaciously for months after death, and are not easily broken. Picking up two of these as he fled, and keeping them dry as he entered the water and swam, Peel had placed them on the dry, rocky part of the bank. Hastily pressing and squeezing as much moisture as possible out of his clothes, he had lifted himself out upon them, and allowed them to receive the droppings from his person. Shifting one before the other, and always keeping upon them, he had ascended the bank, and in this manner reached the tuft of bushes without leaving any moisture or footprint to betray him. We found that the bend of the creek at this spot would hide him from view.

After leaving the tuft of bushes, he had run for some distance at full speed, and again descended into the bed. Upon coming to that part where it approached the mallee sufficiently close to enable the fugitive, had he left the creek, to reach the scrub before the horseman on watch could overtake him, the trackers found that the traces still continued to keep within the banks. By this they were sure that he had not had time to try it, and that Walters had been too quick for him. His resorting to these artifices was another proof, and the trackers now proceeded cautiously, for fear he should double on them and take the back track.

We at length came to a water-hole of great size, being nearly three hundred yards in length, and in parts very broad. Along the side of this the tracks led for a good distance, and then suddenly disappeared. The mallee came closer here than in any other part; and the trooper on sentry there was riding up and down in its front. He examined the ground where he was; and the blacks with us, thinking that by chance he might have dodged in unobserved by the sentry, examined the plain in their own vicinity; but no marks could be seen. The fugitive had evidently taken to the water. But had he left it, and how? was the question; for, search as they would, not a mark to indicate the whereabouts of his exit could be seen. The long, dry summer had sunk the water so much, that on both sides a broad margin of damp clay bank extended, which would have quickly betrayed his passage; and the blacks had soon ascertained that Peel had not repeated his former ruse. They decided, therefore, that he was still in the water, concealed; and that, moreover, there was another black concealed there with him.

The farther end of the larger lagoon was connected by a narrow, shallow strait, a few feet wide, with a smaller one; and on walking round this, one of the troopers had come upon some other tracks, which also led to the margin of the pool, and there disappeared. An examination of these soon led to the decision that they had very recently been made, that they were the footmarks of a black, and that it was *not* Peel. And upon examining the narrow strait of shallow water, they furthermore asserted that the individual, who-ever he was, had passed through it hurriedly on his way to the larger lagoon.

When Walters conveyed this information to the superintendent and myself, who were present, I was much surprised. I could not imagine how it could be possible for the men to be concealed in such a place.

'How can they tell that anybody has passed through this water?' I said to their commander. 'It is only two or three feet deep, but the bottom is invisible, owing to the colour of the clay, and the shade cast by the trees.'

'They examined the edge of it,' he replied, 'and found that a ripple or wave had recently washed over the pebbles, grass, and clay of the bank for several inches. If he had walked *gently* through,

the mark left would have been much slighter than if he had passed
through in a hurry. This fellow rushed through in a hurry,
evidently. Probably just then he caught sight of the troopers
coming over the plain to station themselves by the scrub here, close
by, and made for the larger water directly.'

'Perhaps,' I suggested, 'the tracks are Peel's, made by walking
backwards out of the water, to deceive you.'

'He knew well he could not deceive the blacks that way,' said
Walters. 'No! this is the track of a man running, and running fast.
Doubtless it was one of the head-station blacks, from the public-
house, who had heard or suspected something, and was coming
to give the others warning, but was too late. Whoever he is, he
is hidden somewhere in the water still, and Peel too, most likely.'

'In the water?' I said, astonished.

'Yes; amongst the reeds.'

'But', said I, 'there *are* no reeds, or scarcely any; only those
narrow strips, barely a yard or two in width, round the margin;
and you can see right down into them from the banks, and detect
any man's head above the surface, even if it were in the thickest
patch I see hereabouts; for they are not more than ten or twelve
inches above the water, at most.'

'Yes; if they were such fools as to keep their heads *above* water,'
replied the lieutenant. 'But these chaps are stowed away
underneath.'

'With their heads under water? What do you mean?'

'I mean that you might pass this lagoon, walk round its banks,
and look as closely as you will down upon those scanty reeds
fringing the margin,—you will see nothing, and hear nothing
but the rustling of the wind in the leaves. And yet a hundred
blacks might be lying hidden there all the time! And so closely
will they be concealed that a flock of wild ducks might alight and
see nothing to startle them, so solitary and quiet will be the aspect
of the place.'

'How can they manage it?'

'Simply enough. Almost every one of them keeps about him,
concealed in his thick, bushy hair, a piece of hollow reed tube.
When closely pressed, they take to the water, and, diving beneath,
thrust their heads into a patch of reeds. Turning on their backs first,
they allow their faces to come near enough to the surface for the
tube to project, and they breathe through it. The sharpest eye could
not detect this, hidden as it is amongst the thick growth; and even
without it, it would be impossible to detect their nostrils, which,
in that case, they only allow to project above water. See!' he added;
'they are groping for them.'

Some spears had been brought from the deserted camp for this very purpose; and, walking round the margin, two of the troopers thrust these in all directions into the water, but for some time without any result; the other black continuing his search round the banks for the trail, in case they had after all left it. All at once, however, I noticed one of them, as he was bending forward, and probing with his weapon, slip and partly fall in. His spear had been jerked out of his hand, and a movement in the reeds betrayed the cause. Running up, I caught sight, for an instant, of the twinkling soles of the feet (which are much lighter-coloured than the skin of the rest of the body) of the diver, as he proceeded to swim under water to some other part of the lagoon. But his pursuers had also seen them, and had been able to follow, with their keener gaze, the passage of the dark body itself, which, after the first glimpse, was invisible to me, to its new hiding-place. There was not the slightest disturbance of the surface, or any greater movement amongst the wind-tossed reeds than was observable elsewhere on the water-hole, to betray its whereabouts, yet the blacks unerringly selected the spot, and with poised spears were about to thrust the unfortunate through, whoever he was, when Stevenson interposed.

'No, we must have none of that kind of work, Walters,' he said. 'Get him out alive;' and after poking and following the fugitive to two or three different parts of the lagoon, finding it useless to persist, he at length popped his head above water, revealing to our gaze the features, not of Bobby Peel, but of the boy Pothook, whom we had left at home. Finding a brandy bottle on the shelf of our hut, his custodian had gone to get some water to mix himself a glass, thinking that as the boy was snoring he must be asleep; and the lad had seized the opportunity, slipped out, and made off, and was out of range before the hut-keeper had missed him. But Pothook was too late to warn his friends.

He was in mortal terror at finding himself in the hands of the dreaded troopers, and would not come out of the water until he had made Stevenson and me promise they should not kill him.

'Where Bobby Peel?' asked the superintendent of the lad.

'Him pull away over yonder,' he replied, pointing to the out-station hut, which was invisible, being hidden by some bushes out in the plain.

'Likely story that!' said the lieutenant contemptuously. 'It's no use asking him anything; he wants to get us away from here; and he'll lie till he's white in the face to do it. No! Peel is in this water-hole, I am positive. We shall have him presently, never fear. I *must* have that rascal this time; he has dodged me so often. But I think he won't slip through my fingers now.'

But 'the rascal' seemed destined not to be caught. The blacks stripped and swam about the lagoon, groping amongst the remaining reeds, and now and then diving to take a look below, but in vain. Half an hour had altogether been spent in the search, and still there were no signs of the fugitive.

'I begin to think the boy may be speaking the truth after all,' said the superintendent to me; 'though why Peel should make for the hut, where the men hate him so much, is a puzzle to me. Surely he would not dare. I will ride across and see.'

Just at that moment, however, we observed one of the blacks, who was coursing round the water-hole like a baffled bloodhound, suddenly stop, and look up at the branches of the trees which everywhere surrounded it. These had been examined by them upon first coming, in order to make sure that no boughs hung near enough to the surface for any swimmer to lift himself out by their aid. But the water was so low at this time that every branch was at first sight apparently too far out of reach. Finding no trace, however, on the broad clay margin on either side, the idea again suggested itself, and a more minute examination of the different trees was made; but the bough which approached the water most nearly was five or six feet from the surface, and belonged to a tree which was situated on the side nearest to the hut. Jumping into the creek, however, the black above mentioned swam out until he came beneath it, and, although the water-hole was at least fifty feet deep, to our surprise the man's body presently emerged until he stood up, and, reaching out his hands, grasped the bough and swung himself up on to it. The manner in which Peel had left the water was now made manifest. A large tree was there sunk,[1] a bough of it coming to within a few inches of the surface. From the banks this was invisible, owing to the dark shade cast by the branches above; but the fugitive, who was familiar with every foot of the water-hole from infancy, had availed himself of it, and had landed on the side nearest to the hut, and away from the scrub.

The black scrambled along until he reached the trunk, and, slipping down, looked at the ground at its foot. The grass along the edge of the plain above, for the breadth of a few feet back from the bank, had already been examined up and down the water-hole on his side, but without effect, and no tracks could now be seen at the foot of this particular tree. The black, however, again looking up, observed that a long bough projected out over the plain, and walking out to the end of this he again examined the ground. One glance was sufficient for him, although I could see

1 The Australian woods, with a few exceptions, sink in water.

nothing, and giving a cooey to the rest, who were still hunting in the bed of the creek, Walters and his companions joined him.

'Got it—track belongin' to Bobby,' said the trooper, pointing to the ground, and trotting farther out on the plain towards the hut.

Now what dodge has the fellow been up to?' said Walters. 'If he is skulking in this myrtle patch, hoping to double back to the creek, he is mistaken. Unless he has passed my men on the plain, which isn't likely, we'll soon have him.'

I observed Stevenson looking around for Pothook, but that youth had prudently slipped off. We afterwards questioned him as to what took place when he and Peel met each other. It seems that, cut off from his only chance, the scrub on one side of the creek, and informed, by the way, that the bed of it lower down was guarded, the black had for a few moments given up all hope of escape. He looked in despair between the trunks of the yarra trees towards the out-station hut, which lay a quarter of a mile off, hidden in a belt of myrtle and quandong bushes, some three or four hundred yards long, and extending across the bend so as to shut out the view of the great plain beyond. That plain, he knew, was carefully guarded, and, moreover, it led to the home station. But as he looked he saw an object which excited a gleam of hope, and inspired him with a desperate resolve. The sunken tree was some distance back from where he stood, and to avoid showing his return traces he jumped into the water and swam to it, emerging in the manner described, while the boy took to the creek, intending to remain concealed under the surface until the danger which he fancied menaced himself passed by. In going towards the hut, Peel ran no danger of being seen by the black stationed by the mallee, for on such a level plain the yarra trees which fringed the water-hole completely screened from those at a distance on one side whatever passed on the other side of the creek.

The open space between the part of the banks where we now stood and the belt of small timber above mentioned, was less than a quarter of a mile, and while the blacks who had been swimming in the water-hole were dressing themselves, Walters galloped across it, and through the bushes and on to the large plain beyond, to see whereabouts his sentries were. He could see two, who were riding up and down just within sight of each other, while between and beyond them, far out, was the shepherd with his flock. There was not a bush to conceal the view, and far away, by the edge of the distant timber, the blacks and their guard were still in sight, on their way to the home station. The timber opened opposite to him, and through this opening he could see miles away on to another plain beyond. The road from the punt to the upper part of the river passed that way, and came up to near where he stood, crossing the creek near the out-station hut, and going through a narrow portion of the mallee, which had been cleared for the purpose. On this road, at a considerable distance off, was a solitary horseman, apparently riding to the home station.

Meanwhile the blacks had again taken up the trail, which led straight to the brush in which the hut was concealed. Just before we reached the edge of this, Walters joined us again.

'I can't make the fellow out,' he said; 'he can't have crossed the plain; and if he is skulking here, we shall soon have him.'

The sentry across at the mallee had been called over, and, with another man, now watched in the open, to give notice if Peel doubled out and made back tracks for the creek again; and we proceeded to enter the bushes of quandong and myrtle. All at once there was a commotion amongst the trackers, who sprang to their horses, shouting something to Walters, who thereupon raged and stormed; and no wonder. The distant horseman he had a few minutes before seen was the very man he was after.

'Has either of your men here got a horse?' he asked the superintendent hastily.

'Yes,' replied Stevenson (who, I suspected, had been for some time aware of the trick Peel had played), 'the shepherd has one. He bought it to shepherd his flock with on these level plains, as he was always losing his sheep. He is a very little man, and consequently could only see a short distance.'

'But he hadn't it to-day, had he?'

'No. The fact is, he was taken in, knowing nothing about horses, and bought a thorough buck-jumper, who pitched him off as fast as he got on. And the brute won't let you catch him in hobbles; so, as he expects to sell it again, he keeps it tethered about the hut handy. I am afraid,' added Stevenson to me, as Walters, too impatient to listen further, spurred on after his men,—'I am afraid that vagabond has been up to some mischief. I hope Watkins, the hut-keeper here, is all right. Peel would be desperate, and not stick at a trifle in the fix he was in. I suspected what he had been up to.'

'So I thought,' I replied, as we rushed on after the trackers.

Just as they reached the hut door, a man was crawling out on his hands and knees. This turned out to be the hut-keeper, who was covered with blood, which had flowed from a wound on his head.

'Why, Bill! what's the matter?' said the superintendent. 'Did Peel do that?'

'Oh, is that you, Mr. Stevenson?' said the man, looking up at our party, and raising himself with difficulty. 'Yes, it was; are you after him?'

'Yes, we are; but how came you let him do that?'

'You had best put your men on his track at once, Mr. Walters. He's got King's horse.'

'We know he has, the villain!' said Walters, as he directed the three trackers to follow instantly (Peel was still in sight, but soon disappeared in the timber), while he and the rest waited behind a few moments to hear the hut-keeper's account of the attack made on him, which he gave as I bound up his wound.

It appeared that, while engaged in his usual morning work of shifting the hurdles, after the flock had gone out at daylight, he saw some one riding (as he thought) through the bushes towards his hut, and left his work to see who it was. To his surprise, he found the shepherd's horse, which he himself had tethered out that morning at the edge of the myrtle, tied to the door, but immediately concluded that the man himself had come for it, as he was daily expecting to sell it, and that perhaps the intending purchaser had joined him while with his flock. He therefore entered the hut quite unsuspiciously; but it was apparently empty. While turning round, he was felled by a blow with his own gun; and, staggering forwards, fell close to his bed. He was not entirely stunned, and instantly rolled himself underneath it. At first he thought that Peel (whom he had recognised) was going to drag him out and finish him, but the black was in too great a hurry. He stayed long enough, however, to saddle the horse, and load himself with the tea and sugar bags, as well as the flour and half a damper which was on the table. Moreover, the man found that he had taken down his looking-glass, which hung on a nail in the wall. His object in doing this was that he might whiten his face with the dirty outside of the flour bag. With a cabbage-tree hat and a shooting coat which he put on, at a distance he would not look like a black, and he could pass the sentries unsuspected. In fact, we heard afterwards from them that he went between them, walking, and leading his horse, and pretending to read an old newspaper he had picked up off the table in the hut. It was so natural that a passing horseman coming from higher up the river should call at the out-station, and he turned his whitened, or rather whitey-browned, face towards them both so coolly, that, disguised as he was in hat and coat, and having the horse as well, it was no wonder that, at several hundred yards distance, they should be deceived.

I felt rather queer when I saw the hut-keeper's condition, and reflected that, had he been killed, I should have been indirectly the cause of his death. And what if the black, driven to desperation, committed more murders? There was no chance now of their catching him. He was making straight for the large reed-bed, which extended miles down the river below the head station.

'I don't see the use of following him any longer. He has got off clear!' said Stevenson, after we had gone some miles. 'Upon my word, he deserves his liberty too.'

We at last reached the reeds, and followed the traces along their margin, thick timber with brush being on our right. In passing the head station all but two of the most expert of the troopers were sent away. With these, the superintendent, Walters, and I, continued the chase, although with very slight hopes of capturing the fugitive, now that he had succeeded in reaching the neighbourhood of the reedy swamps, which communicated with the main body of the mallee, extending in the direction of South Australia for hundreds of miles down the river.

'Dodged me once more!' said Walters. 'Oh, if I had only thought of telling one of my men to call as he passed the hut where he stole the horse! We should have had him, for they would have been on the look-out. But now—What's the matter, Doolibut?'

The track had hitherto led for several miles in a straight line, parallel with the river; but now the leading black pulled up his horse and looked about him. The hoof-marks had changed their character, and swerved from their former course, zigzagging in different directions; these signs indicating that a severe struggle had here taken place between the horse and his rider.

'His horse has been playing up!' said the superintendent. 'These are the marks made by his hack jumping about. I wonder the beast went so far with the black on his back without doing so before, for he is a regular brute. No one on the station will ride him.'

It seemed, however, that Peel had conquered, for presently the tracks of the horse once more galloping were taken up, and we followed them on. But again we came to the marks of a struggle; and these increased in number at every mile or so, until we came to a place about half a mile from the scrub for which the black was making, and where the reeds and the timber, mingled with brush, approached each other closely. We were passing along a narrow, winding opening or path between these, having the reeds on our left, when once more the leading black pulled up, and after a brief glance at the ground, dismounted.

The sandy, loose soil on which the trees grew was margined by and intermingled with the soft boggy ground on which were the reeds, here five or six feet in height, and very dense. The spot was thickly overgrown with ferns and small bushes, which in several places were broken and trampled, while the ground was deeply imprinted with hoof-marks. Besides these, however, the blacks evidently saw other signs; for, pointing to one particular place, and speaking eagerly to each other, they stooped down to examine it more narrowly; and then, walking on a few steps, came to the foot of an immense tree, which, growing on the very margin of the swamp, had one portion of its roots bathed by its waters, there being hardly room for a man to pass between the reeds and the trunk on that side. On the other were some bushes, which concealed the view immediately beyond.

'Why, there is the horse!' said the superintendent suddenly, pointing to the right amongst the trees. 'He has left it, and taken to the swamp on foot. He's safe now.'

The two blacks paused and raised themselves up as he spoke; and, following the direction in which Stevenson pointed, one of them walked forward a few paces to look. He stood a single instant, and was in the act of turning to rejoin his companion, when a puff of smoke rose beyond the bushes, we heard a report, and saw him fall to the earth. He was shot right through the heart.

The other trooper, knowing that Peel's gun was a single barrel, and that he had now no charge left, ran round the bushes to fire; and Stevenson and I rode in the same direction. Beyond these bushes was a small open space, margined on one side by a pool of water. Half in this water and half out lay an immense prostrate tree; and sitting on the ground, leaning his back against this, was Bobby Peel. He knew that his last hour was come, for he had evidently made up his mind to die. He had delayed too long leaving his horse, for the animal had at length succeeded in throwing him; and in the fall he came on one of the roots of this large tree, and his leg was broken. He had dragged himself round to the edge of the pool, probably for the purpose of obtaining a drink of water, to assuage the thirst which is always the greatest torture in such calamities.

The dead tree against which he was leaning was that kind of Eucalyptus the bark of which is cellular, and very thick. This bark had peeled off the trunk, and lay in great hard dry flakes by its side; and the black had employed himself in breaking up this heavy, brittle material into pieces about the size of a cheese-plate. Several heaps thus prepared lay ready to his hand on both sides of him. He was busy in reloading his gun; and for a few moments, from my horse's back, I had an opportunity of noticing these particulars, for, owing to the dense brush which surrounded the place in which he was, it was some little time before the troopers could fairly approach him.

'Take him alive, Mr. Walters,' I urged. 'Don't let your fellow shoot him. Tell him to surrender, and lay down his gun, Stevenson.'

But Walters was naturally much incensed at the loss of his man, and felt very little inclination to do anything of the kind; and to the superintendent's summons the black replied by a volley of curses and imprecations against all white men,—in the midst of which the trooper fired, and the ball passed through Peel's chest.

The gun, which was nearly reloaded, fell from his hands, and Walters dismounted and walked forward to take possession of it. But the moment he appeared within the little open space the black, seizing a handful of the pieces of heavy bark, hurled them edgeways at his head and face with a rapidity and certainty of aim perfectly wonderful. The first piece he flung struck Walters across the forehead; and piece followed piece in such quick succession that the lieutenant was compelled to turn his back while he drew and cocked his pistol. For some time he found it impossible to aim, so unerringly did the missiles come rapping at him; but when at length he fired the black fell dead.

Years have passed, but all the incidents of that exciting and tragic chase are still fresh in my memory. The fierce strength of that last terrible effort almost appalled us, and we were loud in our regrets that so much skill and endurance should come to such an end. Times have changed since then, but it remains a reproach to our civilisation that the aboriginal races are fast vanishing before it. At the same time, there is cause for thankfulness that the efforts of Christian benevolence have not been in vain on behalf of the natives. There are still occasional outrages, but reckless treatment of the blacks is now held in check by a healthier public opinion.

THE CONVICT
LAUNDRESS*

Mrs Francis Vidal

ONE EVENING, just before sunset, a young woman was seen leaning
on a stile; she was dressed after the manner of an Irish household
servant, and there was a certain air of coquettish pleasure as she
glanced at her well-turned fair arm, and neat foot and ancle, then
looked anxiously over the fields, or timidly back towards the
house—a handsome building, standing on beautiful ground,
surrounded with every thing that denotes the residence of a wealthy
squire. The substantial chimneys sent up their columns of smoke,
while lights might be seen glancing in the long row of windows
in front. General Montgomery had company that day; and full of
fear lest she should be wanted, had Grace M'Lean stolen out, after
giving a final polish to the spare beds and tables, in the hope of
meeting her English lover. A long sigh escaped her as the moments
flew by and he did not appear. At last there was a whistle, which
made her blush and smile, and in another moment he was at her
side; and passing his arm round her waist, he led her on by the
hedgerow, for a stroll, as he said, this lovely evening.

'Well then, Grace, when I return you'll consent to the marriage,
I suppose? I've spoken for the cottage, and I have some planks
seasoning, to knock up as neat a table as I'll answer for it will please
even your particular fancy.'

Grace smiled, then said, 'No, William; I am only come to say
good bye, and it can't be. You must just forget me, for it can't be.'

'Did you speak to your lady?'

'And that I did, ashamed as I was about it; and you know I told

---

* Note: an introductory passage, which tells how the narrator met Grace, has been
omitted from this story.

you what she would say, good lady as she is. She says I have no right to marry a heretic; and I should work on, as my mother did before me, and not give up to fancies, young as I am. That's what she said, William; and you know my brother Michael is all against it; so indeed, William, I just came to tell you so, and I'm wanting at the house, so I can only have a word or so with you.'

'That's what she said, is it? Then you may tell her, Grace, my darling, that you have no occasion to work on till you're old, for that I have enough to marry decently upon, and can work as well as any one; and as for your religion, can't you be a Catholic, and go to mass and confession all the same? Never a word will I say against it, though I see no sense in it at all. For that matter, I hope I'm honest, and never did any thing to be ashamed of; and I go to church sometimes, because my parents, good souls, did so before me. But I'll never hinder you from doing what you like. And the priest, Grace, Father Donaghan, sure he didn't forbid it?'

'Ah, no, William! because he had the hope I should be the means of bringing you round; and that's why he let Katie marry a Protestant: but you know, William, there's small chance of that with you and me. I'm not the one to lead you, and you're not the one to be led.'

'Led, Grace! I'll promise to go to your chapel two or three times a year. As to being a Catholic, that I shouldn't like; because, as I said before, my father was Protestant, and his father and father's father; but I can't see the great difference—not I! and if you were to pray to all the saints in the calendar, I wouldn't complain. So give up your arguments, Grace, which you will never get me to agree to. Ah, Grace! think of the nice little cottage and the regular work I've got, and the old mother nigh at hand.'

Grace did think of it; and she thought too of him, the handsome English carpenter, about whom every girl in the village was talking; and as she thought, and as she listened, her mistress's warning and advice fell away, like snow in sunshine. Grace had left the house, undecided what answer to give him; wishing to do right, but willing to be reasoned out of it; so after a few turns up and down, with drooping head and blushing face, she gave her promise to be William's wife, and it was settled that when 'the family' went over to Bath for the lady's health, then should be the wedding. William was going to Dublin on business, and was to be absent some weeks, so this was a farewell meeting. They lingered on, till the large clock at the Hall made Grace start, and then they parted. She ran swiftly to the shrubbery, hoping she had not been called for—and from that hour the balance was struck.

Heavily it weighed downwards, and its weight was the world.

From that time Grace thought more of pleasing William Allen than her mistress whom she had served from a child, more than God!

She loved him with a fond, proud, devoted love, and she sacrificed all for him. Her mistress's displeasures—her mother's sorrow—her brother's anger—it failed to touch her; her heart was shielded from all and every thing; there was but one thing in the world for her. Her eye was bright, her steps firm, her voice clear and merry.

Grace made an excellent managing wife. No cottage was cleaner or more tasty, no meals so well cooked. No man turned out so neat and well dressed as William. The rent was always paid, and all things prospered. Grace worked hard; but as evening came, she never failed to be at the garden paling to catch the first look, and if it was fine, they had their evening stroll.

No woman, as she afterwards said, was ever half so happy; alas for the blossom which had no root, and which the first wintry storm crushed to the ground for ever!

The M'Leans were a proud family. The mother had been in General Montgomery's service from childhood, and to the last day of her life considered their word as law to her and hers. Her family turned out well, and all were prosperously settled; the eldest, Michael, was established as a pork butcher, and had a large business, chiefly in salting pork down for shipping. M'Lean's mark on a cask was considered sure warrant that the meat was good. Many a sailor drank his health on the broad seas, while enjoying the well-cured pork which was branded in Michael's name. Michael was 'well to do' in the world, and looked up to as the head of the family. He was wont to boast, with a satisfied smile, that none of their stock had ever been known to darken a jail door for generations back, and they were one and all a thriving, 'rent-paying family.' When his youngest sister, Grace, bestowed her heart and hand on 'handsome Willie,' as he was often called, Michael frowned. He did not like her marrying an Englishman or a Protestant; he knew nothing of William, except that once, on some rejoicing, he had been the worse for liquor and got into an Orange row; and this was a bad prospect, as Michael sagely observed, for whiskey was the curse of Ireland, and as *his* family had always held up their heads and kept out of this bad habit, he did not like the match.

It was with no little pride that Grace, as years passed on, could tell her brother that they were still above the world; that the pig and the garden paid the rent, and that William's earnings were counted into her own hand every week; and even Michael could not forbear smiling at the curly-headed, pretty boy, whom Grace always brought with her. Her eldest child, 'her jewel,' who, as she in after years said, with quivering lips and tearful eyes, 'had something above common in his airs, and any one would have taken him for a real gentleman.' The old mother's cottage was very near Grace; she was skilful in growing and drying herbs for the use of chemists and doctors, she lived to a great age, and on her death-bed she solemnly warned her daughter not to give up her religion, or be slack in her prayers: she said God had prospered her, and she hoped this would bind her the more to Him in gratitude. Grace trembled, for something whispered at her heart that she had forgotten the Giver in the gifts bestowed. She shed a few tears of sorrow by her mother's side, but they were hastily wiped away, and all her best attention was devoted to smoothing her mother's last hours; and never was there a gentler nurse than Grace! But alas! her mother's instructions in the best way of plaiting frills, and the use of herbs for medicinal purposes, were more remembered and practised than all her other advice. Perhaps old Mrs. M'Lean's own example had tended to this. Of what avail are good words, unless we practise what we advise? However it was, Grace went on her way, making a devoted wife and mother. She set up her household gods and worshipped them, and they fell at last, and then there was none to help, none to answer!

Several years of bright prosperity had Grace; her wedded life was as little marred by clouds as is possible in a world of trial. One of her girls was taken into a respectable family, to be brought up as a servant; the other was apprenticed to a dressmaker; her son was still at home, and it was her pride and delight to give him 'learning;' he was quick and clever, and wrote as 'fair a hand as any one in all Ireland.'

There was the comfortable, pretty little cottage, furnished by William's own handy work, its clean sanded floor, its white window curtain, its bright kitchen utensils, and its cheerful old clock; there was the cow, and the pigs, and the poultry all thriving. Roses, and honeysuckles, and jasmine covered the walls; the garden beds had no weeds, and furnished many a dish of vegetables for their own eating, besides bringing in many a penny from market. 'Vanity of vanities! all is vanity!'

Grace had gone to market, and had brought home a good round sum, which she smiled over as she thought of showing it off to William when he came home. She looked at the clock, and almost wondered he had not returned, then she prepared supper, and strolled about the garden, and found her seeds had made a great spring: there was something else to show William! Why does he tarry?

Grace is laughing and joking with her boy in the garden, little dreaming what goes on a mile away.

William was engaged in building a house; he had climbed to the top to place something, when one of his fellow-workmen called out, 'have a care there, Allen, steady!' But before the last word of caution was uttered, there was a tottering of the beam on which William stood, then a crash, a heavy fall, a suppressed groan from the bystanders—Grace was a widow!

The body was raised and carried into a neighbouring house, but no medical aid, no care could bring back life. Everyone knew Grace, and every one knew what she would feel. No one was willing to be the bearer of such news. At length one of the men, one of William's comrades, said he would step down and prepare her. He had been a constant visitor at the cottage; none knew better than he did what this blow would be, and as he walked along, he considered what he could do to help and comfort the widow, and long did he meditate as to how he should break the truth to her.

When he had reached half-way, and was crossing the road towards a stile which led to a short cut, he saw Grace herself coming towards him.

She called out, 'Where's William?' but he stood still and made no answer. Presently she was close to him, repeating her questions.

'God help you, Grace!' was all he could utter, and she staggered against the stile, and held it, for she saw something dreadful in his face.

'Speak man, if you wouldn't kill me!'—and he did speak!—What happened after that Grace never knew. It was all a blank—a frightful dark blank. When she became conscious she found herself in her own bed, with an old woman, a kind neighbour, sitting by her. This woman, Patty as she was called, now rose and brought something in a glass to Grace, begging her 'to take a sup, 'twould comfort her,' Grace did so, and then she asked questions, and Patty answered. Grace heard that the funeral was then taking place; that her brother Michael, and her son, and a great many others were there, and Patty assured her that no one could have a more decent funeral or any thing nicer, and then added such scraps of comfort and condolence as she could think of, and begged Grace to 'take heart and rouse herself.' This Grace could not do for a long time, and, at last, when she left her bed a wasted, stricken woman, she wandered about her house and little garden more like a ghost than a human being, or she sat in a corner, with eyes fixed on vacancy, and moaned, and said she was 'a desolate, forlorn creature; she had nothing to live for.' She tried to pray, but could not, it was all confusion and misery, and not one thought of comfort was there, turn which way she would. It was then that her son stood before her, and spoke gentle words, which, as she afterwards said, 'was the first relief she had, and she cried, which seemed to cure the deadly pain at her heart.' Her son, and he was like his father in form and face, bade her be comforted, for that he was now old enough to do something for himself, and that he dearly loved her, and she must keep up for his sake.

Grace stroked his curly hair, and, still weeping, looked at him, and at last said, 'Sure, and you're your own father's son, and your very words are his.' And from that hour all her energy and love was given to him. To work and toil to get him into a creditable situation was her one object.

She strove to banish thoughts of the past, she put away any vague and dreamy ideas which had arisen in the dark hour for 'a more convenient season.' She must work now!

It seemed indeed as if the poor mother's trouble was repaid; her son was steady, good, and clever, and through Michael's interest he got a situation with some shipping agents at Belfast.

It was with pride, yet with heart-sorrow that Grace saw him dressed in his best, a good suit of clothes which she had got for him; his little box packed, and with a stick in his hand, ready to commence his journey. Long did the last bright smile live in her heart, and the last wave of his hat as he left the garden, and his 'God bless you, mother.' How often did it return in the lonely nights, and the weary days; and in after years, in a foreign land, she would wake out of sleep and listen, for that voice seemed to speak to her by night and day.

Cheerful letters reached Grace very often from her son, saying that he was a favourite with his employer, and should soon be promoted, and receive wages enough to support her as well as. himself; and he always ended with entreating her not to 'slave and toil,' for his only wish was to do every thing for her. But it was not Grace's nature to be any thing but busy. Hers was an active, energetic mind, and she was very clever at many things. No one could excel Grace at mending china, or glass, or even saucepans; no one understood how to manage fowls and turkeys like her; no one contrived to make so much butter from one cow, or to get so much from their garden. Her daughters were doing very well, but she always owned that her chief love was bestowed on the son.

One day Michael brought word that William had been trusted with some important business, and had been sent to England by the agents.

'What, across the water!' said Grace.

Michael laughed, and told her not to look so frightened; that he was all right, and she ought to take it as an honour, and a great compliment, his being chosen, young as he was.

'Very true,' Grace said; yet she sighed, and all that night, as the wind rolled in the chimney, she thought of the stormy sea, and all she had ever heard of shipwrecks, and she tried to pray for a safe return. Very uneasily Grace passed the next few days; she could not go on with her usual employments steadily, but was restless and anxious. She always declared that she had a foreboding that misfortune was at hand,—and yet it came like a shock! Michael brought a letter from the merchant's head clerk—he was drowned—fell overboard when engaged in some frolic, and was drowned! This time Grace did not lose her senses. She sat upright in her chair, she did not shed a tear; but she shrieked aloud in agony, and her own wild voice startled her. Michael was alarmed, and called in Patty, and they strove to reason with her, they entreated her to calm herself; but she said that it was as if she had a raging spirit within her, and for many days 'the breeze among the trees sounded in her ears like a hideous howl, and the blessed sunshine was worse than the darkness.' There was not a shadow of comfort any where; they spoke of God and resignation, but she shook her head; the pain was more than she could bear, and when she lay down in bed, she fancied that she saw her son's body floating on the waves, calling her to come; then she would rush out into the air with throbbing head, and nothing relieved her; she could not cry, she could not sleep. Patty at last persuaded her to swallow a cordial and lie down, and then a heaviness came over her, though it was not sleep, but it seemed to quiet her, and she called for more;—it drowned the grief.

And this was the first coil of the rope which afterwards so tightly bound Grace.

Days passed in alternate agony and stupefaction; and then one morning, when she was all alone, and Patty was gone back to her own home, Grace determined to go to Belfast herself, for she craved for further tidings, and she wished to get everything that belonged to her son. She was glad Patty was away—she wished to go secretly, why she did not know, but she made up a small bundle of linen, locked up the cottage, hanging the key in a particular spot over the door; and, looking on all sides to see if any one were in sight, she set forth for her long journey. Weak and worn as she was, excitement kept her up. She staid a night at a small pot-house on the road, and by the afternoon of the second day she reached Belfast.

When she was fairly in the streets, a stranger not knowing where to go, faint and tired, her heart failed her, and she wished she had never come. She stopped to look about her, and seeing a woman standing outside a small shop-door, she asked her what was the name of the street, and then where Messrs. Panton and Co. lived. The woman said, 'Oh! a great way off,' and proceeded to describe the way; but poor Grace felt she could not take many steps more. 'Could you tell me of a decent and quiet lodging to be had any where near?' said she. The woman said there were several; she herself had a tidy little bed which she often let, and charged low for it: she was a widow, she added, and glad to do anything to turn a penny, for she had four small children to maintain.

Grace sighed. 'You're tired: come, step in, and take a cup of tea; sure you've come a long way seemingly.' Grace followed, and agreed to take the small room which was to let, while her business kept her in Belfast.

Mrs. Cady was active and civil, and very talkative. She told Grace that she sold cotton and lace, and tapes, and pins, and such like things; and sometimes she got a little washing, but it was hard work to make both ends meet, and she had found it a world of trouble, whatever others did. Grace's miserable looks struck Mrs. Cady, and when she heard she could not sleep, she advised her to take the least 'drop of whiskey' just as she stepped into bed: she had found from experience how good it was for sorrow.

Grace did not refuse, and she too found that it 'drove off the pain and brought sleep.'

Mrs. Cady's girl shewed Grace the next day to Messrs. Panton and Co., where she heard many particulars about her son. As she said, they were very kind, and gave her all that was due to him and his clothes, and spoke very handsomely of the lad.

How her fingers trembled and her heart beat as she folded and unfolded the shirts, the waistcoats and neck-cloths; but very few new things were added to his old stock. 'No,' as she said afterwards with glistening eyes but quivering lips, 'he was saving money for his mother; he never thought of himself; it was for me,—for me!'

Could her brother or any of her old friends have seen Grace at this time, they would scarcely have recognised her to be the same person. All her activity, her spirit was gone. She sat staring vacantly out of window, or moved about the room in feverish rest-lessness: her person was uncared for and neglected, she did not mend her clothes, she sat in dirt rather than sweep a room or dust a table.

Mere animal energy, even long practised habits, will fail us under a stunning blow. The most buoyant spirit will sink at last, and woe to us, if, like poor Grace, we have no other support at hand. The tempter, it is said, lurks in glittering scenes, in prosperity, in wealth, in fulfilled happiness. He also hovers over the dim room of agony. He has his weights with which he seeks to crush the bleeding heart.

Mrs. Cady persuaded Grace to remain on where she was for a while: she coaxed and flattered her, and tried to tempt her to eat and to drink; her cordials and her drops were often offered and accepted to still the beating and aching of the heart. She was not pressed to pay for her lodging, but by degrees she was persuaded into investing a small sum in the shop, and at last to take a passive share in the concern. Mrs. Cady was sharp and talkative; Grace doubted her, as she afterwards said, yet she was glad to be led. She shrank from returning home, or from any exertion, and she looked for the evening, the unlocking the corner cupboard, the long-necked bottle, and the dead, heavy sleep which followed, as she had once looked for an approving smile from her husband.

One morning, heart-sick, miserable, feverish and heavy-eyed, Grace stood at the door leaning over that part of it which was shut. Many persons passed;—carriages and beggars, nurses and children, and men going to their work. Shrill cries, laughter, buzzing and rattling, all mingled in confusion, and she looked out on the bright sunshine, and thought of her forsaken home—the little garden. No one had sought her, no one cared a pin for her, she thought. Did they think she had drowned herself in the river! what, if she were to return and find the cottage occupied? The thought roused her. 'I wouldn't like to give it up to ruin—but I hav'n't the strength; if I had, I could pay the bit of rent by washing, and I'd like to die in the old place!' And she shuddered as she thought of a last illness and Mrs. Cady's sharp face over her pillow. She remembered one night feeling a hand under her head, and seeing in the dim light Mrs. Cady's confused face; from that hour Grace placed her money elsewhere. 'She has been kind to me to be sure, but I can pay her now: I've a great mind to go, but I am weak!' and she looked down at her worn shoes. For the first time she felt ashamed at her untidy state. 'Oh! ma'am,' she said in after years, 'it was fate, I was doomed for destruction. Just as I was thinking this way, Mrs. Cady called out from the back room: 'Mrs. Allen, here's some cheap, illegant shoes, jist your very pattern, a rare bargain.' I went in and fitted them on, and paid the money, just half-price. I felt glad, for I thought, 'now I can walk home when I like.' Not three hours afterwards in came some constables. Mrs. Cady and I were seized for buying stolen goods; we were put into jail.'

Mrs. Cady was known as a very doubtful character, which told against Grace. Grace was tried and found guilty. It was clear and just, as she said, she knew she couldn't deny it: she heard her sentence, seven years' transportation, with scarcely a sigh, and with no effort to save herself. She did not write to her friends; she scorned the notion of being the one to bring disgrace to the M'Leans. 'Her daughters,' she said, 'should never know what their mother was, till the broad ocean rolled betwixt them.'

Grace was sent from Belfast to Dublin; and while waiting for the ship, she gained the good will of the matron of the jail. While she was out of the reach of temptation her old habits of industry and her obliging temper showed itself. She made herself useful in the jail and on board the ship: in the latter she was appointed nurse to the sick, and she often showed a Bible, given by the surgeon, with her name written in it; a testimonial of which she was very proud.

From the ship in Sydney harbour she was sent to the female convict barracks at Paramatta, where she says it made her heart sick to hear the horrible language;—old abandoned sinners and quite young girls crowded together. Grace loathed the place, resolved to try and get assigned out, and there to work and to toil, and try to resist temptation,—any thing to be free from such a place. She begged the matron to try and get her a place.

Accordingly, one day the matron called her from the work-room, and told her she had received an application for a laundress in a clergyman's family; she was desired to recommend one, and had chosen her. Grace was thankful at the prospect.

The next day a man came with a cart, received Grace's small bundle, while she herself, in her convict's dress, seated on the straw, soon left the barracks at Paramatta for a new, strange scene.

The roads were edged with wattles in full bloom, their golden blossoms shedding fragrance around. The country was flat and monotonous; the sun hot and burning. The man,—he had been a convict himself,—joked her on her dress, and being sent out at the Queen's expense; and bade her hold up her head, for that 'Government folks were not so bad.' But Grace said her heart sank within her, so forcibly did her shame and situation press upon her. They suddenly stopped at the bottom of a lane, and then the horse slowly mounted the hill, and children's voices rang out clear from the bank,—and as one, a fair-haired boy, reminding her at once of her own child, sprang out to take the whip and reins, she sobbed outright.

The bright stars cast a clear light over the farm that night, and all was still, save the buzzing of insects, and the croaking of frogs. Grace sat up on her little bed, and looked at the rough wooden planks which formed the walls of her room, at her marked dress.

She was once more among respectable people she thought, but she was a convict! Rough were the accommodations of the place, but Grace's spirit revived as the morning breeze rose; she resolved to show that she could work. She went to collect sticks from the wood-heap, as her fellow-servant told her she must light a fire, and prepare for a 'heavy wash.' While so doing, the lady of the house came out and spoke to her; Grace never lifted her eyes from the ground as she answered the questions; the thin, blue lips quivered, the hand was often drawn hastily over the downcast eyes. 'I never forget I'm a convict, ma'am,' she often said.

Grace lived long with that family, to whom she attached herself with that deep devotion which formed so strong a feature in her character; she followed them in their wanderings, was hard-working, and faithful, and gentle, and skilful in sickness and in hours of pain. It was hoped that she would end her days with them, either in that country, or 'at home.' But old recollections came thronging back. Sorrow and bereavement will be received,—it rests with us *how*. If we shut the door for a time, there will be a moment in which they find too sure entrance; we may stifle, stun, and poison them,—they do not die. They came back to Grace, and there were times when the old remedy could be procured. Then followed weeks of remorse—bitter remorse; sorrowful reproaches from her friends; taunts and sneers from those who were inclined to envy the favour shown her by her employers. Grace's bodily strength began to fail, yet she would never give up; she said working was the only way to keep down her sorrows, and work she did for every one. Then came a change from the secluded bush to the suburbs of a town, and it was no longer possible to guard her, as had been done. There were dreadful pangs as she again saw the sea, and its crested waves. She sat like one broken-hearted, gazing at it, or, flinging her arms wildly, saying her son was there, and she must go to him. None but the boy whom she idolized had power to move her; nothing but spirits or opium, which she found means to procure and hide, ever gave her sleep. A veil must be drawn over this latter part of her history.

It would be too painful to write or to read of the struggles and agony which ended in loss of reason—Grace died in a lunatic asylum! She was truly a prey to strong passionate affections, and keen sensibilities, which were unsanctified. She had turned from God to worship idols, and when they were crushed, the pain was lulled by stupifying and intoxicating draughts. May her end be a warning to any of my readers who is tempted 'to drown sorrow,'—often God's last and best gift!

RETRIBUTION

Mrs Charles Clacy

WILL DARLING WAS externally as rough a being as you could possibly meet with. To look at him, you would suppose he had been poacher, housebreaker, prize-fighter, and many other equally ruffianly characters all united in one. People feared him: except his gentle wife and tiny child, all dreaded his approach; but they ever hailed his return from work with delight, violent and quarrelsome though he was. There must have been some kindly qualities hidden beneath that rough exterior, or he could not have retained their affection. And he loved them: his voice might be harsh, his manner stern, but there was a deep love for them beneath it all.

They lived in a comfortable bark-hut, at the Forest Creek diggings. This hut was situated on a gentle slope, at the foot of which ran the golden stream itself, where the busy throng—heterogeneous in its costume, in its language, and its character, but unanimous in its pursuit—worked 'from morn till dewy eve,' washing the once-despised, dirty soil until the pure yellow metal was extracted.

A few of the far-famed gum-trees were scattered here and there, intermingled with some of the stringy-bark. The trunks of the former rose to a majestic height—sometimes two or three hundred feet—their scanty, drooping foliage giving but little shade. All the trees were stripped of their bark up to some distance from the ground, and from this the huts were made.

Will Darling's was a more comfortable one than an outside glance would have led a by-stander to imagine. The interstices were carefully filled up with mud and stones; a sort of fire-place, made also of mud and stone, had been built in one corner; and a barrel on a hole in the roof served as a partial conductor for the smoke.

The interior of this habitation was divided into two compartments by a thick blanket stretching from side to side. There was a round deal table, a chair or two, and many other little comforts scattered about, not often to be met with at Forest Creek.

About a hundred yards from Darling's hut was a large canvas store; and, that no mistake should arise as to the owner's name, 'J. BALL' was painted in large black letters upon it. Above was the flag—the vast variety of which attracts a stranger the moment he gazes on a digging scene; in this instance it was a Union Jack, rather the worse for wear. The store itself was full sixty feet long, and nearly twenty wide. Across the door was a sort of wooden counter, leaving about four feet between it and the entrance, so as to enable the customers to stand under shelter: the large space behind was lumbered with boxes full of goods and other articles connected with the business.

At a store, everything (that is, everything in reason that can be expected at the diggings) is sold: hence there is no need to go to one place for sugar, and to another for a pickaxe or calico; and on this counter a mass of things were lying about, to the great detriment of each other, and to the no small confusion of the people on either side of the counter. There were ten or twelve customers lounging about, and two persons attending to them—the storekeeper's wife and his assistant.

A tall swaggering Irishman entered, flung five shillings on the counter, and asked for three figs of tobacco, value at the diggings about ninepence apiece.

When his wishes had been complied with, he muttered, almost inaudibly to any but the person serving him, 'An' shure, wad yer send me away widout the drap of holy water?'

There was a nod and smile. A tumbler of strong scented, and certainly far from holy, liquid was placed before him, and quickly disappeared. He then left the store, and the five shillings were swept away by the assistant.

No one heeded this little piece of trickery; even had it been observed, they were all too used to it, and too glad to have recourse to it themselves, to draw attention to the fact; but they continued their conversation, discussing the rush here or there. So-and-so's 'find,' etc., as gravely and earnestly as farmers at a country market talk over the price of grain, or money-brokers at a stock exchange the state of the funds.

Another person entered, and commenced the narration of an accident which he had just witnessed—'A child well-nigh killed, and they were a-bringing on him here.'

'Whose child?' asked two or three who were fathers.

'Well, folks say as it's Will Darling's.'

'What!' interrupted he, springing up from an empty tea-chest on which he had been sitting smoking a pipe.

'Only,' replied the first speaker, who, though familiar with Will's name and character, did not know him by sight, 'Only Doctor B— in a hurry rode over a bairn, and folks say it's Darling's.'

'Only!' shouted Darling, infuriated, ready to spring upon and annihilate the unfortunate bearer of ill news; but at that moment the little sufferer, pallid with pain and fright, was brought in.

Darling's lips quivered as he took the boy from the arms of the man who carried him; but he was not allowed to hold him long, for the storekeeper's wife, with a woman's ready sympathy, took the patient child under her own especial charge, and tended him with almost a mother's own tenderness. Soon, however, Mrs. Darling herself and a doctor arrived, when it was ascertained that, though much hurt, no serious injury had been inflicted, and he would soon be able to be moved to his father's hut, where he ought to have been taken at once; but in the confusion of the moment the store had been thought of first.

Darling now inquired into the accident. It was simple, and not an uncommon one. A doctor had been sent for in a great hurry to attend a man who had severely maimed himself whilst working, and in his haste had knocked down little Darling, who was playing with several other lads in the roadway. The child must have been killed on the spot had not a 'mate' of Will's, named John Browning, sprang forward, and, with great presence of mind, swerved the horse aside, and snatched away the boy before the iron-shod foot had descended upon his head; then, taking him carefully in his arms, he carried him into Ball's store.

An acute by-stander—one given to watch the play of countenances, and who could discern the clouds or sunshine that pass over a face as plainly as if gazing on the sky—such a one would have remarked the piercing glance cast by Darling upon a dark, sinister-looking man, who stood a little distance from him; and thence, changing to a look of inquiry, settled upon Browning. It was a rapid glance—so rapid that only an acute observer, as I have said, would have noticed it; but, having done so, would ponder, perhaps, over the meaning of its peculiar intensity.

Let it not be supposed that he was slow to express his thanks for his mate's timely assistance, which he did with a warmth of manner that spoke sincerity.

Will Darling was one of a party of three working together at the diggings. Browning was a poor man, with a wife and family to support—ever ready to deny himself all but the barest necessaries, so as to remit something through the escort for their subsistence. Perkins, the third 'mate,' was of a taciturn disposition, with swarthy complexion, dark, cunning eye, and dissipated habits; yet he had acquired by some means an influence over Darling's mind which he hoped in time to turn to his own advantage.

For the last few weeks, their success in the digging line had been very uncertain: five times a rich vein appeared to have been discovered, but after a day, or even less, of profitable work, it was exhausted. This 'bad luck,' as it is termed, fell most severely upon Browning; and Perkins, to his great surprise, advanced him money to remit to his family, which, for any other purpose, he would not have accepted; but one thought of the eager faces of his wife and children induced him to lay himself under an obligation to a person he disliked—or, rather, *had disliked*—for how could he retain any sentiments of ill-will against one who had treated him so generously, and who, in return for the loan of the money, only demanded a strict promise of secrecy as to who had lent it him? This seemed the more strange to Browning, as he had, before Perkins joined them, related to Will many unpleasant stories against him, which Darling, with his usual straightforward way of acting, had repeated to the new mate, citing Browning as his informer; he had, therefore, expected spite and unfriendliness from Perkins; and, on receiving kindness instead, could not think too highly of him, or too severely blame himself for having been so far duped as to credit the stories in circulation against his character.

On the evening when the accident occurred to Darling's child, Perkins had commenced his insinuations against Browning's honesty; and, by a few cleverly arranged hints, left the impression on Will's mind that their mate had latterly been carrying on a systemic course of robbery, either whilst digging alone, or by abstracting gold from the hole during the night. There was nothing out of the way in this accusation, for perhaps the greatest drawback a steady man will experience at the diggings is the being cheated by his 'mates.' Few can resist the temptation, when working by themselves in a dark hole, of slipping two or three pretty nuggets into their pockets; and with some this is, without attracting suspicion, carried on to an incredible extent.

The conversation between Darling and Perkins on this subject had been broken off by the entrance of the stranger with the tidings of the mishap to the former's child; and there was something so touching to the rough father in the manner in which Browning had rescued his boy from death, and conveyed him to the store, that he felt less inclined than ever to believe anything against him.

In this frame of mind he was not long allowed to remain; before night, his evil counsellor, dwelling particularly on the fact of Browning's transmitting money to Melbourne when they were taking nothing from their holes, had worked him into such a suspicious state, that at Perkins's suggestion, several marked pieces of gold were to be placed in the hole, which he assured Will would never be seen again except by searching Browning for them.

It was two hours past midnight, and every thing was silent at Forest Creek. The revellers had found their tents, or sunk to sleep upon the ground; the weary frames of the miners were at rest; Nature herself was in repose; and the moon and stars—larger and more brilliant in that distant clime than here—flung their soft rays over that wild encampment, and tipped the tents, the stream, and the tall stately trees, as if with frosted silver.

Gradually a gliding figure became visible, cautiously moving as much as possible in the shade, and ever and anon glancing back—like one intent on evil—to see if any human eye were upon him. Cautiously and slowly he moved on till he came to a deep hole, rather removed from the others, down which he descended. He struck a light and then, with as little noise as he could make, he commenced following up a vein of gold which had that afternoon been discovered. For some time he pursued his nefarious work, till the large quantity of gold in his pockets reminded him that it would be wise to discontinue his labour. He now began to replace everything as he had found it—or, at least, as nearly so as he could; this was a work of considerable difficulty and time.

Whilst putting the finishing touches, he thus mused:—'No need to be over particular, if Darling noticed it looked touched, he'd think it was my putting in the marked pieces. Think I've killed two birds with one stone this time—gold for myself and revenge on Browning; soft fool, as if I hadn't a motive for lending him money; laying him under obligation to me, and blinding him as to what I'm about. Now, I've only to hide these bits in some of his things, and Darling will be convinced; shouldn't wonder if he half killed him; well, it won't hurt me. I think I can influence Will into taking a mate of my choosing, and then we'll play into one another's hands, till I've got enough, and then—'

Some loose earth fell upon him, and he looked up; thicker it fell, and thicker; a dark mass came between him and the fair blue sky; it descended, and he was buried alive.

Next morning, Browning and Will came to their work: Browning full of anxiety as to whether the day would yield as well as yesterday promised; and Darling earnestly wishing to discover that the preserver of his boy was an honest as he appeared.

They soon saw that from some reason the earth had fallen in, and on clearing it away the body of Perkins was brought to light. He had ceased to breathe; but the gold found upon him sufficed to prove not only that his insinuations against Browning were false, but that, whilst engaged in the very practice of which he had accused others, this awful fate had overtaken himself.

THE MASTER
AND HIS MAN

John Lang

I HAD OCCASION one day to attend the police office in Sydney. One of my convict servants, a farrier, had purposely 'pricked' and lamed a favourite horse of mine, and I was determined to have him flogged. The reader may naturally ask, how did I know the man had *purposely* pricked the animal? Because he had been heard to say that the next time the horse required to be shod, I wouldn't be able to ride him for some weeks to come. I might, by speaking to the magistrate, have had the culprit put upon the treadmill for a month, or placed in a road-gang, to work in irons, for three, six, nine, or twelve months, or flogged to the extent of one hundred lashes, twenty-five being the minimum. (By the way, there were slang terms applied to these doses of the lash. Twenty-five was called a 'tester'; fifty, a 'bob'; seventy-five, a 'bull'; and a hundred, a 'canary'.) My chief reason for having the farrier flogged was that I should not long be deprived of his services, for I had made up my mind to suggest to the magistrate that he should only receive fifty; and as he was a strong, stout man, that number could not do him much harm, while it would suffice to operate upon him as a punishment. Fifty lashes, administered by the hands of a landsman, who was a convict himself, were not equal to nine administered by the strong arm of a boatswain who can cut 'cross-ways.' Had Captain G., whom Marryat had immortalized, seen a convict flogged at Hyde Park Barracks, Sydney, he might have been justified in exclaiming to the operator—'One would think you were brushing flies off a sleeping Venus, instead of punishing a scoundrel with a hide as thick as a buffalo's! "One!" Do you call that one? It is not a quarter of one! You are only fit to be a fly-flapper at a pork-shop! You Molly Mop! Is that the way you handle a cat? *Where's the boatswain?*

I was walking up and down the courtyard, waiting for the case to be called on, when I was approached and saluted by that prince of Australian thief-takers, Mr. George Flower, who figures so conspicuously in 'The Forger's Wife.'

'It is a beautiful day, sir,' he remarked.

'Very,' I replied.

'And a pretty world it is, sir.'

'Yes. But what leads you to make the remark at this moment?'

'Do you see these two men standing in the doorway of the office, talking?'

'Yes.'

The two men to whom Flower called my attention were habited in fustian trousers, fustian waistcoats, fustian shooting-coats, and black neckties. On their heads were common straw hats; on their feet high-low shoes. Had I been asked to guess their occupation, I should have said that they were constables. One of these men was nearly six feet high; the other not more than five feet four.

'They are "Master and Man,"' resumed Flower. 'The short un is the master—the long un is the man. The short un is a lord—the eldest son of an English earl. The long un is—heaven knows who. He was lagged under the name of Adolphus Frederick Jones. But he is a blood, and there's no mistake about it, sir!'

Here the two men of whom Flower was speaking approached us, and the 'short un' (as Flower called him) made me a very graceful bow and said, 'Forgive me, if I am interrupting you; but I am very anxious to speak to Mr. Flower about a pencil-case which I have lost. It is of no great value intrinsically, but to me it is very precious.'

I signified by a gesture that Mr. Flower was at his entire disposal.

The taller person also saluted me by raising his hat, and his bearing at once satisfied me that he was a man of good birth. I returned his salute, but I evinced no desire to enter into conversation with him; on the contrary, I sauntered away, for it mattered not what might have been his rank or former position in society, since he was then a convict undergoing the punishment of transportation for some criminal offence—in short, a convicted felon.

Ere long my case was called on. I hastened into the office and deposed on oath as follows:—'The prisoner, my assigned servant, farrier by trade, purposely lamed one of my horses while shoeing him.'

'You are satisfied he did it on purpose?' the magistrate asked me.

'Perfectly,' I replied.

'What have you to say to the charge?' the magistrate asked the prisoner.

'Didn't do it on purpose, your worship.'

'It is enough that you lamed the horse.'

Here I made my suggestion as to what the punishment should be, and it was forthwith awarded, the magistrate informing the prisoner that he was fortunate in having so lenient a master. The case did not occupy five minutes. Such cases were always speedily settled.

I have mentioned in a former paper that in 'the good old times' (as they were called) every master who was a magistrate might hold a court and punish his own convict servants. Such, however, was not the case at the time to which this narrative refers. General Rourke then ruled the colony, and the privilege above alluded to having been grossly abused, His Excellency ordered that no magistrate should have any voice in the punishment of his servants, beyond making a suggestion as to the *mode* of punishment, and that all offenders were to be tried in police courts, before *stipendiary* magistrates.

After leaving the court, I mounted my horse and was riding towards my home, some seven miles distant from Sydney, on the Paramatta road, when I was overtaken by Mr. Flower, who, mounted on his famous galloway, Sheriff, was proceeding to a place called Prospect, to effect, if possible, the capture of three notorious bushrangers. He pulled up, and as we jogged along the road together he gave me some further information touching 'The Master and his Man.' In short, Flower afforded me their history, so far as it related to their appearance in the colony of New South Wales. It was thus he ran on:—

'As I have already told you, sir, the short un is a lord—that we know. Who the long un is nobody knows, as he was lagged under a false name. Some say that *he* is the son of a lord; but that's all guess-work. That he was born a gentleman, we don't want a ghost to come and tell us.'

'Certainly not,' I conceded.

'How the long un came to be lagged was this. Two or three years ago, when they were at college, they went to Greenwich, or Gravesend—I forgot which—and they hired a trap to take 'em to London. When they got to London, where they spent all the ready money they had, and both being very fresh, blest if long un doesn't go and sell the trap to a livery-stable keeper, who directly afterwards found out who was the real owner of the trap. Long un was followed, and collared, and given in charge. A clearer case there couldn't be; and as drunkenness is not held as an excuse for felony,

'How did you raise that £335?' I one day asked the thief-taker.

'Well, sir, I did it in this way,' was the reply. 'There was fifty pound reward for Carroty Joe, the bushranger that I shot at Campbell Town and brought in dead. There was fifty for his pal, that I captured and brought in alive. There was five-and-twenty for a bolter from Captain Johnston—a man that had been out two years. That was £125. The rest I borrowed from four Jews, receivers of stolen property, on these easy and quiet terms: my verbal promissory note, payable with interest at one thousand per cent. per annum—the account to be settled on the great day of judgment, and the money to be forthcoming on the day after.'

'And did they consent to those terms?'

'Consent, sir! Why, there is not one of them that I could not transport to Norfolk Island for life, at any moment that I like.'

A few weeks after Mr. Geary returned to England he became an earl, and at this present moment enjoys the title and the estates of his ancestors. He repaid Flower to the full and did not fail to repeat how grateful he felt to him for his 'kindness rendered at a time of such dire difficulty and need.'

MUSIC A TERROR

John Lang

My recollections of Australia relate to some years back, long before the colony had a legislative assembly or a free press—long before emigration had carried to its shores shoals of men and women 'unconnected with the Crown'—long before gold was discovered in the district of Bathurst, or Sir Thomas Mitchell had explored that vast tract of country called by him 'Australia Felix.' I write, indeed, of those times still spoken of by some as 'those good old times,' when the assignment system prevailed and government were glad to get rid of their convicts to masters who would feed, clothe and work them; when 'summary punishments' were the order of the day, and every gentleman was his own magistrate; when the quartern loaf sold for half-a-crown, and beef and mutton for three-halfpence a pound; when the value of a hogshead of rum was £200, and an acre of land five shillings; when money could not be borrowed, even upon good security, for less than thirty per cent, per annum.

In those good old times, I had, in partnership with a gentleman who managed it, a cattle station about 120 miles from Sydney, at a place called Bong-Bong. My partner had formerly held an ensign's commission in the 73rd Regiment of His Late Majesty George III, but shortly after his arrival in the colony he had fallen in love with a very handsome girl of humble birth, whom he married, and then retired from the army, took a grant of land and 'settled' permanently in New South Wales.

My friend and partner, Mr. Romer, was blessed with a numerous offspring—seven sons and four daughters. The eldest was a boy of fourteen and the youngest a baby 'in arms.' They were all remarkably fine children—strong, healthy and intelligent—

but they were uncultivated, of course, like the wilds in the midst
of which they had been born and bred. The only white people
whom they had ever seen were their parents, the convict servants
(some twenty in number) and sundry stray visitors and stockmen
who happened occasionally to pass the station and require shelter
for the night. Nor had their children ever seen any buildings
beyond the mud and slab house in which they lived, and the bark
huts occupied by the servants. Nor had they seen pictures or prints
save those to be found in the old-fashioned spelling-books, by the
aid of which Mrs. Romer, in her few leisure moments, had taught
the elder children to read. The only music they had ever heard was
that which a very rude fife discoursed when played upon by a
hutkeeper, and the only airs that he could compass were 'God Save
the King,' 'Rule Britannia' and 'Poor Mary Anne.' Neither Romer
nor his wife had much 'ear' for melody, and never did more than
hum the words of some old song.

It was my wont to visit the cattle station once a year, and upon
every occasion I used to take with me a variety of presents for my
young friends in the bush. Toys, such as tin-barrelled guns, brass
watches, Dutch dolls, various wooden animals in deal boxes, etc.;
of these they had grown tired, and it now became with me a matter
of great difficulty to get anything likely to please and amuse them.
One morning while walking up George Street, Sydney (the houses
in George Street were in those days all detached residences,
standing in their own grounds), I observed an unusually large
crowd in front of the auction mart. Curiosity prompted me to
ascertain what was the object of attraction. It was nothing short
of 'a piano—to be sold by auction to the highest bidder. Terms,
cash; or an approved bill at three months, bearing interest at 25 per
cent.'

There was not at that time more than five pianos in the colony,
and *this* piano was considered by far the best, inasmuch as it had
once belonged to Mrs. Macquarie, the wife of Major-General
Lauchlan Macquarie, Governor of New South Wales and its
dependencies. At the sale of the general's effects when he was going
home, it had been purchased by the provost-marshal, whose
necessities subsequently compelled him to part with it to a Jew,
who exchanged it with an officer who particularly desired it for an
allotment of land containing eleven acres on the Surrey Hills, near
the old racecourse—a part of which allotment of land has since
realised upwards of £20,000. To trace the old piano through the
different hands into which it afterwards fell would be no easy
matter. Let it suffice that it was now the property of a butcher with
whom I had frequent dealings, and who bought periodically the

fat bullocks which we reared at the cattle station under Captain Romer's superintendence. (I say *Captain*, because everyone called him Captain Romer).

It may be as well to describe the instrument now about to be submitted to public competition. It was three feet two inches long and two feet wide. Its mahogany case had become almost black, and its once white keys were now as yellow as the claws of a kite. The legs were rather rickety, and constant use and frequent removal had greatly impaired and weakened the tone, which in the infancy of the instrument had never been very powerful. However, it was a piano, nevertheless; and there was 'all Sydney' waiting to see it sold, and half of those present ready to bid for it.

An auction room—like love and death—levels all ranks, and on that day were to be seen government officials, mechants who had come out 'free', merchants who had originally come out 'bond' (emancipist), traders, wealthy farmers, Jews, *et hoc genus omne*, straining and jostling to get a sight of, and close to, this (in the words of the auctioneer) 'eligible opportunity of introducing 'armony in the buzzim of a family circle.'

Amongst the crowd was a Frenchman, whose ignorance of the English law relating to chattels (he had 'taken' some valuables belonging to another person) had led to his being furnished with a passage to Botany Bay. This Frenchman had been a teacher of music in London, and at the request of the auctioneer he 'favoured the company' with a few pieces of music, and thus spared the auctioneer—so he said—the trouble of 'hewlogising the instrument, since it could speak for itself.' Had pianos been common in New South Wales, silence on the part of this one would have been more prudent, so far as the interests of the owner were concerned.

No sooner did I witness the delight which the cracked tones of that old piano afforded to so many of the bystanders, than I made up my mind—was determined—to become its purchaser. I was certain that I should be vehemently opposed on all sides; but I did not care about that, especially as I knew that my friend the butcher would have no objection to be paid in cattle instead of coin. I need scarcely say that it was not for myself that I wanted the old piano, although I could play a little; it was for the children of my friend and partner, Romer—whose surprise I longed to witness when they saw me touch the keys and produce a sound—that I craved for the ownership of that antique instrument.

After a brief while, when the Frenchman had ceased to edify the throng, the bidding commenced. 'What shall we say, gentlemen, for this elegant instrument?' the auctioneer enquired. 'Start it at what you please—£150 if you like.'

'Fifty!' said a voice in the crowd.

A roar of laughter followed this ridiculous appreciation of an instrument—a piano—that once belonged to Mrs. Macquarie, while the auctioneer, with an expression of face which plainly betokened how deeply his feelings had been hurt, remarked, very solemnly: 'Those people who come here to joke had better wait till the sale's over, and not interrupt business.' Eventually, it was 'started' at £100, but it was very soon run up to £130. Here it stopped for a while, and I nodded my head. '£140—£140' cried the auctioneer, who refused to take any bid under £10. A very brisk competition now ensued between several individuals and I remained silent, though unshaken in my resolve.

The piano was now 'going for £175—going for £175—once—twice—third, and the ——' I nodded my head.

'£185—£185!' said the auctioneer.

There was 'no advance' for some minutes, and I was in hopes that I should get it for that last bid of mine, but I was mistaken. A gentleman known as Billy Hatcherson—an expatriated highwayman—a very wealthy man, wanted it for one of his daughters who was about to be married, and he roared out, in a very defiant manner, '£200—there!' and, confident that it would be his, he left the room triumphantly and went 'over the way' to refresh himself with a glass of grog.

Another spirited competition now took place, and eventually the piano became my property at £250.

I was quite right in my conjecture that the butcher would be glad to take cattle in payment, and before leaving the auction we concluded a bargain. I was to deliver to him within three months from that date, seventy fat oxen such as I had previously sold to him.

In the days of which I am writing there were no post-offices in New South Wales, much less public carriers, and I had to wait several weeks before I could find a dray going to any station within forty miles of Captain Romer's abode (settlers usually accommodated each other by carrying packages to and from the interior), and it was not until after I had myself arrived at the station that Romer received the news of 'a large box for him at the station of Major Belrington,' another retired officer who had settled in the wilds of Australia.

The despatch of the piano I had kept a secret, and when Romer heard of this 'large box' he could not comprehend it, for he had ordered nothing, and expected nothing, from Sydney. He sent off, however, a cart drawn by a pair of bullocks, and on the third day the large box arrived. 'With Great Care' was painted on the lid, and with *very* great care it was removed from the cart and placed in the verandah.

The advent of a package and the opening thereof was always a great event at the station, even when it was expected. There would be seen Romer with a mallet and chisel in his hands, ready to break into it, no matter whether it was a cask of sugar, a chest of tea, or a case full of slop clothing for the men; while Mrs. Romer, with the youngest child in her arms, might be seen dividing her anxiety touching the condition of the stores with her fears for the children's safety—for they would all flock round their father and frequently go much too close to the implements in his hands. But here was a *special* case—a most mysterious box. Romer said he had dreamt that some of his relations in England had sent him an assortment of saddlery, which would have been particularly acceptable; and he was hoping in his heart that 'saddlery' it would turn out. Mrs. Romer had also a dream—that her father had sent a large box of clothing for herself and the children, and she was hoping for the realisation of *her* dream. It would be in vain to attempt a description of the surprise and disgust of Romer and his excellent wife when they beheld the old piano.

'Such a useless thing!' said Romer.

'Who could have sent it?' said his wife.

While they were thus expressing themselves, the whole of their children, each in a different key, were shouting out:

'Papa! Ma! What's a piano? What's a piano?'

I laughed so heartily at the scene that both Romer and his wife were perfectly satisfied that I had something to do with 'the joke'— for as such they regarded the appearance of a piano in that Australian wilderness—and at last I confessed to them that I had bought the instrument for the amusement and instruction of their young ones.

The piano, which was locked and the key in my waistcoat pocket, had withstood all the attempts of the children to open it in order to see what was inside, and Romer and myself carefully carried it into the room wherein the family were accustomed to dine. (It may be needless, perhaps, to inform the reader that in those remote regions where Captain Romer resided 'drawing-rooms' were dispensed with).

I was just as impatient to witness the effect of music (such as the old piano was capable of) upon the children as were the children to see 'What's inside!' I therefore hastily unlocked it and, placing my foot upon the pedal, swept the chords as vigorously as was prudent, considering the shaky state of the piano.

Alas! instead of delighting the children, I terrified them. Some ran out of the room, shrieking, 'It's alive! it's alive!'—others stood aghast with their mouths wide open. One of the little boys fancied the keys were a row of huge teeth, which would bite me if I continued to touch them, whilst a little girl of four years of age begged of her mamma not to let the baby go near it. The eldest girl, observing that the instrument was perfectly harmless, was approaching my side but was violently pulled back by two of her brothers. Presently, those who had run away returned to the door, and finding that there was no real danger, re-entered the room. By degrees the whole of them were not only reconciled to the belief that the piano was not only inanimate, but vastly pleased with the tunes which I played upon it. Ere long they became both bold and familiar, and, approaching the old instrument, they dealt it several blows with their clenched fists, which, had they been repeated, would soon have silenced it for ever.

When the children had gone to bed—and it was a rather difficult matter to prevail upon them to retire, so maddened had they become with the sound of the music—I played several airs which in former days had been very familiar to the ears of Romer and his wife, but which they had not heard for upwards of sixteen years. Amongst others was 'The Girl I Left Behind Me,' an air which the band of Romer's old regiment—the 73rd—used to play constantly on parade, when the regiment was marching past the colours.

When I had finished playing the air I turned round and said to Romer, 'You remember that, don't you?'

What was my astonishment to find my friend in tears. The large drops were rolling down his sunburnt cheeks. 'What is the matter?' I inquired of him.

'Ah, sir!' he replied, 'you have brought back to me the morning when I embarked for this country, and when, for the last time, I saw my mother and sisters. That old piano makes it seem as though it were only yesterday that I parted from them.'

And Mrs. Romer was crying. *Why?* Because when she knew that Charley really loved her, and they were engaged to be married, she used to go every morning to see the old 73rd paraded, and kept her eyes upon the colours which Charley, as junior ensign, used to carry when the regiment marched past them and played that old tune—'The Girl I Left Behind Me.' And a very happy air it was, and sweet to her ears; for, shortly after it had ceased, Charley and herself had their morning meeting and used to walk round the spot which was called 'the Government Domain.' The tears that were shed by Romer and his wife were not tears of unhappiness; for, although they were not musical, their domestic life had never known a single discord.

'Play it again!' said Romer and his wife, simultaneously—the latter now sitting on her husband's knees, her arm encircling his neck—'Oh! play it again. Do, please!'

I obeyed them, but was soon interrupted by the children, who rushed from their beds to the dining-room and began to dance— or, rather, to 'jump about,' in imitation of the gestures of the aborigines in the act of choral exercises. The boys were clothed only in their nightshirts, the girls in their bed-gowns; and to the best of their ability they followed the air I was playing with their voices. Such a scene! Had the old piano cost me double the number of the fat oxen I had contracted to give for it, I could not have grudged the price.

One of the house-dogs began to bark fiercely and Romer went to the door, whence he saw the whole of the servants, attracted by the sound of the pianoforte, drawn up in line and listening most attentively to the music. Romer, who was one of the most kind-hearted men that the world ever produced, entered completely into their feelings and invited them to sit down in the verandah, and he sent them out two bottles of rum and several ounces of tobacco wherewith to regale themselves while the music was gladdening their souls and carrying them back to scenes in the land which, in all probability, they would never again behold.

It was long after eleven o'clock before we retired to rest that night, and even then the children were frantic for 'more noise,' as they called it.

The next morning, soon after daylight, Romer came into my apartment and, with a smile on his face, said, 'This old piano, it occurs to me, may be turned to very profitable account.'

'How?' I inquired.

'We may make it an instrument of terror to the blacks. Of late they have become awfully troublesome in the matter of spearing the cattle, merely for the fat wherewith to grease themselves, and only last week we lost in this way a very valuable cow. I will send for some of the tribe and frighten them—or, rather, *you* must—by playing on the bass keys.'

I liked the idea vastly. Besides, I was very curious to see the expression of a savage's face when, for the first time, he heard music.

The encampment of the blacks was only three or four miles distant, and a stockman was sent to bring several of them; and at noon, about eight or nine of them, in all their nudity, made their appearance. Mrs. Romer had a strong objection to admit them in or near the house, and so Romer and I carried the old piano out into the open space in front of the dwelling.

The aboriginal native of New Holland—just like the native of India—cannot help touching and examining everything that is strange to him; and no sooner did the 'blacks' whom we summoned observe the old piano, than they moved towards and examined it very attentively.

One of them at last opened the instrument and touched the keys rather heavily, and (like Fear in the 'Ode to the Passions'), terrified at the sound he had produced, recoiled backwards, his spear poised ready to be thrown, and his brilliant black eye firmly fixed on the demon, for as such he regarded the old piano. His companions also poised their long spears and retreated cautiously step by step.

Romer now begged of them not to be alarmed, and with some little difficulty brought them back to the piano, where he represented to them that inside was a fearful demon, who would eat up the whole of their tribe if he were told to do so; but that, if they did nothing to offend or annoy him (Romer), they had nothing whatever to fear.

I corroborated this statement by nodding my head, and, advancing to the instrument, I touched the keys and began to play as loudly as possible. Who shall describe their faces and their attitudes? Some of them grasped their boomerangs, others poised their spears ready to repel any sudden attack that the demon might make upon them. It was a scene such as I would not have missed on any account.

When I had ceased playing, Romer explained to them that I had been telling the demon what he was to do on the next occasion of a bullock, a cow, or a calf being speared on the run; and they must have believed every word he said, for from that day forward the nuisance abated and the tribe very rarely came near the forest where our cattle used to graze; so that the old piano, after all, was by no means dear at the price I paid for it, to say nothing of the amusement which it afforded to Romer's children.

The old piano is still extant. Not long ago I had a letter from Romer, who is now both old and rich, in which he said, 'There are thousands of pianos in the colony now, of all sorts, sizes and prices, from £25 up to £100; but not for any one of them would we exchange our old friend here, which has a place of honour in one of our drawing-rooms, and reposes its tottering legs on a Turkey carpet.'

REVENGE OR JEM DALTON

H. Earle

JEM DALTON WAS as ugly a customer as any one would wish to meet after sunset in a lonely spot. His face wore a cramped, savage expression; one eye possessed a most horrible squint—his brows were shaggy and heavy—his nose broken and large—his form tall, his limbs muscular, and his unkempt hair of a dirty brown. To complete the amiable portrait, his moral character was one peculiarly belonging to such an appearance: his honesty was questionable, and his temper violent. Why Mr. Wootherspoon had engaged such a man, is a riddle I shall not attempt to solve. He filled the situation of shepherd upon the run, a position which, though humble, is one of great responsibility. A shepherd has it in his power to do much harm, from malice or negligence; or he can enhance the value of his charge to an immense extent. How far Jem Dalton studied the interest of his employer, the sequel of my little story will show.

It may not be amiss, before going on any further, to give the reader an idea of the nature of a Shepherd's duties in Australia, and also the character of his life.

He is always, or should be, up before sunrise, so as to get his breakfast over early. He then lets his sheep out of the fold; once out, they require no guiding or driving, the shepherd merely follows with his dogs. They are sure to wander where the feed is best. He should be careful not to permit them to disperse, or enter any thick bush; should they evince any desire to do so, it is his duty to prevent them. This he does either by walking round them, or sending his dogs to drive them back to the right place. About midday he drives them to water, and here they remain during the heat of the day. Meanwhile, the shepherd may be employed in any way he pleases; if he is industrious, he mends his clothes or washes them, should they need it. If it should suit him better, he can occupy himself with his knife, tobacco, and pipe. Just before sunset, he collects his sheep and drives them home. This is no difficulty, as they will generally assemble for the purpose of their own accord. During the night they are folded securely, to preserve them from the attacks of the native dogs, which sometimes do incalculable mischief among the flocks. The sheep are counted generally once a-week, to see whether or not there are any missing. The folds are always visited by the careful shepherd once or twice during the dark hours.

His life is one of extreme solitude, unless he has his family with him. This solitude does not, as a rule, improve his disposition, but renders him taciturn and morose. He is generally an ignorant man, and without either the desire or capacity for improving his mind in any way. He is thus as much a brute as his sheep or his dogs. Liberal settlers usually have a few books, which they lend their servants to read, if they feel inclined.

Mr. Wootherspoon was not a whit behind others in this respect, for he had rather an extensive library of useful and instructive books, especially for the service of those he employed. Our shepherd, Jem Dalton, however, was one of those who looked upon reading and writing as useless to any one except clerks and parsons, and consequently never took advantage of his employer's library.

On one occasion, his rations did not seem to come up to the usual standard of quality; so, after folding his sheep early in the afternoon, and swearing at his wife, as usual, he started off in no very agreeable state of mind to the Home-station, in order to change them for better. The distance was about seven miles. He wandered along carelessly and sulkily, with his eyes fixed on the ground, and his dirty wide-awake hat pressed over his face. As he approached the station, he met several of the labourers and servants, but took no notice, either of them or their salutation. The servants knew his disposition, and merely shrugged their shoulders at his churlishness.

He arrived at length, and with a surly growl complained that his rations were bad, and asked in no very polite language for better. The overseer told him that it was a mistake on his part, and that though he was justified in complaining, there was no necessity for impertinence. 'Now,' he added, 'just get back to your run as quickly as you can—and send your wife the next time you want anything.'

It was quite dark when he reached home, and he had some

difficulty in finding his way. He was guided, however, by the bleating of his sheep; he listened attentively, and fancied he heard the baying of dingoes, or wild dogs, mingled with the sound. He hurried towards the fold, and, to his disgust, discovered half-a-dozen dingoes destroying the sheep as fast as they could. He drove them off as soon as he got at them, but not before considerable mischief had been done. It now occurred to him that he had left one of the hurdles unlashed; the dogs had consequently had easy ingress to the fold.

While he was engaged in collecting the slaughtered sheep, Mr. Wootherspoon, who had been on a visit for some days to a friend on a neighbouring station, happened to pass close by the fold, and, seeing a man employed within, called out, 'Who's there?' Jem, who had no idea that any one was in his neighbourhood, turned round in amazement, and not recognising the voice, replied gruffly—

'What the —— is that to you?'

'Come closer,' said Mr. Wootherspoon, in an angry voice, 'and you'll soon see.'

Jem cautiously approached, prepared for any attack on the part of the—to him—stranger.

'Now, what the deuce are you doing in the fold at this hour?' asked his master, whom he now recognised.

'Doin'!' returned Jem, 'why, I'm a seein' what mischief the —— dingoes ha' done—that's what I'm a doin'.'

'Mischief, you ugly-looking thief!' shouted Mr. Wootherspoon. 'What! have you allowed the —— dogs to get into the fold? You careless fool!—take that for your pains, then.' With this, he gave Jem several smart blows across the shoulder with his riding-whip, which made that worthy start back, and writhe with pain. If Mr. Wootherspoon had seen the hideous glare of Jem's villanous eyes, and the devilish contraction of his unamiable features, he would have paused, after the first application of the whip, and ridden off at once. Jem said nothing, but stood, with his arms folded across his broad chest, trembling with rage. He knew that Mr. Wootherspoon always carried a revolver in his belt, or he would have buried his clasp-knife in his body. Yes, there he stood—hate and revenge as plainly stamped upon his frightful countenance as though it were printed on a sheet of the whitest paper, in the largest type. At length he turned towards the fold, and secured the entrance; and then, without a word or sign, retired in the direction of his hut.

Mr. Wootherspoon was a good sort of man, and, as a rule, a kind and lenient master; but, when crossed or vexed, most violent and hasty. He felt that he had been so in this instance, and would have recalled Jem, to have spoken a little kindly to him—but it was too late.

He rode away home as fast as he could in the dark, pondering upon the late event, and regretting the display of his hasty temper. It was always thus with him—sorrow and regret invariably followed his anger. He reached the house, and calling his overseer to him, narrated what had transpired, and bade him ride over in the morning to learn the extent of the loss.

Meanwhile, Jem prepared for a start, thinking, of course, that he would be discharged; and, with the assistance of his wife—who, by the way, was, in appearance at least, a suitable companion for such a man—packed up his few traps. To his astonishment, however, when the overseer came over in the morning, nothing was said about his going—so far from it, he only received a caution to be more careful in future.

The fact is, Mr. Wootherspoon was so thoroughly ashamed of his part in the proceedings of the previous evening, that he determined to take no further notice of the loss, but to let the thrashing stand against it. Moreover, he determined to ride over in the course of a day or two, in order to have a little quiet talk with Jem—not, of course, on the subject of the horsewhipping, but about other matters connected with the sheep—merely that he might see that he entertained no ill-will towards him, and was inclined to be friendly.

He did so, and, to all outward appearance, Jem was as amiable as he could be; no word relating to the events of that unpleasant night was ever uttered by either party. In fact, Jem was, or appeared to be, much more agreeable than formerly; he sometimes returned the salutation of his fellow-servants when he met any of them; he was also more select in his choice of words when he went up to the station. The sheep were always well looked after, and, although there were a great many wild dogs in the neighbourhood, none were lost. Altogether, the overseer reported that Jem seemed to be an improving man. Once he ventured to borrow a book from the library, but not being a proficient in the art of reading, he kept it for a fortnight, and then returned it—minus a few leaves, which he had extracted to light his pipe with. And so a month or two passed away very smoothly.

One evening, as Jem and his wife sat in their hut, having their tea by the light of a large log-fire, that blazed and crackled merrily in the huge chimney, the sound of a horse's hoofs approached the hut.

'Who the ——'s this, I wonder?' growled Jem; 'the governor come down to see whether any more sheep are killed, I suppose; well, he's sold this time, anyhow.'

The horse pulled up at the door of the hut, and the rider, in a loud gruff voice, shouted—

'Hilloh, Jem! where are you?'

He recognised the voice, and quickly opened the door; and there, in a soft pale stream of moonlight, sat on horseback an individual, who, in the dusk, might have been taken for Jem himself. He sat his strong cob as one used to riding, and bore in his hand one of those whips peculiar to the colony, called stockwhips. As his horse moved carelessly, a gleam of moonlight fell upon a face very little removed from Jem's in point of expression and feature, and scarred in every possible direction. His hair hung in matted locks, of iron-grey colour and wiry texture, over his deep-set eyes.

'What! is that you, Knotty?' said Jem; 'what brings you over here at this time? Has anything gone wrong your way? Jump off and come in. Make your horse fast to that 'ere stump. Well, how are you, old boy? Tip us your flipper.'

He 'tipped his flipper' accordingly, and the interesting pair entered the hut. The light of the blazing fire disclosed to view the tall, gaunt form of Knotty, the extraordinary development of whose joints, which were projecting and large, fully accounting for the oddity of his name. He was Jem's equal in point of height, but inferior in depth and breadth of chest. As the two stood before the fire, side by side, and the ruddy glare fell upon them, an observer would have at once concluded that a more villanous-looking couple never aspired to the glorious elevation of a gallows.

Bet, Jem's wife, now joined them, and after returning Knotty's salutation of 'Well, old woman, how was you?' with a 'Pretty well, matey; how's yourself?' picked up a bucket, and went out to the creek for water. She was a short, stout woman, with a huge, bloated, good-natured face, high cheek-bones, and the smallest possible eyes. Her nose was almost hidden by the rotundity of her cheeks, which were of the sallowest tint imaginable, almost verging into yellow. Her hands were large and fat—so fat, indeed, that the knuckles were entirely hidden. She returned with the water, and poured some into a saucepan, which she placed upon the fire to boil.

'As soon as that water biles,' said Jem, 'we'll have some hot bingo; I've got some stunnin' stuff here; Bill Carter brought it from the hill the other day.'

As soon as the water boiled the grog was mixed, and the worthy pair sat down.

'Well, I didn't expect you over to-night, anyhow,' observed Jem; 'what the —— made you come?'

'Nothin' particular, Jem,' returned Knotty; 'seein' as I'd got nothin' to do, I thought I'd play the swell, and go out a wisitin'. But tip us a gag o' fogus, old boy. I'm quite cleaned out.'

The fogus, as he was pleased to term tobacco, was accordingly given him, and the conversation was renewed.

'How are you gettin' on with your cove, Jem? Have you got over your lickin' yet?'

'Well, you know,' replied Jem, sagely, 'when swell coves get licked, they says as how they must have satisfaction—which means, I guess, a puttin' a ounce or two of lead into a chap, or gettin' one put into themselves. Now, I've a hankering arter satisfaction o' some sort or another, and without the chance of gettin' served out myself, and I don't know how to set about it.'

'Don't let that bother you,' said Knotty, 'it'll all come square some day. The cove's sure to pay for it somehows or another. That lickin' was a reg'lar act of injustice, though, and no gammon. What a hot devil your governor must be, to be sure. I recollect, not many years ago, and not many hundred mile from this yer run, a squatter, who had dropped upon a shepherd for next to nothin' at all, had all, or nearly all his sheep scabbed just arterwards; and sarved him right, too, say I, howsomever it came about; and the runs are all spoiled to this 'ere very day.'*

'Well, now, that was queer,' observed Jem, slily; ''it seems as if it was done on purpose; I suppose you never heard how they got it?'

'No,' returned Knotty; 'our cove—I mean the squatter— supposed they got it from some scabby sheep as was a goin' down from another station; and between you and me, Jem, I thinks so myself, though when and how I don't pretend to know; but, I say, Bessy, my lass, give us some more hot water; and Jem, you shove over the bottle; you keeps it all to yourself.'

Bet, whose temper was considerably soured by ill-treatment at the hands of her husband, and who had sat quietly by during the foregoing short conversation, watching the faces of the speakers, concluded, from Jem's malicious and horrible grin, that he was at no loss to discover who had been the means of introducing the scab among the sheep; neither had she wandered far from the mark when she thought she read, in the aforesaid grin, a determination to effect the same cruel purpose in the sheep under his charge, in

---

* Sheep runs are spoiled if once a flock of scabby sheep pass over them. Others, though sound, feeding on the same ground, are sure to be infected.

revenge for the blows received at the hands of Mr. Wootherspoon. She, however, kept her thoughts (wisely) to herself, and with as agreeable a smile as she could raise upon her face, passed the hot water to Knotty.

'How many sheep was scabbed?' asked Jem, harping upon the subject; 'nearly all, did you say?'

'Yes, precious near,' replied Knotty; 'and a mighty lot o' money he lost by them; he was obliged to send 'em all to town to sell for their taller. I'll never forget the cove's looks when he first yeard on it; he came up to me, and raved and swore tremendous, as if I know'd anythink about it. I told him I was a stockman, and not a shepherd. I believe he thinks I had somethin' to do with it—but not on purpose, though—to this day.'

'And I don't think your cove—for of course they was his sheep; I know'd that, for all your tryin' to hide it—I don't think your cove was far out, neither, Knotty,' said Jem, with a knowing wink.

'Mayhap he was, and mayhap he wasn't, Jem,' returned Knotty; 'but that ain't here nor there. But I must cut it; so good night to yer; good night, Bessy; 'and without waiting for either party to offer an obstacle to his departure, the honest and maligned stockman jumped on his horse's back, and rode off home.

No single word did Jem address to his wife, as they sat on either side of the fire-place, but remained silent and thoughtful. A plan of vengeance had at length occurred to him, and this plan he was resolved to mature; and as he sat there, the fitful gleams of the blazing logs gave him an appearance so revolting and diabolical that Bet shuddered, and rising turned away.

Mr. Wootherspoon was, as I before observed, a kind and good man, and had gained from Bet all the esteem such an individual could be likely to yield; she was therefore at a loss what course to pursue. Should she hasten to the Home-station, and inform him of what she was convinced were Jem's intentions? She cast a side-long glance at her partner, and trembled at the thought of the punishment she would receive at his hands, if detected: and with an approach to a sigh at the awful bonds that encumbered her, and prevented her performing even one good act, she threw herself back upon her bed, and tried to sleep.

A month passed away, and as yet Jem had done nothing towards perfecting his plan of revenge. Bet began to think that he had changed his mind; and so would my reader have thought, had he seen how carefully and cleverly he tended his sheep. So greatly had they improved in every respect, that both the overseer and Mr. Wootherspoon were loud in their praises of him. Jem only smiled as they praised him, and mumbled rather than said, 'Thank you,

Sir; they is lookin' pretty well, I think,' or something to that effect.

Again it is night, and moonlight, too; and again the stockman and shepherd are seated in front of the fire, which lights up the faces of the two; disclosing, in one, the exultation consequent upon a nearly matured plan, and in the other the quiet satisfaction of a successful though coarse Mephistopheles.

'It was a good dodge of yours, and no mistake,' said Jem, 'that of gammonin' to be such a first-rate honest shepherd. Lord, you should o' heard the cove, and Chalmers, the overseer, a praisin' of me this mornin'; I thought I should ha' bust. What a sell for 'em when they finds all their sheep scabbed; I thinks I shall die o' laughin'. I say, though,' he added, with an earnest look at the other, 'you are sure you are not wrong about the part of the run, are you?'

'Wrong, no,' replied Knotty; 'in course I ain't; didn't I do the trick myself? and do you think I'm likely to blunder?'

'You oughtn't to, no how,' observed the other. 'Hush! I thinks I hears my old ooman outside.' He arose, and opening the door, peered out into the moonlight, but saw no one. He closed the door again, and resumed his seat by the fire.

'No, it ain't her,' said he.

'Well, so much the better,' remarked the other; 'it's quite as well that she shouldn't be here just now. Your wife may be all right, but you can't trust a woman; they're too fond of clackin', they are.'

'Bah!' said Jem; 'there's no fear of her; she knows what she'd get if I found her talkin' too fast.' As he spoke, the sound that disturbed him before occurred again. He signaled to his companion to remain silent, and quietly stole to the door. He opened it suddenly, and on her knees, in a listening attitude, he found his wife.

'You ——!' but the pen refuses to record the words he used. He seized her by her shoulders, and drew her savagely into the hut. 'So you've been listening, have you?' and then striking her violently on her face, which laid her senseless on the ground, he added, with an oath, 'there, now, listen again, and I'll cook your goose sharp.'

'Well, Jem,' said Knotty, calmly, as he gazed upon the brutish husband and his unfortunate wife, without, however, moving a muscle of his face, 'well, Jem, you've done for her this time, I fancy.'

'Not I,' growled the other; 'she's too tough for that; besides she's used to it. Why the —— didn't she come in, if she wanted to? I wouldn't ha' minded her bein' here a bit; but when I find her a sneakin' about a listenin' outside the door, I begins to think there's somethin' wrong. And yet I don't think that Bet, as has been with me this gettin' on eight year, would turn round agin me and peach. But what did she want to stand there a listenin' for like that? that's what licks me.'

He paused, and sat without saying a word for a few minutes, evidently at a loss what to understand. At length he roused himself, and looking at Knotty, said:—

'Do you think it's likely, old chap, that the cove has laid her on to watch me?'

'Well,' replied his companion, 'there's no knowin' what chaps is up to, now-a-days. It may be, or it may not be—I can't tell. It looks precious likely, anyhow.'

'If I thought so,' said Jem, opening his huge clasp knife, 'I'd cut her —— throat at once, and make no bones on it.'

'You'd be a fool if you did,' observed Knotty, 'as it 'ud put an end to your plans at once, and you'd be sure to get scragged for it some day. I don't mind usin' my fist, either on man or woman,' added he, closing his hand, and holding it up, as if for inspection; 'but you don't catch me usin' a knife, or any of them things. I'm not exactly what anybody would call a vartuous man, but I'm not quite so bad as that. There, put away your knife, it doesn't look wholesome.'

Jem, with a foolish convinced look, closed his knife and put it in his pocket; then rose and examined his wife, who still lay where she had fallen, and scarcely breathing. From a cut above her left eye a stream of blood flowed, which gathered in a pool by her side.

'Jump up, you treacherous ——!' shouted he, 'jump up, or I'll kick your —— ribs in!' He was about to perform this additional act of brutality, when he was prevented by Knotty, who quietly arose, and putting on his cap made towards him, and seizing him roughly by the arm, swung him round until they stood face to face.

'Now, look here, Jem,' said he, 'you're a sort of man as it's best to leave alone. So now you may just finish your job yourself; it ain't safe to have anything to do with such as you; you might be lettin' the cat out of the bag in some of your tantrums. So, good night, old boy; and be careful and don't murder your wife, as I shall know who did it.'

Jem glared savagely at him, and half put his hand into the pocket where his knife was—but seeing Knotty quietly produce a small pocket-pistol from his coat pocket, and as quietly put it back again, as though he had caught hold of it by accident—he withdrew his hand.

'Sit down, Knotty,' said he, 'I'm a great fool, I knows; but this affair has put me out a bit. I'll have a pipe, that'll set me all to rights in no time.'

Knotty sat down as composedly as though nothing had occurred to disturb them, and lit his pipe. After about ten minutes' silence, during which time each seemed wrapped in thought, Knotty observed—

'Now, I tell you what it is, Jem—the best thing you can do is first to lock up your old woman, and then drive half-a-dozen sheep over into our run, just as though they had strayed there. Do you see?'

'Yes,' replied Jem, in a low surly tone, 'the thing must be settled at once now, in case the old ooman blabs.'

'Which,' interrupted Knotty, 'after the hiding this evening, she's likely to do; and it 'ud serve you right, too.'

'Would it?' snarled Jem, 'and supposin' she did; do you think she wouldn't mention your name?'

'Oh, that's a trifle,' said Knotty, with a half laugh, 'I shouldn't mind that a bit. I can always find a way of gettin' out of a scrape, I can.'

'Well, at any rate,' observed Jem, 'I shall foller your advice, and settle the matter at once, and take precious good care that my missis don't stir out of this 'ere hut.'

'Well, now you've made up your mind,' said the other, 'I'll be off. My nag must have eaten all round to the length of his tether by this time, and won't mind a change; so, good night, old fellow!' With this he shook hands with his companion, picked up his whip, and strode out of the hut. Jem followed him to the horse, and after watching him until he disappeared in the darkness, re-entered the hut.

Poor Bet was still lying on the ground, and although breathing more freely, was still insensible. Jem began to fear, or I should say, think, that he had, if not actually killed her, at any rate given her a blow which would result in her death. He lifted her carefully and placed her upon the bed, and then with some warm water and a piece of rag cleaned the wound. This done, he returned to the fire-place, and re-filling his pipe and replenishing his panikin with grog, sat down awaiting his wife's return to consciousness. She shortly revived, but was too weak from loss of blood to speak. She uttered a faint cry of pain, which aroused her husband and brought him to her side. He poured a little rum down her throat but it did her no good; she merely stared at him with her small eyes, which were opened to their fullest extent, and then closed them again, and went off into what Jem thought was syncope, but which really was a deep sleep. Jem, cursing the obstinacy of his wife in not coming to, threw himself upon the bed by her side, and before long was as sound asleep as she was.

Great was Jem's astonishment when he awoke next morning to find Bet dressing herself as quickly as usual, and as though nothing had happened to her the night previous. His first act was to swear at her, and tax her with intended treachery. She made no reply, but went on dressing herself, and then bound up the wound on her forehead. Jem stormed on, but she said not a word. When her toilet was completed, she walked quietly towards the door; but Jem forestalled her, and thrusting her fiercely back, declared that she should not go out again. She sat down, as if fatigued by over-exertion; and Jem commenced preparations for breakfast, doing everything himself.

When breakfast was over, Jem went out; and gathering all the logs he could find, he piled them up against the door, to prevent her going out. This done, he went to the fold, and releasing his sheep, drove them quietly to the feeding ground.

Meanwhile, poor Bet had fallen back upon her bed, entirely overcome by pain and weakness; she fainted, and some hours passed before she recovered. Evening drew on, Jem's usual time had passed, but he did not return. Night came on—still he came not. The bright moonlight streamed through the chinks in the walls and door, shedding a faint light throughout the hut. Hour followed hour, still no sign of his return.

Fatigued with watching, the poor prisoner fell into a light slumber—so light, that the rustling of the leaves disturbed her. At one time she thought she heard a sound in the direction of the fold, as of the bleating of sheep, but it was indistinct. Dawn at length broke; the sun rose in glorious brightness—but the captive saw it not; she lay stretched upon her pallet in a raging fever.

That day passed, then another night, and the sun again rose. It was near midday, and without was a shouting that would have aroused the heaviest sleeper.

'Jem! holloa, Jem!'

No answer from within.

'Jem! hi, Jem!'

Still no answer.

'Why, what the deuce can be the matter! the sheep in the fold, and this midday! Hilloa! Bet! Jem! is anyone inside? Why, confound it, the door's blocked up with logs. What can all this mean?'

The speaker was Mr. Wootherspoon, who had ridden over to see how the sheep got on. He removed the logs from the door, forced the catch, and after his eyes had got somewhat accustomed to the gloom, discovered Bet stretched upon the bed, with her head bound up, and in a raging fever. He tried to arouse her, but could not; she uttered unintelligible sounds, and threw herself about from side to side. In a fright he hastened out, mounted his horse, and galloped like a madman back to his house. He called the overseer, and ordered a dray to proceed at once to the hut; and after selecting from a medicine chest such restoratives as he deemed most useful, re-mounted, and in company with Chalmers hastened back to the hut.

As nothing could be done for Bet in the hut, they had patiently to await the arrival of the dray. Meanwhile, Chalmers rode over to the neighbouring station to beg the squatter, who was a doctor, to come over to visit the poor woman. On his way he directed another shepherd to take charge of Jem's sheep, and to drive them out to feed.

The dray arrived shortly, and poor Bet was carefully placed therein, and conveyed to the Home-station, where the doctor awaited her arrival. She was pronounced to be in a dangerous state, requiring the greatest possible care. This she received, and within a few days she was able to address a few coherent words to Mr. Wootherspoon. She, being now under no fear of her husband, detailed the whole of the conversations she had heard at different times between him and Knotty. Poor Mr. Wootherspoon stood aghast at the nature of the recital, and leaving Bet in charge of a woman-servant, mounted his horse, and summoning his overseer, who was engaged in the stockyard near the house, galloped in Jem's fold, where he discovered the new shepherd in the greatest possible state of disagreeable excitement, at having observed symptoms of scab among the flock.

'Jem, you devil!' shouted the squatter; 'oh! if I catch you!—if there's a rope and tree left on the station, I'll hang you!'

His rage was so intense that Chalmers began to look for some terrible catastrophe, and increased the distance between himself and employer.

'They've all got it, I think, Sir,' whispered the shepherd to the latter, 'and none of 'em will be worth a farthing.'

Chalmers glanced towards the sheep, and saw them all rolling and scratching in agony.

Every means was resorted to; arsenic and tobacco were expended in hundredweights to cleanse them, but the scab increased, until their bodies were covered with boils, and the wool and hides rendered valueless.

Two thousand sheep, chiefly valuable for their wool, were now condemned, and in a few days driven off to town to be sold merely for their tallow. And thankful Mr. Wootherspoon was, when his temper cooled a bit, that it was no worse; for, had Jem succeeded as he hoped and intended, the whole of the sheep in the station, numbering over thirty thousand, would have been sacrificed.

Poor Bet was taken care of, and retained on the station as an under-servant, for intense as was the squatter's hatred of Jem, it did not extend to her: and although Mr. Wootherspoon was a great sufferer, Bet never had reason to complain of the result of the shepherd's revenge.

MYSTERY AND MURDER

James Skipp Borlase

WHILE IN TASMANIA I met with an adventure of so singular a character, that it has been the subject of much thought during my leisure hours in the intervening space of time, the more so as the mysterious portion of it remains unexplained to this day.

On an evening during one of the winter months I was seated in my quarters in Hobart Town, engaged in making memoranda of my day's occupation, when a gentleman who had requested to see me was shown into the apartment. Although he had not the slightest knowledge of me, I recognised him at once. It was Mr. Longmore, a merchant of Hobart Town, who had the character of being a steady, worthy, and withal wealthy man. He was a widower, the father of an only daughter, and resided on the outskirts of the town, in a handsome residence situated very near to that part of the Derwent which bears the name of Sullivan's Cove; in fact, its waters rippled at the bottom of Mr. Longmore's own grounds.

'I have the pleasure of speaking to Mr. Brooke, the detective officer, I believe,' said he, after having at my invitation seated himself.

'Yes,' I replied, 'and you may spare yourself the trouble of introducing yourself, Mr. Longmore. I have the honour of knowing you well by sight, as well as by reputation.'

'Well, I suppose I need not be surprised at your recognising me,' replied he, with a staid smile, 'although I do not recollect having ever met you before; but it is quite in your way to be observant.'

'It is, sir; and now in what manner can my present services avail you?'

I could not help noticing that the gentleman looked uneasy and hesitant, and not at all easy in his conversation, as I should have expected to find a man of the world as Mr. Longmore.

'I scarcely know what to say to you, Mr. Brooke,' shifting uneasily upon his chair. 'I came with the purpose of disclosing to you something so extraordinary and singular as to be scarcely credible, and now I am doubly inclined to fear that its very singularity may occasion doubts in your mind as to my judgment or want of common sense.'

'You need not be at all afraid, Mr. Longmore,' I responded, encouragingly, 'that I shall draw any false inference from any communication that you may do me the honour of making to me in confidence. Your well-known character as a gentleman of clear judgment and sound common sense is a sufficient guarantee that any information you may give me, or communication you may make, will be well worthy of attention.'

'Thank you!' replied he, 'but in this matter I am positively afraid that my ordinary judgment is at fault; but if you can afford me time I will relate the circumstances, and allow you to form your own opinion upon the matter.' Of course I signified my readiness—nay, anxiety to listen, and Mr. Longmore commenced thus:—

'My house is, as I dare say you know, at this side of the suburbs, and quite near to the river. I reside in it with my only daughter and three servants, one male and two females. The house has no upper story; the front windows are French, all open into the grounds; the back part of the establishment, stables, yard, &c., being separated from the front gardens by a high stone wall. Into the back yard the kitchen and ordinary apartments open, so that unless *through* the house itself no communication can be held by any of the servants with the pleasure-grounds; unless, indeed, they were to go down and approach by the river. I tell you all this so that you may be in the same position as I have found myself, as to the possibility of finding a natural solution of the singular difficulty which I am about to relate to you. The door of communication between the front and back portions of my house I am particularly careful to secure every night myself, my early residence in the colony having made me very cautious in guarding against surprise of any kind, and my daughter's safety is of greater moment than my own, so that I am even more careful in these matters than I might have been.

'This night week I had retired at my usual hour, or perhaps a little later. Everything was quiet, my daughter as well as the servants had gone to their rooms some time before.

'It was a wild, dark night, but as I burn a lamp in my room it is of course lighted, although dimly. For some time I had been asleep, what awoke me I cannot tell; the first thing on which my eyes rested was a form—a figure, or the semblance of one: it was standing at the foot of my bed, and was that of a female! I was not alarmed, for the idea that it was my daughter immediately suggested itself, so I raised myself upon my elbow for the purpose of asking if anything was the matter. As soon as I did so I instantly perceived that the face was strange to me.

'The figure was slight, attired in a white robe; the features had a horrible expression of terror, and their death-like pallor was increased by the contrast presented by the longest and heaviest black hair I ever saw, which hung over her left breast and reached down to her knees. Her dress was of silken material, for I heard it rustling; and all over the front, and also upon the loose sleeves, it was clotted with blood.'

Here the narrator stopped, apparently quite overcome with the recollection of the scene that he had been describing, and I must confess that I could hardly repress a smile at such emotion being felt by a person of Mr. Longmore's sense and experience, about such a piece of absurdity; and I dare say he read the expression of my feelings in my face, for he remarked,—

'I can scarcely feel surprised that you should be inclined to treat the matter as a joke, Mr. Brooke; it is a very singular story to relate, and I do not expect you to give it credence without proving its truth yourself.'

'Oh, I hope, sir,' I hastened to observe, 'you do not suppose for a moment that I doubt your veracity, only to my professional mind the *apparition* looks very like a hoax which some one is playing off upon you; but if you will narrate the facts we can talk of these things afterwards.'

'I have very little to add. The appearance which I have described has visited me every night—in spite of barred doors and windows,—each time waving its hand impatiently, as if beckoning me to follow.'

'And you never followed?'

'No! I must confess that I felt too horrified to attempt moving whilst the figure stood so immediately before me. I felt frozen to the bed, as it were; indeed, I assure you it is a fearful sight!'

'Will you permit me to inquire, Mr. Longmore, are you at all superstitious?'

'In the sense *you* mean I am not superstitious. If I met with anything so peculiar in appearance as to be quite beyond the ordinary run of natural events, before setting it down to be supernatural or apparitional I should certainly do my utmost to find a natural cause or causes for it, as I have done in this instance; failing in that, I am ready to acknowledge there are 'more things in heaven and earth than are dreamt of in our philosophy.' Still, had I been as really superstitious as you appear to think me, I should not have been here to ask your more practised assistance in trying to unravel this mystery.'

'Well,' I replied, laughingly, 'I am inclined to feel certain that we shall easily prove this visitation not to be one from a spiritual kingdom; for in truth, Mr. Longmore, I do not believe in ghosts!'

'Because you have never seen one.'

I did not reply to this observation, as I perceived that his nerves had been much affected, and not without wonder; the appearance of such a figure in one's bedroom night after night, in spite of locks and bolts, was enough to shake any man's judgment; nevertheless, I had not the slightest doubt that the professional cunning upon which I prided myself would expose the trick of some conspiracy, formed, I was sure, for no good purpose.

'Have you mentioned this to any one, Mr. Longmore?'

'No, I have not; I was afraid of alarming my daughter. I do sincerely hope that you will be able to get to the bottom of it. The knowledge of such an unaccountable visitation, such a horrible appearance, being night after night in the immediate neighbour-hood of my unsuspecting child is almost overwhelming me. Now what steps will you take?'

I considered for a moment before I answered, and then mentioned my intention of spending that night in Mr. Longmore's bedroom.

'Could you get in without any one suspecting that you had a visitor?' I inquired; 'and could you manage to let me occupy your room in secrecy also?'

'Oh, easily enough. Only name the hour you will be at the side entrance into the garden, and I will admit you myself. It is usual after dusk for me to smoke my cigar near the river.'

Having made suitable arrangements Mr. Longmore left me.

I sat down and considered the matter on all sides. What was the object in thus acting the ghost in the bedroom of a man of Mr. Longmore's well-known strength of mind? From what I knew of that gentleman's character I was much surprised at the weakness he had shown, the earthly, and I had no doubt criminal nature of which only wanted a little keen-sighted perseverance to be proved.

As to ghosts, and entrances effected without any existing means of ingress—bah! it was all fudge. My intention, in the first place, was to see, if possible, this singular apparition; and while doing nothing more than simply affecting to be the ordinary occupier of Mr. Longmore's bed, for the first night to make good use of my eyes, and be guided in any further attempts at unravelment by my observations. Well, at the appointed time I was conducted by Mr. Longmore into his bedroom, the servants, as well as Miss Longmore, having retired. I was at liberty to examine the room at leisure. The apartment was a good size, perhaps sixteen feet by twenty-two, and had two large French windows that opened on a verandah which ran along the front of the house. These windows consisted each of a single sheet of plate glass in handsome mahogany framework, and faced directly the Derwent, called, as I have before mentioned, at that spot, Sullivan's Cove. With its head against the wall, opposite to the windows, stood a large elegant bedstead, with a canopy at the head, from which depended rich damask curtains, that only formed a shelter to the head of the bedstead, leaving the foot entirely unprotected. On the right hand of the bed was the door opening into a dressing-room, which communicated with the other portion of the establishment. By the wall at the left was the toilet-table; upon it stood a deeply shaded night lamp. There was also a chimney in the room, but as the grate was one of the stove description I did not trouble myself about it. The windows and doors I left entirely to Mr. Longmore's inspection, taking his word that they were fastened as usual.

When this was all right we seated ourselves beside a table, where my entertainer had taken care to have refreshment, and after partaking of a glass of wine I lit my cigar, begging my host to excuse my invariable practice before retiring. It had not escaped my keen observation that the gentleman on whose behalf I had volunteered to encounter a ghost had shown indubitable signs of a mind ill at ease ever since he had ushered me into his house. Taking advantage of the wreaths of smoke that soon curled up between my lips, I watched him as he sat opposite to me more closely than I should otherwise have had an opportunity of doing.

He was gazing down at the floor, occasionally sipping his wine in an abstracted manner, with a thoughtful and troubled expression upon his face, but looking up once, and encountering my eyes steadfastly, and I suspect searchingly, fixed upon his countenance, he became red and pale by turns, and at length addressed me hurriedly.

'I am afraid, Mr. Brooke, that I have done wrong in this business, as I have given you trouble, I think. I believe I should have told you everything.'

'Certainly, Mr. Longmore,' was my reply. 'If you seek my

professional services I think I have a right to learn everything you know in connection with it.'

'It is true; it is quite true. And yet I think you will make allowance for my disinclination to speak of this circumstance. There are some things of the past so painful that I may be excused if I feel a disinclination to allude to them.'

'Well, sir, if you regret having mentioned the subject to me, forget that you have done so, and nobody shall be the wiser.'

'No, no; you quite mistake me. I am anxious to tell you at once of what I should have informed you before, and it is simply that this—this apparition bears the semblance of one with whom I was too well acquainted.'

'May I ask of whom?'

'My wife!'

'Your wife?' I exclaimed, and then checked myself at once as the cause of Mr. Longmore's awkwardness and evident trouble of mind flashed before me. I now remembered having heard a great deal of gossip about this said wife. She had eloped years before from this very house in a most disgraceful manner, and with a most unprincipled, low rascal. I respected my host's feelings of course, and felt grieved that anything should have occurred with which I had any connection to bring the memory of the transaction again before him.

'And you think the figure resembles that person?' I inquired.

'It is herself!' was the determined reply.

'Well, I must say I think it very likely it is. What more probable than that she should be acquainted with some outlet from this room which you do not know?'

Mr. Longmore shook his head.

'It is not she *alive*,' he said.

'Do you then really and positively believe that this visitation is a supernatural one?' I asked, in much surprise.

'I do! I am willing that every means of discovery shall be tried; but when you have seen *it*, I think you will acknowledge that I *must* believe it is supernatural.'

This was very positive and very singular to me. That any man in these days of enlightenment, and possessed of his full allowance of brains, should insist upon the *existence* of a ghost—if I am not making a 'bull' in so saying—was a matter beyond my comprehension; and as I turned into Mr. Longmore's stately bed, after he had taken up his quarters on a couch in the dressing-room, I am afraid I allowed myself to consider for a moment how long in all probability it was likely to be ere this far-seeing merchant should

I rather started at this, as Walter Cuvier was the name of the man with whom the murdered Mrs. Longmore had eloped.

'I was cabin boy in the *Water Snake*, and had been in that brig a couple of years.'

'Can you tell me what Captain Cuvier did with his vessel? In what trade was he?'

'You know, sir, that was none of my business. He traded on his own account, and I think principally in contraband goods. Well, as I said before, I was cabin boy in the *Water Snake*, and all the time I was in her the captain had his wife with him, at least a woman who passed for his wife, and I do believe that the body found in this bill was the woman we used to call Mrs. Cuvier.'

'What makes you think so?'

'I think I am sure of it, and I'll tell you, why, sir. The captain and the missis did not live very comfortable at times, and when he was drunk he was a real brute; and the missis herself I am certain took a drop too much, so they had terrible shindies. Well, we came from Calcutta here, and, tired of being kicked and cuffed, I determined to bolt the very first chance, and give Cuvier leg-bail for it. We cast anchor in the cove last May, and that very night, as I was in the pantry washing up the glasses, I heard such a row between the captain and the missis in their state-room, she insisting on 'going back' somewhere, crying her eyes out all the time, and he swearing he'd kill her first, until at last he told her to 'go back and be ——.' Shortly after the captain ordered the boat to be lowered. He took me into the cabin to help him with a box like the one described in this; and as I went back to get something he had forgotten, I saw Mrs. Cuvier getting ready to go shore. She was dressed very handsome, and it looked like a white silk gown she had got on. She gave me a glass of wine, and shook hands with me, saying she was going to leave the ship and go to her friends. I thought nothing of it, having, as I said before, heard the talk between her and the captain. Well, I and one of the sailors rowed them ashore, and landed them on the beach near some trees. It was a squally, dark night. So Mrs. Cuvier shook hands with the other man, and bid him good-bye. The captain told us to shove off again, and wait for him up at a tavern he pointed out along shore, as he had a few words to say to the missis before he went; and then he gave us the price of a drink or two, so we went off, leaving him and herself sitting on the box that he said had the woman's clothes in. That was the very last time I saw them, for as soon as my mate had a glass or two I took the chance and made tracks, and stowed myself aboard the ship *Chester*, that sailed for Calcutta the next morning; and that's all I know about it.'

'And you never saw or heard of Cuvier or his vessel since?'

'No, sir; and if I had I'd have given both her and him a wide berth.'

And I have never heard of him since. Perhaps he still lives to drag a miserable consciousness of his crime through a wretched existence. Many a time have I pictured to myself the unfortunate and guilty woman returning to the neighbourhood of her husband and child whom she had disgraced, and no doubt still loved and yearned to see! How often, during the abuse and ill usage of him for whom she had sacrificed everything, had her breaking heart prayed for the peace and rest of the home she had left! And then, resolved to brave all—to throw herself at the feet of her injured husband—to beg the intercession of her child—did the demon murder her upon the threshold of her hopes?—within sight of the very window-lights of the home she longed to enter once more? And who can tell who and what was the midnight visitor to Mr. Longmore's bedroom? Was it the bodily presence of some one acquainted with the murder, and who wished the affair to be known without being recognised? To solve the mystery in that manner seemed impossible, considering all the opposing circumstances. And thus it has remained unravelled to this day—a mystery into which I carried the closest investigation without being wiser by the inquiry.

THE ROMANCE OF LIVELY CREEK

Marcus Clarke

CHAPTER I

'Green Bushes'

THE TOWNSHIP OF LIVELY CREEK is not the sort of place in which one would expect a romance to happen; and yet, in the year 18—, when I accepted the secretaryship to the Mechanics' Institute, occurred a series of circumstances which had in them all the elements of the wildest French fiction.

The unwonted impetus given to social relations, which was effected by the 'opening up' of the Great Daylight Reef, brought together those incongruous particles of adventurous humanity which are to be found floating about the gold-mining centres of Australian population, and in six months the quiet village—up to that time notorious for its extreme simplicity—had become a long street, surrounded by mounds, shafts, and engine-houses, and boasting a Court House, a Mechanics' Institute, half a dozen places of (variously conducted) religious worship, and some twenty public-houses.

The thirst for knowledge which attends upon worldly success soon made my office a laborious one, for, in addition to my duties as Librarian I was expected to act as Master of the Ceremonies, Conductor of *Conversaziones*, Curator of a Museum of Curiosities, and Theatrical Manager. The Committee of Management were desirous that no attraction which might increase the funds of the institution should be passed over, and when Mademoiselle Pauline Christoval (of the Theatres Royal, Honolulu, Manilla, Singapore, and Popocatapetl) offered a handsome rent to be permitted to play for six nights in the great hall, I was instructed to afford every facility to that distinguished actress.

Mademoiselle Pauline was a woman of an uncertain age—that

is to say, she might have been two-and-twenty and was not improbably three-and-thirty. Tall, elegant, self-possessed and intelligent, she made her business arrangements with considerable acuteness, and, having duly checked all items of 'gas' and 'etceteras,' announced that she would play the *Green Bushes*, as an initiatory performance. 'I always act as my own agent,' said she, 'and my Company is entirely under my own direction.'

Upon inquiry at the Three Star Brand—where the Company were lodged—I found this statement to be thoroughly correct. Miss Fortescue (the wife of Mr. Effingham Bellingham, the 'leading man') had already confided to Mrs. Butt, the landlady, several items of intelligence concerning the tyranny exercised by the lady manager. Mr. Capricorn, the 'juvenile man' (husband of Miss Sally Lunn, the charming *danseuse*), had hinted vaguely, with much uplifting of his juvenile brows, that Mademoiselle was not to be trifled with, while I found that old Joe Banks, the low comedian (the original 'Stunning Joseph' in the popular farce of *My Wife's Aunt*), had shaken his venerable head many times in humorous denunciation of 'the artfulness of Christoval.'

There was much excitement in the bar-parlour of the 'Main Reef Hotel' at the dinner hour. So many reefers took me mysteriously behind the door, and begged me to bring them casually behind the scenes during the performance, that it was evident that, for the first night of the six, at all events, the improvised theatre would be crowded. The only man who manifested no interest was Sporboy—Sporboy, the newly-arrived; Sporboy, the adventurer; Sporboy, the oracle of tap-rooms; Sporboy, the donor of curiosities to our Museum; Sporboy, the shareholder in the Great Daylight; Sporboy, the traveller, the narrator, the hot whisky swiller:— Honest Jack Sporboy, the richest man, the hugest drunkard, and the biggest liar in all Lively Creek.

'I've seen enough of them sort o'gals,' said he. 'I'm getting old. My hair's grey. Pauline Christoval, of the Theatres Royal, Manilla, and Popocatapetl, eh? Bosh! Hot whisky.'

'But, Captain Sporboy, your influence—'

'Oh, yes! All right. I've been in Manilla. I've eaten brain soup and *basi* in Hocos, my boy. *Human* brains. Devilish good, too. Ha, ha! Another lump of sugar.'

'Human brains, you old cannibal!' cried Jack Barnstaple. 'What do you mean?'

'Just what I say, dear boy,' returned the old reprobate, wagging his Silenus head. 'When I was in Pampalo we made a trip to Pangasinan, and assisted at a native feast. The Palanese had just achieved a victory over the Quinanès, and seventy-five heads were served up in my honour. Gad, gentlemen, the fellows cracked 'em like cocoa-nuts, and whipped out the brains in less time than you would take to disembowel a crayfish!'

'But a theatrical entertainment, my dear Captain Sporboy, merits your patronage.'

'Seen 'em all, sir. Tired of 'em. N'York, Par's, London. No! Jack Sporboy, sir, is tired of the vanities of life, and prefers the noble simplicity of hot whisky. I had the Theatre on Popocatapetl myself once, and lost 4,000 dol. by a *métis* that I hired to dance the tight-rope. Fine woman, but immoral, gentlemen. She ran away with my big-drum-and-cymbals, and left me to support her helpless husband. Never trust a half-caste; they are all treacherous.'

So we left the virtuous old gentleman to the enjoyment of his memories, and went to the hall. My anticipations were realized. The *Green Bushes* was a distinct success. Joe Banks, as 'Jack Gong,' was voted magnificent, and for the 'Miami' the audience could not find words enough in which to express their admiration. Made-moiselle added to the attractions of her flashing black eyes, streaming black hair, supple figure, and delicate brown hands, a decided capacity for the realization of barbaric passion, and her performance was remarkably good. The *Lively Creek Gazette*, indeed, expressed itself, on the following morning, in these admirable terms:—'Mademoiselle Christoval's "Miami" was simply magnificent, and displayed a considerable amount of dramatic power. She looked the Indian to the life, and her intense repro-duction of the jealous wife rose almost to mediocrity in the third act. Indeed, in the delineation of the fiercer emotions, Mademoiselle Christoval has no equal on the Colonial stage, and we have no hesitation in pronouncing her a very nice actress.' After the drama was over, I took advantage of my position to go 'behind the scenes,' and, while Joe Banks was delighting the public with the 'roaring farce' of *Turn Him Out*, to compliment the lady upon her triumph. I found the door of the improvised dressing-room besieged by the male fashion of the township, who (having made Lame Dick, my janitor, drunk) had obtained introductions to the eminent *tragedienne*. Foremost amongst these was Harry Beaufort, the son of Beaufort, of Beaufort's Mount.

'Ah,' said I, 'are you here?'

'Yes,' said he, blushing, 'I rode over to-day from Long Gully.'

'Mr Beaufort and I are old acquaintances,' said the soft tones of the lady, as emerging, cloaked and bonneted, from the rough planking, she melted the crowd with a smile, and turned towards me, 'Will you join us at supper?'

I looked at Harry and saw him blush again. It struck me that he was only two-and-twenty; that his father was worth half-a-million of sheep, and that Mademoiselle Christoval was not a woman to marry for love.

'Thank you,' said I. 'I will.'

We had a very pleasant supper, for though I was evidently a skeleton at the banquet, the actress was far too clever a one to let me see her uneasiness. Harry sulked, after the manner of his stupid sex, but the lady talked with a vivacity which made ample amends for his silence. She was a very agreeble woman. Born—so she told me—in the Phillipines, she had travelled through South America and the States, had visited California, and was now 'doing Australia,' on her way to Europe. 'I want to see Life,' she said, with extraordinary vigour of enjoyment in her black eyes, 'and I must travel.'

'Why don't you take an engagement in Melbourne?' I asked.

'Can't get one to suit me. I don't care about sharing after everything a night but the gas. Besides, I only want to pay my way and travel. I should have to stop too long in one place if I took a Melbourne engagement.'

'And don't you like to stop in one place?' asked Beaufort.

'No,' said she, decidedly. 'I am an actress, and actresses, like fine views, grow stale if you see them every day.'

'But did you never think of leaving the stage?' asked the young man.

'Never. I was born in a theatre. My mother was a ballet dancer. My father was an actor. My grandfather was clown in a circus. I have played every part in the English language that could be played by a woman. I could play 'Hamlet' to-morrow night if the people would come and see me. Why should I leave the stage?'

'True,' said I, 'but you may marry.'

Oh! the vicious look she gave me!—a dagger sheathed in a smile.

'I never intend to marry. It is growing late. I am an actress—the people will talk. Good-night.'

We parted with mutual esteem; and, as she shook hands with us, I saw, lurching up the passage, the whisky-filled form of the Great Sporboy. His eyes, attracted by the light from the room, fell upon us, and—surprised, doubtless, at the brilliant appearance of Mademoiselle Pauline—he started.

Mademoiselle Pauline grew pale—alarmed, perhaps, at the manner of the intoxicated old reprobate—and hastily drew back into her chamber.

'Go away. You're drunk!' said Harry, in a fierce whisper.

'Of course I am,' said Sporboy, advancing diagonally, 'but that's my business. Who's that?'

'That is Mademoiselle Pauline,' said I.

'Ho!' cries Sporboy, his red face lighting up as if suddenly illumined by some inward glow. 'Ho! Ho! That's she, is it. He, he! A fine woman. A fair woman. A sweet woman.' It was a peculiarity of this uneducated monster to display a strange faculty for mutilated quotation.

'Ho, ho! I wish ye joy o' the worm. So a kind good-night to all.'

CHAPTER II

The Mystery

Busy all next day, I found in the evening that the *tragedienne* had been indisposed, and had kept her room. Harry Beaufort, who informed me, said that she had intended to throw up the engagement and quit the town, but that he had persuaded her to remain. 'I do not want her to do anything that may appear strange,' he said. Then, sitting in the little room off the bar, underneath the picture of the Brighton Mail, he told me the truth. He intended to marry Mademoiselle Pauline. 'But,' said I, 'do you know anything about her? I will tell you frankly that I don't like her. She is a mystery. Why should she travel about alone in this way? Do you know anything of her past life?'

'No.'

'So much the worse. One can always obtain the fullest account of an actress's life, because she is a notable person, and the public takes an interest in the minutest particulars concerning notable people. If, as she says, she is the daughter of an actor, fifty people of the stage can tell you all about her family. Have you made enquiries?'

'She came from California,' said he. 'How should they know her? Come, let us go into the theatre.'

I went in, and saw, to my astonishment, the cynical Sporboy seated in the front row, applauding vehemently, and sliming 'Miami' with his eye as a boar slimes a rabbit it intends to devour.

'Capital!' he was exclaiming, 'Capital! What a waist! What an ankle! What a charming devilkin it is! Black blood there, boys! Supple as an eel. Ho, ho! Good! Our Pauline shall receive the homage of her Sporboy in the splendid neatness of a whisky hot!'

The stage, being of necessity but three feet from the front seats, these exclamations were distinctly heard by the actress, who seemed to shiver at them, as a high-bred horse shivers at the sight of some horrible animal. But she never turned her flashing black eyes to where the empurpled vagabond wheezed and gloated. She seemed, I thought, rather to avoid that fishy eye, and to feel relieved when Sporboy went out for that 'splendid neatness,' and did not return. I complimented her—in my official capacity—upon the success of her performance, but she seemed tired and anxious to get to the hotel. I offered to escort her, and when on the steps was met by Sporboy.

He lifted his hat with a flourish which made the rings on his fat hands flash in the gaslight. 'Introduce me!—Nay—then, I will introduce myself. John Sporboy, madam, late of Manilla, 'Frisco, Popocatapetl, and Ranker's Gully. John Sporboy, who has himself fretted his little hour upon the stage, and has owned no less than ten theatres in various parts of the civilized world. John Sporboy craves an introduction to Mademoiselle Pauline Christoval.'

She paused a moment, and then—probably seeing that opposition might expose her to insult—said to me: 'Pray introduce your friend, if he is so desirous.'

'Spoken like a Plantagenet,' cried Sporboy. 'Mademoiselle, I kiss your hands. If you will permit me, I'll sing the songs of other years, of joyful bliss or war, and if my songs should make you weep, I'll touch the gay guitar!'

'Pray come upstairs,' said she, coldly; 'all the people are staring at us.'

The Great Sporboy was never greater than on that well-remembered evening. He talked incessantly, and when he was not devoting himself to the 'elegant simplicity of whisky hot,' he was singing Canadian boat songs to his own piano accompaniment, or relating anecdotes of his triumphs in Wall Street, his adventures on the Pacific Slope, or his lucky hits in every kind of speculation.

'I have been through fire and water. I know most things. I have been up some very tall trees in my time, and looked around upon some very queer prospects. You can't deceive me, and my advice is, don't try, for, if you do, I'm bound to look ugly, and when I knock a man down, ma'am, it takes four more to carry him away, and then there's five gone! Tra-la-la! Pu-r-r-r!' And he ran up and down the keys with his fat fingers.

'I think Mademoiselle Pauline looks tired,' said I.

'Oh, no,' she returned, uneasily. 'Not at all. Captain Sporboy is so amusing, so vivacious—so young, may I say?'

'You may, Mademoiselle,' said Sporboy, 'say what you like.'

To lovely women, Sporboy was ever as gentle as the gazelle.

'Pray'—suddenly wheeling round upon the music-stool and,

liquorishly, facing her—'have you heard lately from your sainted MOTHER, ma'am?'

They say that a creature shot through the heart often leaps into the air before it falls dead. Mademoiselle Pauline must have received at that instant some such fatal wound, for she leapt to her feet, standing for an instant gazing wildly at us, and then sank back into her seat, speechless and pale.

'What do you mean? I do not understand you,' she gasped out at length; and then, as though her quick intellect had assured her that deceit was useless—'I have not seen my mother since she left me, seven years, ago, at St. Louis.'

'As she left *me* once before!' said Sporboy, with savage triumph in his bloodshot eyes. 'I thought I knew you, Miss Manuelita. "Should old acquaintance be forgot?" eh? I hope not.'

I rose to go, faltering some lame excuse, but Sporboy stopped me. 'Nay, my young and juvenile friend (as I used to say in Chadband), be not hasty. This lady and I are old friends. "We met, 'twas in a crowd;" and I thought she would shun me, Ho, ho! Let us drink to this merry meeting! For "when may we three meet again?" I will order Moet and Chandon.'

'I think, Sporboy, that you have drunk enough.' (She was sitting motionless, waiting, as it seemed, for the issue of events.) 'Let us go home.'

'Home. It's home I fain would be—home, home, home, in my ain countree! Eh! Miss Pauline, "I'd be a butterfly born in a bower." EH?'

'If you have anything to say to me, sir,' (the dusky pale of her cheeks illuminated by two spots of crimson) 'you had better say it.'

'I, my enslaver? No, not I, not I, not I! Was it Vestris used to sing?' (humming it) '"I'll be no submissive, wi-fe, no, not I, no, not I!" Would you like to be a submissive wife, ma'am? God help the man who gets you! Adieu, adieu! "Hamlet, r-r-remember me!"'

'Good heavens, Sporboy,' said I, when I got him outside, 'what on earth did you go on in that way for? What do you know of her?'

'Ho, ho!' chuckled Sporboy, with thickening utterance. 'What do I know of her? Tra-la-la! Tilly-valley! No good, you may depend.'

'Tell me what you do know then. Young Beaufort wishes to marry her.'

'I know,' said Sporboy, with another chuckle; 'he told me. He's gone to Melbourne by the night coach to make arrangements.'

'When will he be back?'

'The day after to-morrow. Tra-la-la! Oh haste to the wedding, and let us be gay, for young Pauline is dressed in her bridal array. She's wooed and she's won, by a Beaufort's proud son, and Pauline, Pauline, Pauline's a lady.'

'But, Sporboy, if you know anything absolutely discreditable about her, you ought to tell me.'

'Not to-night, dear boy. To-morrow! "To-morrow, and to-morrow, and to-morrow, creeps on this pretty pace from day to day, and all our yesterdays have lighted fools away to dusky death." Where's the brief candle? So to bed, to bed!'

All night I tossed uneasily. The strange mystery of this hand-some and defiant woman affected me. Who, and what was she? What did the profligate old adventurer know of her? Was she innocent and maligned, or a guilty creature to be unmasked and abandoned to her own fortune? The hot morning steamed into my window, and woke me from some strange dream, in which such conjectures as these had taken visible shape to torment me. I sprang up and opened the window. Presently I heard voices approach the lattice-work, and distinguished the tones of Sporboy and Mademoiselle Pauline.

'Why do you wish to persecute me?' said she. 'I am not inter-fering with *your* schemes. This boy is not a friend of *yours*. I have not seen you for years.'

'No, my charming child, you have not. You thought me dead, eh?'

'I had *hoped* so often,' said she, slowly.

'But we don't die young in our family, my dear,' he laughed. '"We live and love together through many a changing year"—ay, and *hate* together! Ho, ho!'

'What do you want to do then?'

'To make you suffer for your mother—for your infernal wretch of a half-bred, Spanish-blooded, treacherous devil of a mother—my young lamb.'

'How?'

'By waiting until your lover comes back with his licence in his pocket, and then telling him as much of your history as I know, and as much more as I can invent.'

She fell upon her knees.

'O, no, no! You will not do this. I will go away to-night, to-day, this hour. I never injured *you*. If you knew the life I have led. I am weary, weary. This boy loves me. He is honest, and, and ——'

'And *rich*, my Manuelita?'

'I cannot marry a poor man. You should know that. I have suffered poverty too long.'

'But have you not your Profession? Are you not an eminent *tragedienne?* Do not the diggers throw you nuggets? I am ashamed of you, my Manuelita,' and he began to whistle as though intensely amused.

She rose to her feet. 'My profession! I hate it! hate it! hate it! I never wished to belong to it. I was forced into it. Forced by my mother, and by you ——'

'And by others, my pigeon!'

'When I was thirteen you sold me. When I was fifteen I was a woman. I am thirty now, and do you think that fifteen years of sordid cares and desperate strifes have led me to love my art—as you call it? An art! It *is* an art. But you, and men like you, have made a trade of it—a trade in which bare bosoms and blonde hair fetch the highest prices.'

'Gently, sweet Manuelita! Tra-la-la-la! Tum-tum! Tra-la-la-la!' And he stopped his whistle to hum, beating time with his hand on the verandah-rail.

'All my life I have been told to get money—money—money—money. Good looks are worth—money. Health is worth—money. I am taught to sing, to play, to dance, to talk, that I may bring—money. Well, you have had your profit out of me. Now, I am going to sell myself for my own benefit!'

He stopped whistling and caught her by the wrist.

'I tell you what you are going to do. You are going to do just as I tell you, until this time to-morrow morning. You are going to stop acting, for I won't let you out of my sight. (Don't start; I will pay the salaries of your people.) You are going to remain with me all day. We will visit the claims, the shops, the museum, the places of interest, and this time to-morrow your lover will arrive, and I shall have the honour of relating to him the particulars of your lively career in the United States, Mexico, California, and the Great Pacific Slope.'

'I will not obey you. Let me go.'

'Does my Manuelita wish that I relate her history to the world, then? That I print it in the local paper; that I tell my friend Craven, the police-magistrate and warden that ——' and he approached and whispered something in her ear which I could not catch.

There was silence for a moment, and then the sound of suppressed sobs. Sporboy had conquered, for he walked away humming, and in a few minutes I saw him pass out of the door below me, and—with no trace of the debauch of last night upon

him—call out to the waiter, 'Mademoiselle has asked me to breakfast, Chips. When the heart of a man is oppressed with cares, the
mists are dispelled when a woman appears! Rum and milk, Chips.'

CHAPTER III

The Sumpitan

I WENT about my business that morning rather more satisfied than
I had been. It was evident that, however infamous, from a moral
point of view, might be the behaviour of Sporboy, the woman was
an adventuress who merited exposure, and that the action proposed
would liberate my foolish friend. I resolved to wait events.

The first event was the arrival of Sporboy to pay me for the Hall.
'Our charming friend—I knew her poor dear mother in 'Frisco—
is unwell and cannot play. Genius, dear boy, is often a trying
burden. I have taken upon myself to show her about the township,
to take her for a drive to the dam—to amuse her mind in fact. Is
that whisky in that bottle? No? Ink! Ah, I will not trouble you.
Till we meet, dear boy! Ho, "let me like a soldier fall." Tum, tum!
Te, tum! Tum, tum!'

The second was the report started at the 'Main Reef Hotel,' that
Sporboy was going to marry Mademoiselle Pauline, and that he
was taking her down his claims to show her his wealth.

The third was the appearance of the pair themselves in Merry-
jingle's new buggy, to 'look at the Museum.' 'We have done the
dam, seen the claims, been down shafts, and exhausted nature
generally,' said Sporboy. 'Ma'amselle is almost expiring.'

In truth she looked so. She was very white and nervous, and
glanced about her with the stare of a hunted animal. Knowing that
which I did know, I thought that Sporboy might esteem himself
fortunate in not having been precipitated down a shaft by the little
hand which so nervously twitched at the magnificent shawl of
Angora goat's hair, which had been the envy of Main Street for
the last three days. I almost pitied the poor creature.

'Show us the wonders of the Museum,' cried the vivacious
Sporboy (smelling strongly of the elegant simplicity of hot
whisky). Let us see your fossils, your emu eggs, your Indian
shields, and your savage weapons of war! Ho, ho! Here is a canoe,
Ma'amselle. How would you like to be floating in it away back to
your native land? Here we have a model of the Great Lively Creek
Nugget. How would you like to have that now, and live in luxury
all your days?'

If this was the method of torment he had put in practice since morning, she must have had more than human patience to endure it in silence.

'Here we have a club from New Caledonia. How nice to cleave the skull of your enemies! Our charming friend, Pauline, if she *has* enemies, might long to be able to use so effective a weapon! Or this spear! Adapted even to a woman's hand! Ho, ho! Miami, would you like to draw this little bow, and spit your foe with this arrow? By the way, how goes the time?'

It was two o'clock, and I told him so.

'The coach for Melbourne passes at three; would you like to go by it?' he asked her. 'But no, I would not recommend it. And yet the company is paid a week in advance. They would not stop you. Shall we make a trip?'

She turned to him half hopefully, as though deceived by his tones, but catching the malignant glance of his eye flushed and turned away.

Skipping from case to case like an overgrown bee, he paused at last.

'Ho, ho! What have we here! Oh! *my* gift. *The Sumpitan, or blow-pipe, the weapon of the natives of Central America, presented together with a case of poisoned arrows, by John Sporboy.* Tra-la-la! Observe this:—The fellow takes one of these little wooden needles stuck into a pith ball, puts it into the pipe, blows, and puff!—down falls his dinner!'

He commenced capering about with the long reed to his lips, swelling out his cheeks as in the act of blowing, and looking—with his big belly and tightly-buttoned coat—like a dissipated bullfrog.

Mademoiselle seemed roused to some little interest by this novel instrument.

'But how can they eat poisoned meat?' asked she.

'The poison does not injure the meat,' I replied, with the gravity proper to a Secretary. 'It is the celebrated Wourali poison, and effects no organic change in the body of the animal killed by it. You fire at him; he feels the prick of the needle, and, as Captain Sporboy says—puff—he falls dead in a few minutes!'

'Ho, ho!' cries the exhilarated Sporboy from the other end of the room. 'See me slay the Secretary with his own weapons,' and wheeling about, he blew at me a pellet of paper, propelled with such force that, narrowly missing my face, it struck and knocked to the ground a little Indian figure, which shivered into fifty pieces.

The gross old villain was somewhat sobered by this incident, and taking the quiver from the hands of Mademoiselle, replaced it, together with the reed in its accustomed rack.

'I am an ass,' he said. 'Let us return to the hotel and see the coach come in. We may have news of absent friends, who knows? My Pauline, thy Sporboy awaits thee!'

Paler and colder than ever, she allowed him to lead her away, and they departed. The manner in which Sporboy treated the wretched woman whom he had vowed to unmask disgusted me. It was unmanly, cruel. That she should be prevented from ruining a young and wealthy fool was right and necessary, but there was no need to torment her, to play with her as the cat plays with the mouse. Surely the best thing to do with her would be to let her go her own ways back into the great world out of which she had come. I determined to see Sporboy, inform him of that which I had overheard, and beg his mercy.

At four o'clock, the hour for closing the Museum, I went down to the hotel. At the door I saw Stunning Joe Banks.

'I was coming to see you,' he said; 'I want to take the Hall.'

'Oh certainly, but I must see Mademoiselle Christoval first.'

'She's gone!'

'*What?*'

'Gone to Melbourne.'

'When?'

'By the three o'clock coach. It's all right. *We*'re all square.'

'But,' said I bewildered, 'what about Sporboy?'

'Which?' asked Joseph, with one of those fine touches of humour for which he was so distinguished. 'What?'

'Excuse me a few minutes,' I said. 'There is something strange here,' and I hastened down Main Street. 'Captain Sporboy in?' I asked Chips.

'He was here this afternoon, sir.'

'When did Mademoiselle Christoval leave?'

'She came down with the Captain in his buggy, and went upstairs with him. Presently she rang the bell and told me to take her passage by the coach. She paid her bill, sent down her boxes, and was O.P.H., sir.'

'And was not Captain Sporboy with her?'

'No, sir. Didn't see him after he went upstairs with her. P'raps he's in his room.'

I went upstairs and knocked at the Great Man's door. No answer. I opened the door, and nearly fell over Sporboy's body. He was lying on the floor, just inside his room—DEAD!

My hurried summons filled the room with people in a few seconds. We lifted the corpse from the ground. There was on it no mark of violence, save that in falling the dying man had struck his nose against the floor, and the blood had slightly spotted his shirt front, and that his right hand doubled under him was bruised and discoloured.

'I wonder,' said the Coroner, taking his 'Three Star' afterwards in the bar, 'that a man of his habits was so apparently healthy. He drank whisky enough to have killed a regiment of dragoons. Those sort of subjects almost always die suddenly.'

Suddenly, indeed, when he was last seen by Mr. Butt, in perfect health, shaking hands with Mademoiselle Christoval at the threshold of the room that was his death-chamber.

The romance of Lively Creek was over, buried in the grave of the friendless adventurer. No one ever knew the nature of the secret which bound the Great Sporboy to the travelling actress, for when Harry Beaufort returned by the morning coach, he found a letter awaiting him, containing three lines of farewell from the unworthy woman he had hoped to marry, and who disappeared into the unholy mystery out of which she had emerged.

★

Was it accident or murder which removed the profligate prosecutor of Pauline or Manuelita so opportunely and so suddenly from her path? In common with the rest of the world I believed the former—until yesterday.

Despite the strong motive for the crime, the absolute absence of all testimony, medical or circumstantial, against her had compelled me to adjudge her innocent of the deed. I thought so then—I hope so now—but the reason I have recalled upon paper the details of this unfinished history is, that upon taking down yesterday, for some official purpose, the Sumpitan quiver, which had hung upon its accustomed nail for the last ten years under the noses of all the world, I found that the tiny, poisoned, thorn-point of one of the wooden needles had been broken off, and caught by a splinter in the little cane ring which sustained the mutilated shaft was a fine white thread—the hair of the Angora goat.

HUMAN REPETENDS

Marcus Clarke

WE HAD RETURNED from a 'Seance,' and were discussing that which
every one discusses without being anything the wiser—the future
of the soul.

'Come,' I cried at last, 'our thinly-clad intellects will take cold
if we venture so far up the mountain. Let us hasten to take refuge
at the fireside of the great DON'T KNOW.'

'Ay,' said Hylton, the surgeon, 'it is best. The secrets of the
grave are in safe keeping. Who has held parley with one risen from
the dead?'

'You are sure, then, that the spirits of the dead do not re-visit
us?' asked the sad voice of Pontifex, from out the gloom.

'Ay, as sure as of anything in this unstable world. But *you* are
no convert to the "spiritualistic" doctrine. You are no believer in
the ghost of Benjamin Franklin's small clothes.'

'I speak of spirits clad in flesh—ghosts who live and move
amongst us—ghosts who, tenants of bodies like our own, mingle
in the practical life of a methodical age, fulfilling a destiny, in the
accomplishment of which some of us, all unwittingly, may be
involved.'

'What do you mean, man?' asked Hylton, frowning down an
involuntary stare of alarm.

'Did you never meet one of these embodied ghosts?' said
Pontifex. 'Have you never, when dining in a public room or
walking in a crowd, been conscious of the presence of something
evil? Have you not known men, whose voice, silence, attitude,
gait, feature, gave token of crime undetected? These are the ghosts
of our modern day. They are with us, but not of us. We turn to

look after them, and yet avoid them, or meeting them, shrink from contact, shuddering we know not why.'

'Pontifex,' I cried, urged to utterance by the tones of the speaker, 'we have all known that you have a story. Tell it to us to-night.'

The young man fixed his hollow eyes upon the fire and laughed low.

'I have a story, and I will tell it to you, if you like, for the occasion is a fitting one. Listen.

'Most men, however roughly the world has used them, can recall a period in their lives when they were absolutely happy, when each night closed with the recollection of new pleasures tasted, when the progress of each day was cheered by the experience of unlooked for novelties, and when the awakening to another dawn was a pure physical delight, unmarred by those cankering anxieties for the fortune of the hour which are the burden of the poor, the ambitious and the intriguing. To most men, also, this golden time comes, when the cares of a mother, or the coquettish attention of sisters, aid to shield the young and eager soul from the blighting influences of worldly debaucheries. Thrice fortunate is he among us who can look back on a youth spent in the innocent enjoyments of the country, or who possesses a mind moulded in its adolescence by the cool fingers of well-mannered and pious women.

'My first initiation into the business of living took place under different auspices. The only son of a rich widower, who lived but for the gratification of a literary and political ambition, I was thrown, when still a boy, into the society of men thrice my age, and was tolerated as a clever impertinent in all those witty and wicked circles in which virtuous women are conspicuous by their absence. My father lived indifferently in Paris, or London, and, patronised by the dandies, artists, and scribblers who form, in both cities, the male world of fashionable idleness, I was suffered at sixteen to ape the vices of sixty. Indeed, so long as I was reported to be moving only in that set to which my father chose to ally himself, he never cared to inquire how I spent the extravagant allowance which his indifference rather than his generosity permitted me to waste. You can guess the result of such a training. The admirer of men whose successes in love and play were the theme of common talk for six months; the worshipper of artists whose genius was to revolutionise Europe—only they died of late hours and tobacco; the pet of women whose daring beauty made their names famous—for three years; I discovered, at twenty years of age, that the pleasurable path I had trodden so gaily led to a hospital or a debtor's prison, that love meant money, friendship, an endorsement on a bill, and that the rigid exercise of a profound and calculating selfishness alone rendered tolerable a life at once so deceitful and barren. In this view of the world I was supported by those middle-aged Mephistopheles (survivors of the storms which had wrecked so many argosies), those cynical, well-bred worshippers of self, who realise in the nineteenth century that notion of the devil which was invented by the early Christians. With these good gentlmen I lived; emulating their cynicism, rivalling their sarcasms, and neutralising the superiority which their existence gave them, by the exercise of that potentiality for present enjoyment which is the privilege of youth.

'In this society I was progressing rapidly to destruction, when an event occurred which rudely saved me. My father died suddenly in London, and, to the astonishment of the world, left—nothing. His expenditure had been large, but, as he left no debts, his income must have been proportioned to his expenses. The source of this income, however, was impossible to discover. An examination of his banker's book showed only that large sums (always in notes or gold) had been lodged and drawn upon, but no record of speculations or of investments could be found among his papers. My relatives stared, shook their heads, and insulted me with their pity. The sale of furniture, books, plate, and horses brought enough to pay the necessary expenses of the funeral, and leave me heir to some £800. My friends of the smoking-room and the supper-table philosophised on Monday, cashed my I.O.U.'s on Tuesday, were satirical on Wednesday, and "cut" me on Thursday. My relatives said that "something must be done," and invited me to stay at their houses until that vague substantiality should be realised. One suggested a clerkship in the War Office; another a stool in a banking-house; while a third generously offered to use his interest at head-quarters to procure for me a commission in a marching regiment. Their offers were generously made, but, *then*, stunned by the rude shock of sudden poverty, and with a mind debauched by a life of extravagance and selfishness, I was incapable of manly action. To all proposals I replied with sullen disdain; and, desirous only of avoiding those who had known me in my prosperity, I avowed my resolution of claiming my inheritance and vanishing to America.

'A young man, with money and a taste for *bric-à-brac*, soon gathers about him a strange collection of curiosities, and at the sale of my possessions I was astonished to find how largely I had been preyed upon by the Jews, print-sellers, picture-dealers, and vendors of spurious antiques. The "valuable paintings," the curious "relics," the inlaid and be-jewelled "arms", and the rare "impressions" of old prints were purchased by the "trade" for a third of the price which I had paid for them, doubtless to be re-sold to another man of taste as artless and extravagant as myself. Of the numberless articles which had littered my bachelor-house I retained but three or four of the most portable, which might serve as remembrances of a luxury I never hoped again to enjoy. Among these was a copper-plate engraving, said to be one of the first specimens of that art. The print bore the noted name of Tommasco Finiguerra, and was dated 1469. It was apparently a copy of a "half-length" portrait of a woman, dressed in the fashion of that age, and holding in her hand a spray of rue. The name of this *grande dame* was not given—indeed, as I need hardly say, the absence of aught but the engraver's signature constituted the chief value of the print.

'I felt constrained to preserve this purchase, for many reasons. Not only had I, one idle day, "discovered" it, as I imagined, on the back shelves of a print-shop, and regarded it as the prize of my artistic taste; not only had it occupied the place of honour over my mantelshelf, and been a silent witness of many scenes which yet lingered fondly in my memory; not only had I seemed to hold communion with it when, on some lonely evening, I was left to reflect upon the barrenness of my existence, but the face possessed a charm of expression which, acknowledged by all, had become for me a positive fascination. The original must have been a woman of strange thoughts, and (I fancied) of a strange history. The *pose* of the head was defiant, the compressed lips wore a shadowy smile of disdain, and the eyes—large, full, and shaded by heavy lashes—seemed to look through you, and away from you, with a glance that was at once proud and timid, as though they contemplated and dared some vague terror, of whose superior power they were conscious. We have all, I presume, seen portraits which, by accident or design, bear upon them a startling expression rarely seen upon the face of the original, but which is felt to be a more truthful interpreter of character than is the enforced composure which self-control has rendered habitual. So with the portrait of which I speak. The unknown woman—or girl, for she did not seem to be more than three-and-twenty—revealed, in the wonderful glance with which she had so long looked down upon me, a story of pride, of love, of shame, perhaps of sin. One could imagine that in another instant the horror would fade from those lovely eyes, the smile return to that disdainful lip, and the delicate bosom, which now swelled with that terror which catches the breath and quickens the pulse, would sink into its wonted peacefulness, to rise and fall with accustomed equanimity beneath its concealing laces. But that instant never came. The work of the artist was unchangeable; the soul which looked out of the windows of that lovely body still shuddered with a foreknowledge of the horror which it had expected four hundred years ago.

'I tried in vain to discover the name and history of this strange portrait. The artists or men of taste to whom I applied had neither seen another copy of the print, nor heard of the original painting. It seemed that the fascinating face had belonged to some nameless one, who had carried with her to the grave the knowledge of whatever mystery had burdened her life on earth. At last, hopeless of discovering the truth, I amused myself by speculating on what might, perchance, have been the history of this unknown beauty. I compared her features with the descriptions left to us of women famous for their sorrows. I invented a thousand wild tales which might account for the look of doom upon her fair face, and at last my excited imagination half induced me to believe that the mysterious print was a forged antique, and represented, in truth, some living woman to whom I had often spoken, and with whom my fortunes were indissolubly connected.

★

'A wickeder lie was never uttered than that favourite statement of colonial politicians—more ignorant or more impudent than others of their class—that in Australia no man need starve who is willing to work. I have been willing to work, and I have absolutely starved for days together. The humiliation through which I passed must, I fancy, be familiar to many. During the first six months of my arrival I was an honorary member of the Melbourne Club, the guest of those officials to whom I brought letters of introduction, the welcomed of South Yarra tea-parties, and the butt of the local *Punch*, on account of the modish cut of my pantaloons. I met men who 'knew my people,' and was surprised to find that the mention of a titled friend secured for me considerable attention among the leaders of such second-hand fashion as is boasted by the colony. In this genial atmosphere I recovered my independence. Indeed, had my social derelictions been worse than those incurred by poverty, I was assured that society would find in its colonial heart to forgive them all. I was Hugh Pontifex, who had supped with the Marquis of Carabas, and brought letters of introduction from Lord Crabs. Had Judas Iscariot arrived armed with such credentials South Yarra would have auburnised his red hair and had him to dinner. To my surprise, instead of being cast among new faces, and compelled to win for myself an independent reputation, I found that I was among old friends, whom I had long thought dead or in gaol. To walk down Collins-street was like pulling up the Styx.

On either side I saw men who had vanished from the Upper World sooner than I. Tomkins was there to explain that queer story of the concealed ace. Jenkins talked to me for an hour concerning the Derby, which ruined him. Hopkins had another wife in addition to the one whom he left at Florence; while Wilkins assured me, on his honour, that he had married the lady with whom he had eloped, and introduced me to her during a dinner party at a trading magnate's. The game was made in the same old fashion, only the stakes were not so high. The porcelain was of the same pattern, only a little cracked.

'For six months life was vastly pleasant. Then my term of honorary membership finally expired, and I left the Club to live at Scott's. By-and-bye my money ran short. I drew a bill on England, and the letter which informed me of its payment contained a stern command to draw no more. I went on a visit to the "station" of an acquaintance, and, on returning to town, found that my hotel bill was presented weekly. I retired into cheaper lodgings, and became affiliated to a less aristocratic club. Forced to associate with men of another set, I felt that my first friends remembered to forget met. My lampooned trousers began to wear out, and I wondered how I could have been once so reckless in the purchase of boots. I applied to Wilkins for a loan, then to Tomkins and Hopkins. I found that I could not repay them, and so avoided those streets where they were to be met. I discarded gloves, and smoked a short pipe publicly at noon-day. I removed to a public-house, and, talking with my creditor-landlord at night, not unfrequently drank much brandy. I discovered that it is possible to be drunk before dinner. I applied for a clerkship, a messengership, a "billet" in the Civil Service; I went on the stage as a "super," I went up the country as a schoolmaster, I scribbled for the newspapers, I wrote verses for the Full and Plenty eating-house. I starved in "genteel" poverty until fortune luckily put me in the way of prosperity by suggesting coach-driving and billiard-marking. Thanks to an education at a public school, a licensed youth, a taste for pleasure, and the society of the "best men about London," I found myself, at three-and-twenty, master of two professions, driving and billiard-playing. You will understand now that my digression concerning pictures was necessary to convince you that all this time I never sold the mysterious print.

'One Sunday evening, towards the end of August, when the windy winter had not yet begun to melt into sudden and dusty spring, I was walking up Bourke-street. All you folks who have made a study of Melbourne city know what a curious appearance the town presents on a Sunday evening. The deserted road, barren of all vehicles save a passing cab, serves as a promenade for hundreds of servant-maids, shod boys, and idlers, while the pavement is crowded with young men and women of the lower middle class, who, under pretence of "going to church," or of "smoking a cigar," contrive to indulge their mutual propensities for social enjoyment. Those sewing-girls who, at six o'clock in the evening, are to be nightly seen debouching from Flinders-lane or Collins-street, frequent these Sunday evening promenades, and, in all the pride of clean petticoats and kid gloves, form fitting companions for the holiday-making barbers or soft-goods clerks, who, daring rakes! seek a weekly intrigue in the *Peacock* on the unsavoury strength of a "Sunday" cigar. Examining these groups as I walked, I found myself abreast of Nissen's Café, impeding the egress of a lady. I turned with an apology, but the words melted on my lips when, beneath the black bonnet of the stranger, *I found the counterpart of my unknown print.*

'For an instant surprise rendered me incapable of action, and then, with a beating heart and bewildered brain, I followed the fleeting figure. She went down Bourke-street, and turned to the left into Swanston-street. When she reached the corner where the Town Hall now stands, a man suddenly crossed the moonlit street and joined her. This man was wrapped in one of those Inverness cloaks which the slowly travelling fashion of the day had then made imperative to the well-being of the Melbourne dandies. A slouch hat of the operatic brigand type shaded his face, but, in the brief glance that I caught of him, I fancied that I recognised those heavy brows, that blunt nose, and that thin and treacherous mouth. The two met, evidently by appointment, and went onward together. It was useless to follow. I turned and went home.

'I passed the next day in a condition of mind which it is impossible to describe. So strange a coincidence as this had surely never happened to man before. A woman has her portrait engraved in the year 1469; I purchase the engraving, try in vain to discover the original, and meet her face to face in the prosaic Melbourne of 1863. I longed for night to come, that I might wander through the streets in search of her. I felt a terrible yearning tug at my heartstrings. I burned to meet her wild, sad eyes again. I shuddered when I thought that, in my wildest dreams, I had never sunk that pictured face so deep beneath the social waters as this incarnation of it seemed to have been plunged. For two nights I roamed the streets in vain. On the morning of the third day a paragraph in the *Herald* explained why my search had been fruitless. The body of a woman had been "found in the Yarra." Society—especially unmarried society—has, as a matter of course, its average of female suicides, and, as a rule, respectable folks don't hear much about them. The case of this unfortunate girl, however, was different. She was presumed to have been murdered, and the police made investigations. The case is sufficiently celebrated in the annals of Melbourne crime to excuse a repetition of details. Suffice it to say that, against the many persons who were presumed to be inculpated in the destruction of the poor girl, no proof was forthcoming. The journals aired Edgar Poe and the "Mystery of Marie Roget" for a day or so, but no one was sent for trial, and an open verdict left the detectives at liberty to exercise their ingenuity without prejudice. There was some rumour of a foreigner being implicated in the deed, but as the friends of the poor outcast knew of no such person, and as my evidence as to seeing a man of such appearance join the deceased was, in reality, of little value (for I was compelled to admit that I had never seen the woman before in my life, and that my glimpse of her companion was but momentary), the supposition was treated with contempt, and the "case" dismissed from the memory of the public.

'It did not fade so easily from my mind. To speak the truth, indeed, I was haunted by the hideous thing which I had been sent to "view" upon the coarse table of that wretched deadhouse which then disgraced our city. The obscure and cruel fate of the unhappy woman, whose portrait had so long looked down upon me, filled me not only with horror but with apprehension. It seemed to me as if I myself was implicated in her fate, and bound to avenge her murder. The fact of my having speculated so long upon her fortunes, and then having found her but to lose her, without a word having passed between us, appeared to give me the right to seek to know more of her. The proud queen of many a fantastic dream-revel: the sad chatelaine of many an air-built castle: had this portrait leapt to life beneath my glances, as bounded to earth the nymph from beneath the chisel of Pygmalion? Had the lost one, who passed me like a ghost in the gloaming, come out of the grave in which they had placed her four hundred years ago? What meant this resurrection of buried beauty? What was the mysterious portent of this living presentment of a dead and forgotten sin? I saw the poor creature buried. I wept—no unmanly tears, I trust—over her nameless grave. And then I learned her history. 'Twas no romance, unless the old story of a broken home and the cold comfort of the stony-hearted streets may be called romantic. She was presumed to have been well born—she had been a wife—her husband had left her—she was beautiful and poor—for the rest, ask Mother Carey, who deals in chickens. She can tell you entertaining histories of fifty such.

'At the inquest I met Warrend—you remember old Tom, Hylton?—and he sought me out and took me home with him. We had been schoolfellows; but although my taste for prints and pictures had now and then brought me into his company, I had seen but little of him. He was—as we know him—kindly, tender, and generous. He offered me his help. He was in good practice, and could afford to give me shelter beneath his bachelor roof. He wrote for the *Argus*; knew the editor, would try and procure work for me. That meeting laid the foundation of such independence as I now claim. Shaken in health by my recent privations, and troubled in mind by the horrible and inexplicable mystery upon which I seemed to have stumbled, I was for some weeks seriously ill. Warrend saw that something preyed upon my spirits, and pressed me to unbosom myself. I told him the story and produced the print.

★

'I must beg your grace for what I am about to tell you. You may regard the story as unworthy of credit, or sneer at it as the result of a "coincidence." It is simply true, for all that.

★

'Warrend became grave.

'"I have·a copy of that print," said he, in a tone altogether without the pride usual in a collector. "I think a unique copy. It is the portrait of a woman round whose life a mystery spun itself. See here."

'He opened the portfolio, and took out the engraving. It was an exact copy of mine, but was a proof after letters, and bore, in the quaint characters of the time, the name, *Jehanne La Gaillarde*.

'I fell back upon the sofa as if I had been struck in the face. The name of the poor girl whom I had buried was Jenny Gay.

'"Warrend," said I, "there is something unholy about this. I met, a week ago, the living original of that portrait, and now you, a man whose name re-echoes that of the Italian artist who engraved it, tell me that you know the mystery of her life. What is it, then? for, before you speak, I know *I* figure in the scene."

'Warrend, or Finiguerra, took from the book-shelf a little book, published by Vander Berghen, of Brussels, in 1775, and handed it to me. It was called *Le Coeur de Jehanne La Gaillarde*, and appeared to be a collection of letters. In the advertisement was a brief memoir of the woman whose face had so long puzzled me. I glanced at it, and turned sick with a nameless terror. Jehanne La

Gailliarde was a woman whose romantic amours had electrified the Paris of Louis XI. She was murdered by being thrown into the Seine. "All attempts to discover the murderer were vain, but, at length, a young man named Hugues Grandprête, who, though he had never seen the celebrated beauty, had fallen in love with her picture, persuaded himself that the murderer was none other than the Sieur De la Forêt (the husband of the beautiful Jehanne), who, being a man of an ill-life, had been compelled to fly from Paris. Grandprête communicated his suspicions to none but his intimate friends, followed De la Forêt to Padua, and killed him." As I read this romance of a man who bore a name which reflected my own, I shuddered, for a sudden thrill of recollection lighted up the darkness of the drama as a flash of lightning illumes the darkness of a thunder-cloud. The face of the man in the cloak was recalled to me as that of a certain gambling lieutenant, who was cashiered by a court-martial, so notorious that the sun of India and the snows of the Crimea have scarce burned out or covered the memory of his regiment's nickname.

'As Jehanne La Gaillarde was the double of Jenny Gay: as Hugues Grandprête lived again in Hugh Pontifex: as the Italian artist was recalled to life in the person of the man at my side, so Bernhard De la Forêt worked once more his wicked will on earth in the person of the cashiered gambler, Bernard Forrester. If this was a "coincidence," it was terribly complete.'

'But 'twas a mere coincidence after all,' said Hylton, gently. 'You do not think men's souls return to earth and enact again the crimes which stained them?'

'I know not. But there are in decimal arithmetic repeated "coincidences" called *repetends*. Continue the generation of numbers through all time, and you have these repetends for ever recurring. Can you explain this mystery of numbers? No. Neither can I explain the mystery of my life. Good-night. I have wearied you.'

'Stay,' cried I, rashly; 'the parallel is not yet complete. You have not yet met Forrester?'

'No,' cried Pontifex, his large eyes blazing with no healthy fire; 'I have prayed that I might not meet him. I live here in Melbourne at the seat of his crime because it seems the least likely place again to behold him. If, by accident, in the streets I catch sight of one who resembles him, I hurry away. But I *shall* meet him one day, and then my doom will be upon me, and I shall kill him as I killed him in Padua 400 years ago!'

THE PREMIER'S SECRET

Campbell McKellar

I DO NOT KNOW what it was that first attracted me toward Edward Benson. He was more than thrice my age, and our positions, occupations, and mode of living were totally different. Without being able to give any reasons for it, it was, however, a fact that from the moment we first met I felt a strong liking for him, and it was evident that he was drawn toward me in an equal degree, so we gradually drifted into an intimacy. Intimacy is, perhaps, not the right word, as, though my whole life was laid bare before him—all my thoughts, aspirations, temptations, and woes poured into his willing ears—yet of his own life he seldom spoke, and the history of his youth was a subject on which his lips were always sealed. He was a man one did not dare question, nor could one imagine him making a confidant of anyone. That he had sprung from the people, and risen to his high station by his own genius and energy, were facts known throughout all Australia; but as to what he had been originally, or where he came from, no one knew, nor did anyone care to question.

When I first knew him he was Minister of Railways, and afterwards he became Premier. There was probably no public man in the same colony who possessed talents so great, and at the same time so little culture and general education. In those subjects to which he devoted himself none could approach him, but he often betrayed his humble origin in the most open ignorance of other subjects, and also in his rough speech and odd habits. In a land where so many of his contemporaries among the prominent men of the day were known to have risen from very humble origins, and been the carvers of their own destiny, his lack of general culture, and his unknown past, passed almost unobserved, and he was accepted simply for himself. Of his private life the world knew nothing, as he never went into general society or mixed with any people save a few of the most prominent politicans. He was unmarried, and was said not to possess a single relation in the world, hence some little curiosity was occasionally manifested as to what would be done with his vast fortune after his death.

That part of the world which professes to know all its neighbours' affairs whispered dark stories of what his private life really was—of wild orgies and scenes of terrible sensual dissipation. These stories, however, were not generally known. I, who knew the man better than most people, knew that many of these stories were true, and indeed fell far short of the mark. A man mentally and physically very strong, possessed of fierce passions, there was so much of the animal in his nature that at times it broke beyond his control. Friends warned me of this and that; spoke angrily of our growing intimacy; but with no avail. I saw plainly all that was wrong in his life and nature, but I also saw plainly all that was great and noble.

They who sin deepest and seek the lowest depths of degradation have sometimes more of what is great and noble, and best worthy of reverence, in their natures than the pitiful moral world-fearing mob, who, though they may do no action which the world may censure strongly, most assuredly do no action which is worthy of great praise. I knew that this man, who had worked his own way to the highest position his chosen country could give him, and to great wealth, yet was one of the most lonely and miserable beings amongst men—no friend; no wife, no child—he was utterly alone.

What availed position, wealth, all worldly success, with the awful hunger of heart which was there? His political career had been stainless, and he gave largely and freely to many charities. He was generally acknowledged to possess great mental gifts, yet he could not claim to be popular with any person or party. The reserve of his life and manner told against him.

I, who know myself so well, and am accustomed to search deeply my own heart and my own motives, did not feel any claim to question anything in his life.

My partiality for odd friendships has always been one of the most striking points of what people are pleased to call my eccentric character.

There are words of Holy Writ which have always seemed to me most solemn and to be carefully heeded; these are:—

'Judge not that ye be not judged.'

One of Edward Benson's most marked peculiarities was a strong aversion to Chinese. He was a strong supporter of all measures for their exclusion from the country, and the sight of an innocent John Chinaman selling fruit or fish seemed to annoy and disturb him immensely. When I tell you the story of his life you will not wonder at it.

I had often promised to visit him at one of his stations where he usually spent a few months every year, and at last managed to find time to fulfil my promise.

Bengalee, as the place was called, was a much more imposing mansion than bush houses usually are. It possessed a fine library, and the numerous rooms were filled with treasures of pictures and sculpture. There was a collection of China unequalled probably in Australia, delicate figures, vases, and cups of Rose du Barri Sèvres. of Meissen, of Nymphenburg, of Chelsea, of Bow; grotesque bronzes from Japan; wonderful porcelain and terra-cotta plaques and jugs, which might have been the work of Lucca della Robbia himself; fragile glass of Murano; Florentine mosaics and brasses; a wonderful table of Sèvres and ormolu, which had belonged to Marie Antoinette, and might have caused the heart of Mr. Jones, of South Kensington fame, to burn with envy in his grave, and I do not know what other rare and beautiful and priceless things that house held.

All these treasures were seen by almost no one save their owner. They had been collected during a long tour in Europe.

It was the last night of my visit. I was to leave at the unearthly hour of two in the morning, having a long drive to the nearest railway station.

It was about eight o'clock, and Edward Benson and myself had just finished dinner, but were still lingering over our wine, reluctant to leave the glorious fire which blazed and crackled on the hearth, when a servant entering, said that there was a swagman outside who wished particularly to see Mr. Benson. 'Send him round to the window,' said Mr. Benson, pointing towards a long French-window which opened into the verandah. He was reluctant to leave the fire, and supposed the man was only wanting a billet or something of that sort.

The servant opened the window, and shortly afterward the swagman, a rough, unkempt specimen of his rough, unkempt class, appeared on the verandah.

'Beg pardon, boss, but I jist were a-wantin' to tell you that there's a cove up in woolshed, as comed there to-night, and I'm thinkin' he's off his head, or got the horrors, or going to kick the bucket, for he's a-goin' on a-ravin' that awful that I'm blowed if I could stand it, and I'm a-goin' to clear on. I thought I would let you know, m' happen you can do something for him.'

'Drinking, I suppose,' muttered Benson peevishly. 'Well, I'll have it seen to. You can go;' he added coldly.

The man shrugged his shoulders, and turned sullenly away. The night was wet and cold, the wind howling through the trees; he would have a long tramp to the next station, and no doubt the sight of the brilliantly lit dining-room, with its wealth of plate and glass, the profusion of fruit and flowers on the table, and last but not least the blazing fire, and the shining decanters with their ruby and amber contents, would awaken many a bitter thought in his mind, to console him during his long wet night journey. The contrast between his own life and this must have been rather painful.

It surely must have been something out of the ordinary that drove him from the woolshed; swagmen as a rule are not thinskinned.

A rather unaccountable curiosity came over me to go up and see for myself what ailed the man. Perhaps I too wished to experience the effect of the contrast between the luxuriant comfort of the brilliant firelit room and the spectacle of the dingy woolshed with its occupant dying in the horrors. Perhaps a little touch of intense pity possessed me. Having made up my mind to go, I did my utmost for a long time, without avail, to persuade Benson to accompany me.

The shed was quite close to the manager's house, and he would send word up to have the man attended to—it was absurd our going up. After some time, however, he consented with a very bad grace to go with me. I remembered then that one of his peculiarities was a great dislike to even enter a woolshed, the smell and look of the place, he said, made him faint. This night, however, something—fate perhaps—took us to the Bengalee woolshed.

Wrapping ourselves in waterproofs, and taking a lantern with us, we walked up through the drenching rain to the shed, which was at some little distance from the house.

The building was large and looked very eerie as our lantern but dimly illuminated our immediate surroundings, and left the rest in total darkness. We stood inside the doorway for a moment, not knowing whereabout the man would be. All was silent, save for the scratchings of the native cats and 'possums in the shingle and iron roof.

Suddenly from close to where we stood, there rang out a peal of wild demoniacal laughter, with an effect that was absolutely startling.

For a moment I felt unmanned, then recollecting what we had come for, turned the light of the lantern to the corner from whence the sound had proceeded.

On his back on a couple of greasy sheepskins lay the tramp. His swag was under his head as a pillow, and his tin billy lay by his side.

I placed the lantern on the floor, and kneeling down bent over him. Edward Benson slowly approached, and mechanically knelt down on the opposite side of the man, who was but a mere wasted skeleton consumed by disease and drink. He seemed conscious of our presence and lay silently regarding us.

Dying? There was no doubt of it.

The lantern shone on his face and on our two faces, making a little circle of light round us, and here and there bringing into relief a beam or rail of the shed. We must have made an odd picture— a subject for a Rembrandt—we two kneeling in that small circle of light by the dying man.

Suddenly the eyes of the tramp seemed to light up with fire; drawing himself up on his elbow he gazed as if fascinated into Benson's face, then with wild frenzy seized him by the arm.

'Bill Adams, by the Lord! Bill Adams!' rang the hoarse cry through the shed. 'Bill Adams!' again he shrieked, with a burst of laughter.

A unearthly pallor had crept over Benson's face; he knelt immovable, gazing blankly down into the face of the swagman.

'Bill Adams—old pal—I knows you, Bill. Hist! see there;' he pointed out into the darkness; 'don't you see him, Bill—Jimmy the Chinaman.—Hah! there, don't you see him, man? Press him down, boys—stop his yelling mouth! You'll never peach no more, will you Jimmy?—Sing louder, boys, sing louder! He's yelling in my ears—he's always a-yelling in my ears! Why won't he go away?— Blast him! press him down, boys—see there he is again!'

Despite myself, I could not resist glancing where the man pointed, though knowing well he was only raving; then I glanced at Benson's face.

His face was half turned over his shoulder, his eyeballs gleaming red as he gazed out into the darkness as if he too saw something there; great drops of perspiration stood on his brow. Never in all my life have I seen such a face of horror as that.

'Don't you see him, Bill?' The man raved on, tossing wildly about, and pointing with frenzied hands before him. 'See him grinning there! Damn you! You —— Chinaman, sneak again, will you? Turn the screw of the press, boys, that's it. Sing louder, sing louder! Don't let me hear his voice again. It's in my ears, boys, always in my ears—Jimmy, the Chinaman. Bill, your sin will find you out. Hist! Bill, he's never left me all my life—but you'll stop his mouth, Bill. I cannot bear to hear him yell like that. Sing louder—louder, boys—louder!'

I cannot render all his wild frenzied ravings, the torrents of fierce imprecations which he poured out with wild excitement.

At last he fell back exhausted, and lay breathing heavily. His face was growing more ghastly and blue, and I knew he was dying. Opposite me, silent and immovable, knelt Benson, with wild horror imprinted on his face. I spoke to him, but he did not answer me, he seemed unaware of my presence. So, for a few minutes, we remained.

Then, as I fancied, I heard distant music, but supposed it to be but imagination, a gust of wind blew open the door by which we had come in, and, with the wind, entered a burst of glorious melody—someone playing the piano at the manager's house— some strange, beautiful march, full of gladness, and graciousness, and solemness. The dying man heard, and over his face there came a look of wonderful rest and peace, his lips moved in a gentle murmur, but I could not catch what he said.

Then the music changed into a tender, simple old ballad, and a woman's voice joined in. One could scarce distinguish the words, but the sweet old air came echoing softly through the shed.

The man listened with a smile of glad recognition.

'It's Bess, a-singing in the garden—Bess, as I loved so well! I can see thee, lass, in the old apple orchard. It war'nt me as done it, Bess, so help me God, girl! I wouldn't touch a hair of his head. It war'nt me, girl. I have been a bad un, Bess, but I didn't touch nothing you loved. It were someone else as stole on him, Bess, by the little gate o' the orchard, and struck him down—struck him down when he were a courtin' you, Bess. Twar'nt me, Bess, though they lagged me for it. Bob Simmons won't ne'er hurt nowt you cares on, girl. Bess—Bess Dale—you'll not be hard on me, girl? Good-bye—I'm a-goin' now, Bess. I've been a bad un, but— good-bye, girl—good-bye—.'

The music died away, and I laid the dead man's head down on his swag again.

'Come—come out of this. He is dead!' I said, touching Benson's arm.

'Dead!' he repeated, and then, with a gesture of utter despair, he threw his arms out before him. 'Bess Dale—Bess Dale!—Bob Simmons!—Ah! my sin *has* found me out!'

There was such a weary, utter despair in the hoarse cry, that I shuddered as I drew him from the shed. Once outside he seemed to recover himself somewhat.

'Go to the manager's house and tell them!' he said, briefly and sternly. 'Let them do all that is needful!'

I went at once, without question; nor did it strike me as odd that he should order me, his guest, to do so.

I knew that with the dead man lay the secret of Edward Benson's life.

I directed the manager to do everything that was necessary, and then slowly went down toward the house. I found Benson waiting for me, and we walked down together, without speaking.

Now, indeed, I saw the contrast between the scene just left and the beautiful luxurious dining-room, with its light and warmth.

'Sit down!' he said gravely; 'after what you have heard you must listen to the story of my life.'

He blew out the waxlights on the table, and turned down the crimson-shaded lamp. I did not answer, I could not; something held me silent. He came and leant on the mantelpiece, looking down on me. At this moment a servant entered, and said a China-man wanting work was without. With a fierce imprecation, Benson told them to drive him away from the place—Why did they come to him, instead of the manager?

I wondered the servant had the courage to speak to him of a Chinaman, his aversion to them being so well known; and this night I learnt the reason of this great aversion, and yet I wonder at the odd coincidence which brought that Chinaman there that night of all others.

When he had somewhat recovered from the evident distress this interruption had caused him, he sat down. Leaning his head on his hand, he seemed to see before him in the fire the incidents of his life, as he told them. I sat with my back to the window, and he sat opposite to me.

So, sitting by the hearth, I listened to this tale of horror:—

'You have always known, I suppose, that I can boast of no ancient lineage—that I am a self-made man. My father was a small cottar, on the estate of a certain great English nobleman. It is not necessary for me to tell you his name, or even what county I came from. My father brought us up by blows and curses, and our whole family were continually in trouble, for poaching and other pecca-dilloes. What good was in me never had the chance of showing itself.

'When I became old enough to consider myself a man. I fell desperately in love with a farmer's daughter, who, though of humble enough station, was yet a cut above me. Her name was Bessie Dale—she whom the dead man up yonder raved about. It was no wonder that he and I and many others loved her, for she was no common country wench, but I know now even better than I did then, that she was wonderfully beautiful and gentle and pure and good. I can picture her as I often saw her in the very orchard he talked about, with her chintz gown tucked up, standing amongst the tall grass with bare arms upraised above her head, plucking the apple-blossom, or going singing through the orchard that song we heard to-night, calling now and then to the cows which followed at the sound of her voice. Such a beautiful, calm, restful life that was—but why tell you all this? Know only that to none of us who wooed her then would she have anything to say. I, fierce passioned and jealous natured, vowed that none but myself should ever possess her.

'In one spring time there came a gentle man—an artist—and he too loved Bess Dale, and she, we could all see, was flattered and glamoured by her fine lower.

'All day he would lie at her feet in the apple orchard, making pretence to sketch her, or the trees, or feeding cattle around them, and instilling God knows what poison into her ears. Perhaps I am wrong, he may have meant no harm to her, he may have wooed and loved her honestly, but he was a gentleman, she a farmer's lass, so we judged him by ourselves and thought the worst. Then I got to know that she met him at night by the orchard gate, and I stole secretly to watch them.

'Maddened by bitter hate and jealousy, one night I stole softly on them in the dark, and struck him down—stabbed him in the dark, and left him lying dead at her feet in the long grass.'

He paused for a moment and sighed heavily.

'Her terrified screams brought all the inmates of the farmhouse to the spot, and the light of their lanterns shone on the terrified girl, the murdered man, and another man crouching low, with fear in his eyes and a bloodstained knife in his hand.

'It was Bob Simmons, whom we have just seen die. He had been near and seen a man rush out from the shadow of the apple trees and stab the girl's lover at the gate, and then rush swiftly away. Horrified, he, Bob Simmons, had rushed forward and pulled the knife from the breast of the murdered man. This was the tale he told. No one believed him. It was known he hated this man who had won the heart of Bess Dale. Many things went to prove him guilty. He was tried for the murder, found guilty, and sentenced to penal servitude for life. I think he was transported to Western Australia, but I am not sure.

'I, who had done the deed, escaped even suspicion, but it did me no good, for I had to watch Bessie Dale grow whiter and more sad and frail day by day, till one day I followed, with many others, the coffin that bore her to her last resting place.

'It was *my* sin killed her, and *my* sin wrecked and ruined Bob Simmons' life—he had to suffer in my place.'

The tall old oak clock ticked away loudly, the ruddy firelight shone over the room, the logs crackled and blazed, but otherwise there was silence.

I sat in a trance, I could not have spoken to save my life. The expression of terrible despair and remorse on the man's face haunts me yet.

'You little thought there was blood on these hands—blood on the hands of your friend,' he went on bitterly. 'When Bess died, all that was bad in me came to the surface, and I went from bad to worse. Ah, me! how I suffered—such awful shame and remorse! Do not think I have not been punished.

'I eventually came out here. I knocked about under many different names, trying my hands at many a different things, now striving to live cleanly and retrieve my past, and then giving way to terrible bursts of ill-doing and badness—herding and living with the scum of the country—and you know what that is here.

'One year I went as shearer to a certain station, of which I need not tell you the name. The shearers at the place that year were as vile and low a crew of men as it was possible to get together. Like takes to like perhaps, but, anyway, there was not a man amongst us who was not capable of every species of iniquity. There were several old lags, whose whole lives had been criminal and spent in criminal thought and deed—for this was many years ago, remember, when yet there were many convicts and ticket-of-leave men knocking about the country. The race has almost died out now. There were, of course, several boys amongst us, employed in various ways in the shed, and it was one of our chief amusements debasing and corrupting these boys as much as in us lay. As the men got to know each other, and find kindred spirits, they learnt they need not fear revealing their past life in any way. A rougher, more utterly bad and reckless lot of devils it would not be possible to bring together, and the two worst among them were Bob Simmons—whom we have just seen die, the man whose life I made what it had become—and myself. Bill Adams, I called myself then, and he bore some other name also, so I never knew he was Bob Simmons, we never recognised or suspected each other. Since then, I have heard no word of him till to-night.

'The shearers' cook that year was a Chinaman, who was always called "Jimmy, the Chinaman." He was a sneaking hypocritical specimen of his sneaking hypocritical race. The men hated him, and were continually grumbling at and tormenting him. There were wild fierce orgies, when Jimmy, the Chinaman, was always the object of rough horse-play and bad treatment. I would be afraid to tell or even hint at what went on amongst us then—those who were weakest and least able to protect themselves were made to wait on and slave for the others, and were brutally treated. Some of our doings reached the squatter's ears. There was a great uproar, and some talk of getting the police out to us. Someone had peached on us, and, instinctively, we all hit upon the Chinaman as the culprit. We watched him, and again we found him spying on us, and sneaking off to the manager with tales of our doings. The men determined that on the last night of shearing he should be paid off for his sneaking. He was a cringing, cowardly creature, and used to grovel at our feet in terror if we threatened him.

'Never can I forget that awful night. It haunts me always. That first crime of mine has seemed to me nothing in comparison to it. I had a motive then—jealousy. I have never repented that deed—but its effects? Ah, yes! the death of gentle Bess—the life-long wreck and ruin of the dead man up there—these have been with me always, such remorse and horror! You cannot picture it, but they seem as nothing to the crime we perpetrated that awful night. It has haunted me as it haunted him.'

He stopped with a violent shudder, and remained silent for a while, gazing into the fire with a face of awful remembrance and fear—then, pulling himself together, he went on:—

'Shearing was over—it was the last night—in the morning we were all to leave.

'Can I describe to you, or can you picture to yourself, the scene that night in the shearers' hut?

'The long narrow building, with its rough slab walls, along which ran rows of bunks, mere shelves, with bundles of straw and nondescript bedding and frowsy blankets tossed on them in disorder. A fireplace, with huge fire of blazing logs, at either end of the hut. The long table, round which sat and sprawled the shearers, drinking, swearing, cursing and quarrelling. A few lay in their bunks, others crouched over the fire; some were playing cards, others tossing with dice; all were smoking. The air reeked with tobacco smoke, and the fumes of whisky and rum intermingled with the odour of cooking. On the table lay broken plates and scraps of meat—everything in careless disorder. All, without exception, were drunk—some sullenly drunk—others maudlin or quarrelsome. Jimmy, the Chinaman, alone was sober, for the simple reason that they would not give him anything to drink, nor allow him to leave the hut. He crouched in the corner, his opium pipe in his mouth, shivering with fright, for he knew that there was little chance of his getting through the night unmolested.

'The shearers had made up their minds that they would be revenged on him that night, though they had no particular plan. Deeper and deeper they drank, and I—Oh, cursed hour!—drank deeper and longer than most. We all became quarrelsome and mad with drink—reckless what we said or did. Cards were thrown aside, broken bottles flung about recklessly.

'"Let's take Jimmy to the shed and try him there, boys," I yelled.

'In a moment, Jimmy, the Chinaman, yelling with terror, was seized and dragged off to the woolshed, which was close by, followed by a mob of men, singing, laughing, shouting, and cursing—mad with drink. Some had seized up the lanterns off the table, others carried bottles of whisky—whatever they could lay their hands on. Mounting on a wool bale, I—I, who am now an Australian Premier—I, who was then Bill Adams, the vilest and most reckless of that hellish crew—I, I say, was judge and jury and all. *I* tried Jimmy, the Chinaman, amidst the yells and jeers of the shearers who sprawled drunk on the bales and wool-fleeces round me—I tried and condemned him to death!

' "Put him in a wool bale, boys, and ship him out of the country!" I cried, with drunken glee.

'None of us knew what we did, surely; for no sooner were the words out of my mouth, than the Chinaman, yelling and gibbering with fright, was seized and tossed into the woolpress. There was some wool in it, and, on top of the struggling wretch, they pressed down more; and then, all the wild beast that is in all men's natures, woke in them—in us, I should say, for I too lent a hand.

'With yells and blasphemous cursing and singing—a chorus, surely, of devils—we turned the screw of the press. Lower and lower it went—agonising yells came from the suffocating wretch—lower and lower it went, and louder and louder we sang to drown the cries!—Lower and lower pressing the wool down, crushing and suffocating the Chinaman beneath it!'

With gasping breath and shuddering hands held out before him, as if to ward off some dreadful sight, he paused. Great drops of perspiration streamed off his face—he seemed to see the scene all before him.

In my chair I crouched, dumb with horror. I could not speak or move. I waited for what came next.

'We sewed the wool bale up; we branded it, and tossed it amongst the other bales of wool; and on the morrow it was taken away in the drays, and afterwards shipped to England—that bale with the dead man in it.'

His voice had sunk to a hoarse whisper.

'Night and day—night and day—through all these years, the dying yells of that Chinaman have rung in my ears. In the glare of day I see his cursed face. I see it when I stand in my place in the House and the people cheer me. I see it in the faces of all his cursed race—one so like another. At night he yells by my pillow— he is ever with me.

'My God! See there—there! Do you not see his cursed grinning face?' and he leapt to his feet and gazed in a paroxysm of horror towards the window. Such a picture of fear and despair!

The blood seemed to curdle in my veins, and, thrilled with fear, I, too, sprang to my feet.

There, pressed close against the glass of the window, was the ghastly grinning face of a Chinaman!

Before it had scarcely dawned on me that it was no weird apparition—no creation of fancy—but the face of a living man, Benson strode forward with a terrible oath and thrust his hands through the glass, as if to grasp the face. Whether he did see the glass or not I cannot say, but the shock recalled him to himself. His hands were cut and bleeding, and the Chinaman had fled.

He came back to the table, drank half a tumbler of brandy as if it were water, and, rolling his bleeding hands in a serviette, sat down again. He seemed scarcely aware of the damage to his hands.

'You see it is no fancy of mine that his face haunts me always,' he said hopelessly.

'Oh, but this was no fancy,' I said, 'it was the Chinaman they told you of, wanting work; he was probably attracted to the window by the bright light.'

'Ah no,' he answered, '*you* may think so. I know the cursed face too well; or, even if you are right, does it not show that their faces are ever before my eyes?'

It was useless to reason with him, and he went on:

'That bale of wool, I tell you, was shipped to England with its ghastly contents undiscovered, but'—

'Oh!' I exclaimed. 'this is surely a mad dream. It is not possible men could do such a thing in sport. You are playing on my credulity.'

Surely, indeed, it was some grotesque joke. I even seemed to see a certain ludicrousness in it.

'You do not mean to tell me that it passed undiscovered; that this really took place? But when the wool reached England, or on the ship, it must have been discovered. No! I cannot believe it.'

'It never reached England. The ship foundered at sea, and all her cargo of wool went to the bottom. The sea holds the horrible secret. The ship was the *Loch Fennich*. You may have heard of the wreck, and the terrible sufferings of some of her passengers, cast adrift in an open boat. I swear before God that every word is true. Do I look like a man who jests?'

I *did* remember to have read an account of this wreck, which had happened long before my day. I doubted no longer; indeed, I had never doubted at all.

'Do you know,' he said, 'I have often feared that the bale might have floated to the top of the sea, and the crime be yet discovered. My life has been a hell upon earth.

'The day after this event, sobered and terrified with fear of detection, the shearers left the station, all of us avoiding each other and many, I believe, leaving the colony for some other part of Australia. In all these years until to-night, when I saw the face of Bob Simmons, I have heard no word of, nor seen any of my accomplices in that awful deed save one. I know not whether they are living or dead. I did not dream that anyone could ever recognise me, but see now, even in his delirium. Bob Simmons knew my face. It is strange—strange—for this other whom I have met, has seen me often daily for years; and has given not the faintest sign of recognition—him, I could not mistake, for he has marks and scars on his face which admit of no doubt as to his identity. He too is known to you—he has reached high station and great wealth, and his charities are boundless—his life flawless. His name is ————!' and he mentioned a name which filled me with unutterable surprise, the name of a man whose good deeds and charities had made him known to all—who stood high in his country's favour. Yet his life, too, held this hideous secret!

'My life,' went on Benson, 'after that was a continual success. I by degrees acquired lands and wealth, and worked my way up till I am Premier of this great colony, and I believe I am regarded with respect; and—but he and I, you know us both now. What is his life or mine? A hideous lie! Oh! do not think I have not been fearfully punished. I am alone in the world, ever haunted by my crime, and living in awful fear of the punishment which—escaped perhaps on earth—awaits me twofold beyond the grave.

'Is it not a strange world? The wisdom and justice of God? Can there be such things? Can there be a God? The man who suffered unjustly for my sin, whose life was wrecked and ruined through me, dies an outcast, friendless and unregretted at my door—whilst I—*I*, whose sin has been too great for atonement, am surrounded with everything wealth can give me, with the honour and respect of my country. Ah! there is no justice in Heaven or on earth. God himself cannot undo what has been done. For such as I there can be no forgiveness—no atonement. And if there be punishment beyond the grave, how great, indeed, must be mine? I am like a little child, I know not what to believe or trust in. I am full of doubt and fear—dreadful fear of that awful thing we call death. Oh! if it only meant rest—eternal rest—if the grave were but the end of all! Hateful as my life is I dare—Oh! I dare not die, I am not fit!'

The terrible hopelessness and despair of the man woke all my pity—the horror that had risen in me as he told his tale left me, to give place to intense sympathy and pity. I understood what the loneliness, the misery, the remorse of his life had been. I dared not add to it by *my* blame, for before me rose the words:—

'Judge not, that ye be not judged.'

When it was yet dark, in the early morn, I left Bengalee. I left doubting whether I ought not to have stayed beside this man, consumed with misery and fear and despair. But what could I have done?

I never looked on Edward Benson's face again, for a few days afterwards the telegraph spread the news from end to end of Australia that Edward Benson had been found dead in his bed—accidentally killed by an overdose of chloroform. The world never doubted it was accidental, and I, who guessed differently, held my tongue.

He was given a great funeral, and paeans of praise were sung in his honour. His wealth was left to different charities, and his splendid collection of pictures and other art treasures went to a colonial museum.

I follow yet the course of that other life with curious eyes—that life of charity and fair renown covering a hideous secret.

But a year ago I visited the spot on Bengalee, where the outcast swagman Bob Simmons had been buried. The post and rail fence which had marked his lonely bush grave was gone—the wild flowers bloomed amid the tall grass which waved over the spot—few could guess it was a grave.

I wonder if *he* finds peace and rest there—surely it is quiet and still enough.

Standing by the grave, words I have heard somewhere came back to me:—

Perhaps that better 'tis, life's sorrows past,
Flower-crowned, forgotten, so to lie at last;
The goal of life's long earthly quest,
Undreaming sleep—Nirvāna—Rest.
But is there sleep and rest.—Who can tell?

MISS PALLAVANT

Rosa Praed

AN EPISODE

Waye House, Woodfordshire, *June 28th*.

I CAME DOWN HERE a few days ago on a visit to my friends the
Laudes. One always says 'down here,' though, in reality, 'here' is
a Midland country to the north of London. Mr. Laude is both
rector and squire of Waye, a combination described by Sydney
Smith, I think, under the term of 'squarson.' Mr. Laude is more
of the squire than the parson. He pays a curate to perform his
clerical duties, and devotes himself to the management of his farms,
most of which he has upon his hands, to hunting and shooting, to
pottering about the garden, and to other occupations befitting a
country gentleman. He considers that he fulfils his priestly obli-
gations by cottering a few favoured sick people, and preaching one
sermon on Sunday. Mr. Laude frankly owns that it was not his
vocation to become a clergyman. He likes farming much better
than preaching. He enjoys his mild hunting in winter, and his much
milder shooting—for Waye is in a shoe-making county where
poachers abound—in September. He enjoys, too, his month in
London during the season, when he and Mrs. Laude and their
daughter Sissy go up to an hotel in Albemarle Street, and to the
picture galleries and the Row and the more classical theatres—Mr.
Laude draws the line at the Gaiety and Ascot and Sandown; he does
not object to the Lyceum and Hurlingham. They always go to
London in the middle of May. Mr. Laude likes to be back at Waye
before the hay is ready for cutting and the strawberries are ripe.
No one ever thought of finding fault with Mr. Laude for neglecting
his duties. He pays his curate at a higher rate than most rectors, and
Waye is only a small parish. Besides, everyone knows that Mr.
Laude is very fairly off, and it is not to be supposed that a
gentleman with an income of three thousand a-year will be

contented to grind away among poor people. He is very popular with the neighbouring gentry, and he always has a cheery word for the farmers. He is a short, spare, wiry old gentleman of between sixty and seventy, with a clean-shaven face, a Roman nose, and snow-white hair, riding as light a weight as a boy, and taking his fences as pluckily as his son, Captain Tom. Mrs. Laude is large, stout, placid, comely, and well preserved. I never knew her utter a cross word, and yet I am quite aware that she rules her husband and her household. She walks about the lawn with a little spud, uprooting plantains as she goes, and she too is interested in the farms, but in a distant, superior sort of fashion, and takes great pride in her roses and her grape-house. She is on excellent terms with their nearest great neighbours, the Lord-lieutenant and his family, and lets us know it in a well-bred manner. She never says anything clever, and she finishes up most of her remarks with a little fat laugh, designed, it would seem, to give them point. She frequently takes Mr. Laude to task for small social lapses.

The Laudes' only daughter, Sissy, is a fresh, frank specimen of the English country miss, who, I confess, does not inspire me with any particular enthusiasm. She is slim and fair, and has been enough in London to have studied the approved fashion of squaring out her elbows and buckling in her waist. Mrs. Laude has done her duty to Sissy. She presented her last year, though they were only their usual month in London, and then she took her abroad for three months. Sissy came home with a large bundle of photographs, a travelled air, and a store of tourist anecdotes, in which the inevitable Italian count figured, and in which there were many jokes about papa's John Bull tendencies. The Laudes, however, rather prided themselves upon being persons of light and leading, above paltry prejudice, not in the least Philistine or insular. Of course they are Tories. No one in Woodfordshire—no county person, that is to say,—could possibly be a Liberal, 'on account of that dreadful Bradlaugh and the shoemakers and dissenters, don't you know?' So they have very strong anti-Irish views, and Mr. Laude talks of Mr. Gladstone as if he were an arch-fiend set loose to work the ruin of country squires and of England.

Sissy does not go in for politics. She has two or three dear little families of geese and goslings, which she tends most carefully, and she has her dachshunds and fox terriers, and she has also the flowers to arrange for the dining table and the drawing-room; anti-macassars to see to, and then she teaches in the Sunday school, and is great on lawn-tennis, and has all the summer garden parties to think of and sundry penny readings to organise. Sissy is a very busy young woman.

The Laudes have two sons. The youngest is on a cattle-ranch in America. I mention him first to get him out of the way. There is more to say about the eldest, Captain Tom Laude, who is in a cavalry regiment, and had been engaged for the last six months to the Honourable Henrietta Pallavant, daughter of General Lord Pallavant, who was commandant at Gibraltar or some place where Tom Laude's regiment was stationed.

Miss Pallavant is said to be a beauty, and has been very much admired. I have often heard of her, and was surprised that she should content herself with so comparatively insignificant a *parti* as Tom Laude; but she is over thirty, as Debrett testifies—rather older than Tom—and no doubt thinks it is time that she settled herself. The Laudes were at first very pleased at the engagement, especially when, through the Pallavant influence, Tom got a staff appointment; but now that the wedding is coming near, and the settlements are being prepared, I fancy they are less delighted. The marriage is fixed to take place a month hence, but the settlements are not signed yet, and from what I hear, there is little probability of the respective fathers coming to an agreement. Mrs. Laude looks a good deal worried over the business. She was alone when I arrived the other day, and I could not help telling her that I feared her London dissipations had been too much for her. They had just returned from the annual month's season.

'Oh, my dear, it isn't that,' she said.

We were in the cosy hall, with its big Japanese screen shutting off the entrance door, its cane chairs, and couches carefully covered, so that dirty boots should do no injury, its litter of news-papers, old gloves, gardening implements, parish basket, and so forth, which gives it a homely, comfortable appearance. Waye House is quite a type of English middle-class comfort and respect-ability. It is one of these modern-old houses, square, with case-ments and mahogany furniture—a cross between a rectory and a hall, and which would be ugly if it were not so homelike and so unpretentious. The whole establishment is in keeping. There is one man-servant, and the coachman comes in to wait when there are visitors. The china is old Chelsea and Worcester, and there are two or three ancestral portraits of worthy-looking squires and dames, which don't go back further than the Third George; and they are always very particular about dressing for dinner, except when there is a school treat or a penny reading or an early service which the rector is obliged to attend.

Mrs. Laude began to pour out the tea, carefully creaming and sugaring the cup she handed me. 'One lump or two, dear? It's this engagement of Tom's. How could one possibly enjoy London with one's boy's happiness at stake, and the lawyers bothering one all the time?'

'I hope there's nothing wrong,' I said. 'Settlements are always tiresome when it comes to the point.'

'It's Lord Pallavant who is tiresome,' replied Mrs. Laude. 'He seems to think he is to get everything and give nothing. We are to provide for his daughter, and to be content with nothing more than the honour of the connection! Mr. Laude's back is up, and he won't give in. Lord Pallavant won't give in either, and really things are at a deadlock. It's fearfully hard on Tom, who is wildly in love, and is all for taking the law into his own hands and marrying without any settlements.'

'There's no fear of Miss Pallavant agreeing to that,' said Mr. Laude, who had come in while his wife was speaking. 'How do you do, Mrs. Ellison. Very glad to see you again at Waye. Hope the last book was a success. Now, don't you go making us the text of a philosophical essay—British Philistinism in the county—that sort of thing, you know,' he added, parenthetically, as he dropped a lump of sugar into his tea. 'You may do that if you like with Miss Pallavant. I should say that there's material for a dozen novels and a hundred essays on our social system in her.'

'I'm longing to see her,' was my reply. 'I am told she is so handsome.'

'Oh yes, she is very handsome,' grudgingly assented Mr. Laude; 'and she has a way with her that takes you whether you like it or not. She makes you think about her. But between ourselves, Mrs. Ellison, I suspect that Miss Pallavant is playing her own game and not Tom's.'

'Oh, Thomas!' said Mrs. Laude with her uneasy little laugh, 'I don't think it's fair to say that; and she is staying in the house too.'

'Well, well!' said Mr. Laude. 'You know that you think the same, wife, and you are dying to open your heart to Ruth Ellison, who is like one of the family, and as safe as a house. Take my word for it, Miss Pallavant will get a telegram in a day or two saying that she had better be at home till the settlements are arranged, and she will go. I don't know that I shall break my heart if this difficulty about the money upsets the marriage. I shall be sorry for Tom, of course, and for the wife who thought it a fine thing for her boy to marry Lord Pallavant's daughter; but it always went against the grain with me to think of my son having to say "Thank you" for another man's leavings.'

I knew to what, Mr. Laude alluded. Three or four years ago Miss Pallavant had been engaged to the Earl of Lackford, and had been jilted by him. The affair had taken place at Rome, and had made a good deal of talk. Lord Lackford had been blamed, but there were people who insinuated unkind things about Miss Pallavant. In general she was the object of contemptuous pity. The charitable declared that mischief had been made by the gentleman's mother, who wished him to marry another lady. Anyhow, the engagement had been suddenly broken off, and with very little explanation. Lord Lackford went abruptly away from Rome, leaving a letter behind him. Miss Pallavant was stricken with brain fever, and before she got well again Lord Lackford had married the lady of his mother's choice. I had almost forgotten the story. It came suddenly to my mind now, and I said, thoughtlessly, 'Oh, I saw in the *Morning Post* a few days ago that Lady Lackford is lying dangerously ill in her house in Bruton Street.'

Mr. and Mrs. Laude exchanged glances. 'She is in a galloping consumption,' said Mrs. Laude, gravely. 'It has been known for some weeks that she could not live. But that could not make any difference to Miss Pallavant—after Lord Lackford's behaviour ——'

She stopped suddenly. There was a sound of voices outside. Sissy Laude ran in, carrying a tennis-racquet. 'We have come back,' she said. 'Henrietta was tired, and Tom insisted on our leaving before anyone else. Engaged people are so tiresome. Oh, Mrs. Ellison, how do you do!' and there was a buzz of greeting and a fresh brew of tea, in the midst of which Miss Pallavant and Captain Tom entered.

She was certainly a striking-looking woman—tall, dark, slow in movement, and extremely graceful. She had soft, deep, violet eyes, jet black hair, a clear, pale complexion, and a fascinating, mysterious smile. She had a look of high fashion, and the air of expecting admiration as her due, though her supreme indifference to it was also remarkable. I have never cared much for the 'professional beauty' type. Miss Pallavant distinctly belonged to it, but she was very much more than the conventional 'beauty.' She was full of suggestiveness. Her face and manner indicated drama.

We were introduced to each other. She looked at me with more interest than I could have supposed myself capable of arousing, gave me a sweet smile, and said one or two pretty things about my books, and her pleasure at making my acquaintance. Then she subsided into a chair, and gently patted Sissy's dachshund. Captain Tom, a fine, soldier-like fellow, with a curled moustache, and, just now, a fiercely melancholy expression, hovered about her, waiting upon her, bringing her tea and strawberries, and receiving hardly a glance, and only a languid word of thanks in return. Presently she looked up at him. 'Would you mind asking if there are any second-post letters for me?'

He obeyed. There were some. They had been given to Miss Pallavant's maid.

'Why weren't they put here?' he said, rather angrily.

'Henrietta always likes to have her letters taken to her room,' softly replied Mrs. Laude; and just then they were brought in.

Miss Pallavant read them through, all except one, which she laid on her lap. Tom was watching her with ill-concealed anxiety. I watched her too, and saw her give a little start as she tore open an outer envelope, and looked at an inner one, which she did not open. She vouchsafed no comment on the other letters.

'I think I'll go and take off my things,' she said, rising. 'It must be nearly dressing-time.'

Tom opened the door, and said something to her in a low tone.

'Oh, no, nothing,' she answered, and moved away.

It still wanted an hour to dinner, and Mrs. Laude suggested a stroll. To my surprise Tom came out with us, and attached himself to me. He evidently did not imagine that Miss Pallavant would return. We had once been great friends, Tom and I; indeed, about five years ago, in the earlier time of my widowhood, Tom was in love with me, as young men have a knack of being with women considerably older than themselves. It was a phase, and Tom got through it, and was none the worse, but perhaps rather the better, and we had always been good comrades since. This was the first time I had seen him since his engagement to Miss Pallavant, and I saw from his manner that he wanted to talk to me confidentially. Mrs. Laude was soon at work digging up plantains on the lawn. Tom and I walked along a beautiful old-fashioned border set against a red brick wall, in which columbines, peonies, lavender, flaring gigantic poppies, and all the dear old flowers flourished.

'Well, what do you think of her?' was his first question.

'I think she is very beautiful,' I answered; 'and I am sure she must be very charming, or you wouldn't care for her so much.'

Tom gave his moustache a wild twirl. 'You are only talking platitudes,' he said. 'Of course she is beautiful; of course I adore her. That wasn't what I meant. Do you think she cares for *me*? Do you think the marriage will come off?'

'Oh, Tom, how can I say? I have only been five minutes in her company. I am very sorry to hear that there has been any difficulty,' I added; 'but that can be of very little real importance if you and she understand each other. The elders will squabble, but you are both old enough to take your own line.'

I felt as I spoke that I was offering weak consolation, and Tom seemed to feel it also. He uttered an impatient sort of groan.

'We don't understand each other,' he cried; 'I don't understand her. Oh, what wouldn't I give to be able to read her own soul! You don't mind my opening out to you like this, Ruth? I feel as if I must talk it out with someone who is safe and sympathetic.'

'Tell me anything and everything you will, Tom,' I said. 'You know, at all events, that you may count upon my sympathy.'

'You can make "copy" of us afterwards, if you like,' he said, with a grim attempt at gaiety. 'I don't mind who knows about the whole thing. When it's at an end, one way or the other, I don't care what becomes of me if she throws me over.'

'Tom,' I said, earnestly, 'you would rather that she threw you over than that she married you without loving you, or loving someone else. If I were a man and loved a woman, I'd let her go rather than torture myself with doubts.'

'And I, loving her as I do, would hold her to me even against herself,' he exclaimed, passionately. 'I'm waiting for my sentence, Mrs. Ellison. I know it's coming. I feel as if the rope was round my neck now.'

'But, Tom, if what you fear were likely to be true, Miss Pallavant would tell you. She could not be here now, staying here as your future wife. I am sure, my poor boy, that you are making yourself miserable without just cause.'

'Am I?' he said. 'We shall see.'

He was silent for a few moments. 'I won't let her go,' he cried. 'She could not—and we are to be married in a month! It's not that she says anything, Mrs. Ellison,' he went on more quietly, 'or that she cares about the money any more than I do. What does it matter to me about the settlements—whether, if I die, she takes all the money from the estate, and leaves Lionel without a penny of income? Lionel is nothing to me, and she is everything. It drives me wild—this sordid calculation, and these legal provisos about death, and children, and all the rest. She doesn't care either, but she won't stand out against her father. Sometimes I think—and the thought makes me mad—that she is waiting, hoping that there may come a deadlock. It isn't that she has said anything,' he repeated. 'She is always the same—gentle, and indifferent, and cold. She is much more distant now than she was at the beginning. She says it is right, when things are still unsettled. She is very kind, but she won't let me come near her. Why, it is weeks since she has allowed me to kiss her. What am I saying? What must you think of me?' said the poor young man, with a bitter laugh.

We had paused opposite a bench, which was placed in the angle of the kitchen garden wall.

'Let us sit here for a minute, Tom,' I said, 'and talk quietly. If Miss Pallavant really wishes to draw back, there must be some motive for it. What is her motive? You say it isn't money.'

'No; she is not mercenary. She doesn't care. There's another man in the question, Mrs. Ellison; that is the truth. I daren't speak of it to her; I can't ask her; but I know it.—I feel it. I think of it every time she takes up the morning paper, and reads the list of births, marriages, and deaths. You know what I mean. It's horrible, isn't it?'

I could not help saying, 'Yes, it is horrible.'

'Ah!' he went on, 'you mustn't blame her. She told me about it when I asked her to marry me. She said she had never loved any other man, and that she never could. She said that there had been some terrible mistake, and that it could not be put right in this world without a wrong to an innocent person. To that she would never consent. Mrs. Ellison, she told me that she had only once in her life known what it was to be tempted of the devil, and that was when he tried to make her run away with him, after he was married.'

'Stop!' I said. 'You ought not to tell me such a thing as that.'

'It doesn't matter,' he answered. 'She said to me, when she heard you were coming here, that some things you had written made her long to open her whole heart to you. Mrs. Ellison, if she does talk to you, be nice to her, for my sake. Try and make her understand how much I love her.'

At that moment Sissy came running to us. 'I suppose you don't know that the dressing-gong went some time ago?' she said.

'Go away, Sissy,' exclaimed Tom, impatiently, 'There's plenty of time.'

'Oh, no, there isn't,' returned Sissy. 'The old man's back is up, and he mustn't be kept waiting, Two messengers came over from Waybridge a little while ago. One brought a packet from old Johnson—(our lawyer,' added Sissy, turning to me in an explanatory manner)—'and the other was a telegram for Miss Pallavant.'

Tom started up. Sissy gave a little laugh—the laugh of unthinking, unsympathetic youth, which must have irritated Tom to the last degree.

'That fetches you at once, Tom; but there's no use in hurrying. Miss Pallavant hadn't begun to dress when I went up to her room just now with the telegrams. There were two of them. She was reading letters still.'

The atmosphere of Waye House that evening was decidedly electrical. Everyone was late, though the dressing-gong had been struck rather after its regular hour. Mrs. Laude seemed nervous and anxious. Mr. Laude reminded me of a ruffled turkey-cock; the collar of his shirt appeared to chafe his neck, he moved his head about so uneasily. Tom looked most unhappy. Sissy, in her white frock, and with her little 'ways' and laughs, was the only person present who did not look as if something had happened.

'Another disagreeable communication from Lord Pallavant's lawyers,' whispered Mrs. Laude. 'I really don't see how things can go on. The demands are perfectly exorbitant and unreasonable. In justice to Lionel it would be quite impossible for us to meet them even half-way. Tom is obliged to admit that.'

Tom gnawed his moustache and watched the door eagerly. Miss Pallavant did not make her appearance till some time after we were all assembled, and dinner had been announced. She came in with a peculiar gliding movement, in which there was much resolution but no haste. She was very pale. Her lips were set, though she smiled with mechanical sweetness; and there was an odd smouldering gleam in her eyes. Seeing her in evening dress, her beauty and fascination struck me far more than they had done in the afternoon. There was something magnetic about her, and I could not wonder at Tom's infatuation. I pitied him from my heart, however, for instinct told me that his doom was sealed.

Miss Pallavant went straight up to Mrs. Laude. 'I am so very sorry to be late,' she said. 'I had to send off an answer to the telegram, and the fact is that I was obliged to think a little while.'

Mrs. Laude gave a nervous stiff laugh. 'I hope your people are quite well,' she said.

'Yes. It isn't that.' Miss Pallavant hesitated, and looked round in a half-defiant, half-imploring way, as if she were trying to gather in strength. 'My father telegraphs to me that I must go home to-morrow,' she said. 'I am extremely sorry,' she added, turning to Mr. Laude, 'but I am afraid that I must ask if you can send me to the station early in the morning.'

'The carriage is at your service, Miss Pallavant,' he replied.

'No, no,' cried Tom, coming forward; 'Etta, you don't mean it?'

She let her eyes rest upon his face in a mournful, reflective manner for a moment or two before answering. 'I have no choice,' she said simply. 'My father thinks that under the circumstances I had better be at home.'

'We have had a communication—indirectly—from Lord Pallavant. We expected something of this kind,' said Mrs. Laude stiffly.

Miss Pallavant made a gesture with her hands, as if she would sweep the whole matter from her. 'I don't know anything about business details. I don't want to know. I have always said that everything of that kind must be arranged without reference to me. I do what I am told; and when my father tells me that it is advisable I should be at my own home till—till things are arranged, I yield to his judgment without question. I am extremely sorry,' she repeated, as if conscious of self-contradiction. 'I did not send off my answer without having considered it.'

'I have no doubt that Lord Pallavant considered the matter also, and that he is right from his point of view,' said Mr. Laude, rather grimly. 'Tom, you can talk it over later. I think that now it is time we went in to dinner. The carriage is at your service, Miss Pallavant, for whatever train you wish. Come, Mrs. Ellison,' and he offered me his arm.

The meal was awkward and constrained. As if by common consent, allusion to Miss Pallavant's departure was dropped. Mrs. Laude talked in a perfunctory manner about my London life, about common friends, and about my literary undertakings. Miss Pallavant joined in sometimes with a show of interest. I fancied that her eyes sought mine every now and then, and that there was a sort of questioning appeal in their glance, as if she wanted me not to judge her harshly, and was wondering what I did think of her. She hardly spoke to Tom. He was trying to mask his misery by a spasmodic effort at gaiety. He started one or two heavy bucolic jokes with his father, laughing at them immoderately, and chaffed Sissy about her admirer, the Italian count. . . . Sissy, to a certain extent, acted the part of a buffer. It was a relief when we rose from the table. Tom remained to talk to his father, and we ladies went back to the drawing-room. The windows stood wide open. I seated myself in one of the window-seats, and presently Miss Pallavant joined me.

'I am sorry that I am going away to-morrow, Mrs. Ellison,' she said. 'I have wanted to meet you for such a long time. I like your books. I am not going to gush about your knowledge of human nature, because you must get rather tired of that sort of talk; but they are "real" books, I think, and I have always had an idea that you must be a real woman—above petty prejudices.'

I thanked her for her good opinion, and said that I hoped she was not going to qualify it by saying what so many young ladies said to me—'I like your books, Mrs. Ellison, but why do you always write about dull philosophy and religion? Why don't you write novels?'

Miss Pallavant shrugged her shoulders contemptuously. 'I am

not a young lady,' she said; 'I'm past thirty, and I like philosophical books far better than novels. The people who are most interested in novels are those who have nothing interesting in their own lives.'

'I understand,' I said. 'Your life is so interesting that you don't need novels to amuse and excite you. I can well believe that.'

She looked me straight in the face. 'It is quite true,' she said. She seemed to be thinking. 'I've had a great deal of excitement in my life, and a good many experiences; and I've come to one conclusion, among several.'

'I should very much like to know what that is,' I said, really interested.

'Well, I'll tell you. Everyone wants to know what sort of investment pays the highest interest, in the shape of happiness, don't they?'

'Ah! Your opinion ought to be a valuable one—on that subject, Miss Pallavant.'

'I am not sure. I can't speak from personal knowledge except in the negative way. Some people think riches pay best; others, rank; others, fame. I suppose you'd say the last?'

'No, indeed, though I'm afraid my personal knowledge doesn't count for much either. I believe that the most celebrated men and women in the world, if you asked them their honest conviction, would say that fame is—husks.'

'Almost everything is—husks. I'm certain the only thing that pays steady interest is—friendship.'

'Friendship!' I repeated.

'You thought I was going to say love. Does love pay? No; no; no! Do you know what love really is, Mrs. Ellison? It's an infinite capacity for being miserable. It's more than that; it's an infinite capacity for anomalies—for being dishonourable and quixotic at the same time; milk-soft and cruel; passionately revengeful and passionately forgiving—' She stopped abruptly. The door opened. Mr. Laude, more like a diminutive turkey-cock than ever, came in, followed by Tom. He went up to his wife and daughter, and Tom made for the window. Miss Pallavant smiled a curious smile as she made a little motion of her hand, waving him off for a moment as it were. 'Our subject isn't a very appropriate one for discussion just now,' she said to me. 'I wish I were going to see more of you, Mrs. Ellison. It is too bad that we cross each other "like ships on the sea," in this way. I don't think I'm given to gushing; but I do want to talk to you. Will you let me come and see you in your room this evening?'

'With the greatest pleasure in the world,' I rejoined.

Miss Pallavant smiled now at her lover, thus giving him permission to approach.

'Etta,' he said, 'I want you to come out into the garden. I have brought you a wrap.'

She took the wrap from him, a light woollen cloud, and held it thoughtfully for a moment or two. Then she said, 'Yes, I will come,' and they went into the garden together.

We indoors had rather a dull evening. Mr. Laude went to his study, and Mrs. Laude, begging me to excuse her, and murmuring something about an important letter which had to be written and sent to Mr. Johnson, the lawyer, in the morning, followed him. It was evident that they had some private business. I guessed that it was connected with Tom's marriage, about which they wished to take counsel together. Sissy brought out her bundle of photographs, and we talked guide-book for a little while. At ten o'clock Mr. and Mrs. Laude came back, and the servants were called in for prayers. The lovers, if they may be called so, had not returned. When the candles were lighted and I had bidden Mr. Laude good-night, Tom entered by the hall door alone. He looked haggard, and a little wild, I thought, but he spoke composedly enough.

'Good-night, Mrs. Ellison; good-night, mother. We shall have rain to-morrow. You had better get your hay up, father—all that in the meadow down there. It's packed too close to the water. I've just been down by the river, and if the floods are out ever so little you'll lose a lot of it for ever.'

'You've been down by the river!' said his mother. 'Was Etta with you?'

'No; Etta went in some time ago. She asked me to say good-night to you. She was tired, and she had packing to do.'

Mrs. Laude put her hand out with a quick gesture of sympathy. 'Etta is going away to-morrow, then, Tom?'

'Yes, mother, by the eight train. That was another message I was to give. I'll see Roote about the carriage. You needn't mind.'

'Things are not wrong, are they, Tom?' I heard Mrs. Laude say anxiously, though I moved on up the stairs so that they might not be embarrassed by my presence.

'About as wrong as they can be, mother—for me,' Tom answered out loud.

I did not wait longer, but went on to my room. Sissy followed me and saw that I was comfortable for the night, but I did not see Mrs. Laude again. I wondered whether Miss Pallavant would come as she had suggested. I almost hoped she would not. I had put on my dressing-gown, and was reading, as my habit is, before getting into bed, when there came a knock at the door, and she softly entered. She wore a long white robe, with a great deal of lace about it, and wide sleeves. The sleeve fell back from one round white arm as she held the candle up before her face. She looked picturesque and tragic. Her dark hair was unbound, and hung in a thick plait behind. I got up and pushed forward an arm-chair. She sat down, but for a minute or two she did not speak. Suddenly she threw back her head, and, fixing her great serious eyes upon me, said—

'You are very fond of Tom?'

'Yes,' I answered. 'I have known him for a long time. We are great friends.'

'I know that. He wanted to marry you once and you refused. I wish you had not done so. In that case he would not have been so mad as to think of me for a wife. I am not going to marry him, Mrs. Ellison, and I have told him so to-night.'

'I guessed as much,' I answered drily. I was very angry with her.

'I suppose so. He told me that he had been talking to you about me. He told me what he had said. They were things he had no right to say. Still I do not mind. I am going to tell you the truth. I shall not care who knows it, or if the whole world knows it . . . after six months. You can try your hand on a novel then, Mrs. Ellison, and take me for a heroine.'

I was disgusted with her flippancy. 'Doesn't it strike you, Miss Pallavant,' I exclaimed, 'thatt you have been playing a heartless and unwomanly part?'

'I don't know what you mean by "unwomanly,"' she returned, in a placid manner. 'It is a word that is used in so many different senses; and I am not heartless. I wish to God that I were,' she added, passionately.

'You have acted cruelly to poor Tom,' I said.

'Ah! Tom!' She seemed to be thinking again, and roused herself as if with an effort. 'I am not so cruel as you may think. He went into it with his eyes open. He said he preferred running the risk to losing me altogether. I told him when he asked me to marry him that there was only one man in the world whom I loved or could ever love.'

I was silent. There was nothing I could say. I waited for her to tell her own story. She went on after a minute.

'I told Tom this. He knew his risk. I told him that I didn't love him, that I should probably make him a bad wife, that I was only marrying him because I was tired of my life, and of being pointed at as that Miss Pallavant whom Lord Lackford had jilted. Well, he didn't care. He wanted me in spite of all that. I didn't even give him a definite promise. It was conditional. I said that I would marry him, unless one thing happened before our wedding-day. I was reckless. I threw a challenge to Fate. That one thing has happened. You shall know what it is.'

She had been holding one hand closed. She opened it now. Within it was a crumpled piece of pink paper. She unfolded the paper.

'It is true that I got a telegram from my father, bidding me go home,' she said, quietly; 'but that was not the only telegram I received, nor was it that which made me determine upon leaving this place early to-morrow. I got another telegram as well; I expected it. A letter came to me by second post, which told me that I might expect it. You may read.'

She smoothed out the paper, and handed it to me. The telegram was sent from a London office. It had no signature, and consisted only of these words:—

'Lady Lackford died at three o'clock to-day.'

I could not repress a cry of horror. She was looking at me intently, leaning forward, her chin upon her hands.

'What if this had come a month after your marriage instead of a month before?' I asked, with grim emphasis.

'I don't know. I ran that risk. It might have been worse for Tom,' she said, in a low voice.

We were both silent. It was a curious position. I folded the telegraph paper, and laid it on the table by her side.

'You are horrified,' she said. 'You think that I am a very wicked woman.'

'I am horrified that you can plan the future; calculate on this; act deliberately, while the woman for whom you were forsaken lies still unburied. In common decency—'

'Oh, I know all that you would say,' she interrupted. 'You would have me go about with a lie on my lips, deceiving these good people, torturing poor Tom, for the sake of "common decency." I thought you were greater than that. You are nothing but the British Philistine after all, and I made a mistake in coming to you to-night.'

'Indeed, no,' I exclaimed.

'I felt that I must speak to someone,' she went on, passionately. 'I felt that I couldn't bear it alone any longer. I have never had a woman friend in my life; perhaps that is the reason why I said friendship was the best moral investment one could make. I know what I would give for a friend now, from whom I might hope for a little sympathy.'

'My dear,' I said, deeply moved—the girl's self-abandonment touched me to the heart—'I wish that I could help you. I would sympathise with you, if I could—if I knew. I see that you are very unhappy. I am certain that you feel more for Tom, of whom I cannot help thinking, than you will let me believe. I could not wish you to be true to an engagement which you have found out to be a mistake. It is all the circumstances'—I hesitated. 'It is what you have just shown me that is repellent to me. I am doing you injustice, perhaps. This terrible news has awakened you to the real state of your feelings? It has convinced you that you cannot marry a man whom you do not love?'

'It has convinced me that I must marry the man whom I do love, and, who is free,' she answered, solemnly. 'I will marry Lord Lackford as soon as he pleases—as soon as decency permits.' She laughed in hysterical fashion. 'Oh, I hardly know what I am saying,' she cried. 'I am not myself.'

Her bosom heaved. She flung her hands suddenly across her face, and burst into sobs. Her whole frame was shaken with the violence of her emotion. I slipped down on the floor beside her, and tried to soothe her as best I could. Presently she grew calmer.

'I have loved him for so long,' she said, between her sobs. 'I have suffered so much. Oh, you don't know what the strain of the past few months has been. I felt that only a miracle could save me—and the miracle has happened. You would pity me if you knew.'

'I do pity you, from my heart,' I whispered.

'You wouldn't think so badly of me,' she said, brokenly, 'if you knew. I don't know whether I am glad or sorry that she is dead. Death isn't such a frightful thing. I have often wished that I might die; and she died in happy ignorance. I made him promise that she should never be told, and he was a man to keep a promise, except that one promise which he broke.' She said this with infinite pathos. 'He didn't trust me enough to keep his promise and be true to me, when that would have saved us both; but I forgave him that.'

'You forgave him!' I repeated, in bewilderment; 'and you could trust him after that?'

'A woman always forgives the man she loves—when he loves her. He always loved me. Appearances were against me. His mother made him believe things. I will try and tell you how it was. You know we were engaged in Rome. It's five years ago. I wasn't very young then—I was six-and-twenty—and I had led a fast sort of life, allowed to do what I pleased, and to flirt as I pleased. We had no mother, and you can imagine how things were in garrison towns. I was made so much of, and all the men were in love with me, and my father angry because I threw away the good opportunities, and *would* compromise myself with men I couldn't marry. I did it out of bravado, and because I hated the idea of marrying for a livelihood. We have no money, and it has always been dunned into us that we must marry. I wasn't a marrying girl. I liked my liberty too much, and I liked flirting. I did the maddest things. I thought I could hold my own, and that a look from me would keep a man at a distance. I didn't care for one of them, but I enjoyed the excitement. You can understand?'

'Yes,' I said, pressing her hand. The clasp seemed to embolden her to confidence. 'There was a man on the staff—it was at Malta. He used to boast, I believe, that he could make me do anything. He had a sort of fascination for me. It is quite true that he made me do things I shudder now to think of—not actually wrong things, but dangerous. It was like walking along a precipice. He was a married man too. His wife was in England. One night I met him. I don't know why, unless it was in a fit of madness. He persuaded me to go with him to what he told me was a place of entertainment. . . . You can imagine the rest. I was fatally compromised. My reputation was at his mercy. This was the story which old Lady Lackford made use of against me. She showed her son proofs of what he believed to be my guilt. He gave me no chance of clearing myself. He went away, and the next thing I heard of him was that he had married as his mother had wished.' She stopped.

'But you met again? He learned the truth?'

'Yes; we met in Paris a year ago. He believed me. He told me that he had always loved me. He wanted to leave his wife and take me away. It was not the fear of the world that kept me back. I would have gone joyfully. I would have given him everything, and thought it no shame—yes, it is true. Think me a wicked woman if you choose! But I wasn't wicked enough to stab another woman who had done me no wilful wrong, and who was more innocent than I—who loved him too. I couldn't do that. But, oh, the struggle!—and the awful blank when it was all over! That was why I engaged myself to Tom. I wanted to place a real barrier between him and me—between my love and me. We never met again after that struggle, nor have I had a line from him of any kind till to-day. He told me when we parted that if he was ever free I should know it from himself, and that that should be a sign to me that he was mine for ever. The sign has been given. Thank God! it has not come too late.'

She rose as she spoke. Her agitation was so great that she was obliged to lean heavily against the mantel-piece to keep herself from tottering. She trembled in every limb. Presently she mastered herself, and came to me, holding out her hand. 'Mrs. Ellison, will you try and make it easier for Tom? He knows the truth. I told him last night. I'm going by an early train. I have asked that the carriage might take me to the station before breakfast. I can't see Tom again, or any of them. They have every reason to think badly of me, and to hate me. I have written to Mrs. Laude. Mrs. Ellison, I'm going to leave you a legacy. I daresay we shall never meet again. I leave you the right to console Tom. Good-bye.'

She laughed a dreary laugh, and taking up her candle, went out without another word.

In the early morning I heard the carriage drive off, and when I went down to breakfast Miss Pallavant had gone.

MR AND MRS SIN FAT

Edward Dyson

MR SIN FAT ARRIVED in Australia in the year of grace 1870, a poor and friendless man. He entered the great city of Melbourne, a stranger in a strange country, possessed only of a blue dungaree suit that had served him long and faithfully in his distant home, ninepence in coppers and as much of his fatherland spread over his surface and deposited in the cracks and crannies of his gaunt person as he could conveniently carry.

Sin Fat was not tall and athletic, nor fair to look upon—in truth, he was stunted, and as plain of face as the pottery gods that he had learned to revere at his good mother's knee. His complexion was so distraught by an uncongenial climate that it possessed less bloom and beauty than the inside of a sundried lambskin; his features were turned and twisted and pulled awry till they resembled excrescences and indentations on a pie-melon, and his lank, lean limbs were mute evidence of a life of privation and toil. In point of fact, Sin Fat was so ungainly and so sparing of personal attractions at this period of his existence that his homely visage soon became the theme of popular comment, and 'ugly as Sin' is an aphorism which will survive as long as the English language is spoken.

The humble immigrant paid no poll-tax; he was a duly certified subject of Her Gracious Majesty Queen Victoria, towards whose throne and person he possessed an ardent and undying affection, as he told the Customs officer in mutilated English and accents tremulous and low. For Sin was by nature bashful and conciliatory, his tones were unctuous, and his humble carriage excited the derision of a distempered and woe-worn dog which had its habitat amongst the lumber on the wharf—a vagrant, craven mongrel, that lived in a perpetual state of cringe, yet which assumed something of dignity in the presence of a still meaner creature, and boldly pursued Sin Fat as he ambled away, and assailed him in the rearmost parts of his frame. But the lowly foreigner continued on his road with downcast eyes and an expression of religious meekness, till, as if guided by instinct or the power of affinity, he slunk into the nest of pestilence between Little Bourke and Lonsdale streets, and was lost amongst the hordes which there do congregate.

Fifteen years ago the Chinese Camp at Ballarat East was a large and populous suburb. Thousands of prosperous, but unkempt and wasted, disciples of Confucius lodged in a nest of tottering, vermin-ravaged, smoke-begrimed hovels, of which no independent hog would accept a protracted tenure. The area extending from the main road to back beyond the old Llanberris was almost covered with the broken-backed tenements of squalid, immoral heathens, who followed various light and remunerative callings—peddling tea, gimcrack fancy goods, and moonstruck fish; fossicking on the Yarrowee and Black Hill Flats; or prowling round with a pair of shabby baskets strung on a stick, collecting rags, bones, and bottles, or any movable items of intrinsic value which could be reached through the fence when the proprietor's attention was otherwise engaged, and each and all supplementing their income by deeply-planned nocturnal raids on distant poultry yards, fruit farms, wood-heaps, or sluice-boxes. A couple of serpentine streets, inhabited by grimy pagans, still remain, but the majority of the Chows have migrated to other diggings, some have returned to the homes of their childhood, and some have gone to heaven. The staggering shanties which still remain are a good sample of the sties that littered the flat in '73—decrepit dens, reaching away in all directions for something to lean against, indented on one side, bulged on the other—compiled of logs, stones, palings, flattened tins and battered pans, and roofed with sugar-mats. The common Chinaman glories in these little snuggeries. When by some chance he becomes possessed of a home with a respectable exterior he straightway hews a hole in the roof, boards up the windows with borrowed planks, and disfigures the front with scraps of tin and old battens—whether in accordance with a perverted taste or out of a guileful desire to mislead the tax-assessor is beyond Caucasian comprehension.

It was evening, after a day hot enough to blister the ear of an elephant. Sin Fat's work was done, and he jogged homewards along a little side-street in Ballarat East. He bore the orthodox Chinese baskets, a pair which had evidently been in active business for some considerable time, and, judging from the hooked stick in his hand and the grateful aroma of old bones and such things which clung to him like a brother, Sin was following the calling of a 'Rag John.' S. Fat, as we now see him with the eye of faith, is physically much improved since he landed in Australia; he does not appear to have missed meals so regularly of late, and his predatory success has lent him an air of confidence and self-esteem, though he smiles with his old deference and still clings with superstitious awe to the dirt of his fatherland, now cemented by grit of Australian origin.

Our hero has disposed of his day's collection of rags and rottenness, gleaned from the gutters and rubbish-heaps of the city, at a local marine-store, and he now hies him to his humble home and merited repose. But he is not lost to a sense of duty; his ever-watchful eye is open to detect an opportunity, however trifling, of increasing his diurnal income, and when he espies a goose, obese and matronly, making frantic endeavours to squeeze her portly form through a small aperture in a fowl-house behind a private residence, his soul is instantly fired with a desire to possess her—to call her his own, if only for a few hours.

Sin is a man of action; dropping his baskets, and casting aside all reserve, he enters the yard, and in a moment the well-conditioned bird is in his power. Tucking her under his arm, and stifling her noisy clamours, he turns to vacate the premises; but, alas for his circumspection, the door of the residence opens, and a fat woman, with a baby dangling over one arm, comes out to swear at a neighbour's boy who is throwing stones at a cat on her roof. She has not noticed the enterprising Mongol, but 'he who hesitates is lost,' and Sin's native wit serves him well. Advancing boldly to the stout female, smiling obsequiously the while, and covering the brands and birth-marks of the goose with his jerkin, he blandly queries:

'Buy em goose, missee? Welly good, welly fat.'

'Naw!' snaps the woman, eyeing him suspiciously.

'Muchee fine goose, welly fat!' persists Sin, coyly smiling.

'Don't want it; go away!'

'All li; some odder day, eh?' So Sin retreats, still smiling, and as he trots on his way congratulates himself, gibbering aloud in his rapture.

Sin had a bijou villa, built in his spare time from plans and specifications of his own making, and composed of old palings gleaned from neighbouring fences on moonless nights, and multitudinous other scraps and patches which were within the reach of a poor Chinee. The residence was a very comfortable one for summer wear; it had openings to catch the breeze from every point of the compass, and if the rain did come in at the roof—well, it ran out at the sides again. Standing at the front door one commanded an excellent view of a creek, embedded in whose thick yellow clay lay the decomposing remains of many domestic fauna. The house was within two minutes' walk of a fantan-table and a Joss-house; it abutted on a stagnant pool, and received the balmy westerly breeze as it bounced off a candle-factory. Our hero was content with these few advantages for the time being, but by steady industry and frugality he hoped one day to run a gambling-hell of his own, and move in the best Celestial society in imported wooden boots. Sin was ambitious.

Sin Fat parted with his feathered prize to an epicurean fellow-countryman at a high figure before he reached his humble home. He knew that, had he not done so, Mrs Sin Fat would have seized the earliest opportunity of converting the bird into square gin. Mrs Fat was possessed of a deplorable habit of thus transmuting all kinds of personal property into liquor, in consequence of which it was part of her industrious husband's policy to carefully place all articles readily saleable beyond her reach.

It was dark before Mr Fat reached his own roof-tree. He groped his way into the parlour, which was also kitchen, bedroom, drawing-room, and outhouse, and lit a candle (candles were another of Mrs Fat's extravagances). The glare awoke a woman who was sleeping, sprawling amongst a few filthy rags on a low bunk at one end of the hut. She lifted herself on her hands, and gazed at the Chinaman with stupid, drunken eyes. A great shock of unkempt black hair fell about her sallow face, which, despite the ravages of drink, and that faint, strange Mongolian look which surely comes to the woman who consorts with Chinamen, still possessed something of beauty. Under earlier and more favourable circumstances her eyes had been full, dark, and luminous. Her features were well cut, the nose somewhat aquiline, the mouth large and sensual. A virago surely, with the temper of fifty devils—a woman abandoned to the filth and utter loathsomeness of a Chinese camp. About thirty-four years of age, tall, round with the unnatural obesity of a heavy drinker, intensely hating all about her—aye, and hating herself worse than all as she wallowed in the very dregs and slime of the social system—such was Mrs Sin Fat.

'Home again, sweetheart!' she muttered; 'home again to your true love, my tall, beautiful—— Bah, you ugly thief! Get out or I'll brain you!' And a list of profane ejaculations was smothered as she fell with her face amongst the rags once more, clutching vacantly for the empty bottle wherewith to assault her submissive husband.

This was Sin's only weakness—this she-fiend, from whose bursts of passion he had often to fly for his life. He had found her one cold, wet night, stretched in the mud at the door of his hovel, and had taken her in. She was haggard, ragged, and so fearfully emaciated that the men turned from her with wry expressions, and this seemed her last chance. She and Sin Fat 'got married.' She was possessed of one husband already, a portly Melbourne mechanic, but she had left him and her child years before—left him because he was a 'fat old fool,' an opinion based on the fact that he did not kick her down and jump on her with his working-boots when she flew into a tantrum. Other men had done this since, and she respected them. Sin fed her up, dressed her well, and then she left him, only to return again, worn with debauchery, to be dressed and fed, and to 'clear' once more. She repeated this course several times, and her dutiful lord always received her with open arms; but at length an idea occurred to Sin: he refused to provide fine clothes, and then she stayed with him, and made merry by occasionally cracking his head with a gin-bottle—an empty bottle, of course, for she would rather that her dear lord should escape correction altogether than waste a 'nobbler' of her favourite nectar. Sin bore his cross patiently, but it was not affection entirely that restrained him from dropping something unhealthy into her gin. We have said that he was ambitious; he had many plans, and this woman could dress well and ape the lady. He foresaw the time when she would be useful to him.

Sin had no intention of remaining a toiler and moiler all his life. He had done well in the rag-and-bone business, but it was laborious, and our hero had gentlemanly instincts—he wanted to acquire riches and fatty tissue without expending any more of the sweat of his brow than was absolutely necessary, and he but waited to increase his available capital before embarking in business. By a dispensation of Providence, the fulfilment of his laudable ambition was brought about earlier than he expected.

Midnight. The white moon floated low in the eastern sky, and thrust her sheeny beams like sword-blades through the caray walls of Sin Fat's home. A tall, willowy cat, with swan-like neck and attenuated frame, bestrode the ridge-pole, and stood black against the pallid orb of night, and lifting up her voice recited her woes to the listening spheres in accents wild and weird. All else was still. The camp lay like a cluster of islands in a lake of light. Sin's sleep was calm and child-like, and his wife had ceased to toss and breathe half-uttered curses in his deaf ear. The moon rose higher and higher, and the long black shadows slowly folded towards their base. Suddenly and stealthily the ground opened like a yawning giant; Sin Fat's villa trembled, tottered, and sank quietly into the black abyss, and where it had stood gaped a deep, dark pit—and a dusty cat, with a broken tail and a coat of many colours, tearing madly across the battery sands, seemed to be the only creature that quite realized the extent of the catastrophe. The Chinese camp at Ballarat is situated chiefly over 'old ground.' The country has been worked so thoroughly that sections of the earth's crust often settle down abruptly into the caverns below, accompanied by sundry Mongolian residences, to the exceeding discomfort of their greasy inhabitants.

At break of day the squalid denizens of the camp gathered about the chasm, at the bottom of which lay Mr and Mrs Sin Fat buried in the ruins. The Chows appointed a chairman, and discussed the situation with characteristic clamour and gesticulation, finally resolving by a large majority to call in white men to undertake the rescue. When there is work to be done which entails the probability of a broken head or the unearthing of a corpse, the heathen Chinese is sure to have a sore hand or an important engagement at some distance. White men came, and Mr and Mrs Sin Fat were fossicked out of the debris, full of dust, old nails, and wooden splinters, but not much the worse for their premature interment. Mrs Fat thanked her rescuers, as she was hauled up through the roof of the hut, with a few well-chosen objurgations, terminating with a heart-felt wish that they might be instantly consigned to a region where frost and snow are unknown.

Sin stood on the brink of the aperture for some time after the thoughtless herd had dispersed, dolefully surveying the fragments of his late home. His mind was made up at last—he would not build again, he would go into business.

The year 1876 A.D. Little Bourke Street, Melbourne, Sunday morning. On both sides of the narrow thoroughfare were groups of sleek-looking Chinese, arrayed in imported clothes, their hands buried in their long sleeves, debating politics and theology, or more likely cavilling at the absurdly low price of 'cabbagee' and 'gleen pea,' the conversation occasionally eliciting a shrewd ejaculation from a dun-coloured philosopher a hundred yards off, or from a hoary, half-dressed pagan at a third-storey window. They were a fat, comfortable-looking lot, and they aired their Sunday best on a fine Sabbath 'allee same Eulopean.' In front of a smoky little shop, possessed of only one window, in which a roast fowl, beauti-fully browned and highly polished, hung suspended by a string, and served as a roost for half the flies in the lane, was congregated a particularly verbose and noisy crowd, attracted evidently by the brilliant conversational powers of one of their number—a short but enormously fat 'John,' who leaned in the doorway. His stoutness was phenomenal; it would not have discredited the treatment of those wily men who prepare prize hogs for agricultural shows. Layers of blubber bulged about his eyes, leaving only two conical slits for him to peer through; his cheeks sagged below his great double chin, and his mighty neck rolled almost on to his shoulders, and vibrated like jelly with every movement. But his corporation was his greatest pride—it was the envy and admiration of all his friends; it jutted out, bold and precipitous, and seemed to defy the world. This Celestial phenomenon was dressed in the very latest Chinese style; gorgeous silks of many colours bedizened his capacious person; his feet were encased in the richest stub-toed wooden shoes; his hat was a brilliant building direct from the Flowery Land, and his proud tail swept the floor. A dandy dude was he—a heavy swell from home—oily and clean, looking as if he had been well scraped and polished with a greasy rag. He was jolly; his smiles went from his ears to his toes like ripples on a lake, and succeeded each other like winking—in fact, he was brimful of a wild sort of Chinese humour. We have read that the Chinese delight in punning; this man must have been the king of Mongolian punsters, judging from the merriment his every remark was wont to evoke. He was brimming with irony, sarcasm, and sparkling repartee. A white man could never grasp his witticisms; after translation they sounded much like childish nonsense, but anyone who listened to him would feel confident that he was a comical dog all the same.

In compliance with a suggestion from the portly host, the Chows streamed after him through the dark, dirty 'shop' into a long, low room on the left, where were a number of tables covered with matting. Seating himself at the head of one of these, and producing the 'tools,' the fat man prepared to preside over the game, his small eyes twinkling keenly enough now from out of the depths of his head; and soon all were enthralled in the mysteries of fantan. The Chinaman, stoical under all other circumstances, gambles like a fiend; these men were soon worked into a delirium of excitement, but the fat Mongolian was always cool, and whilst the sums of money before the players fluctuated, his increased steadily, surely.

A sign over the door of the little smoky shop translated into English implied that Sin Fat, Chinese cook, lived and plied his trade within, and was prepared to fulfil all orders with promptitude. That sign was a bold and brazen lie. Sin Fat was no cook, and the burnished fowl which hung in the window was only a 'blind'—a window-blind, so to speak—intended to beguile 'him foolee white feller.' Sin Fat ran a gambling-hell and something worse. Sin had attained his ambition; while making flesh he was also making money rapidly. Our hero, the poor broken Chow who had landed in the city not many years before without a shilling or a change of raiment, had, by patient industry and steadfastness of purpose, acquired an extensive business and a quantity of capital at interest. The colonial climate agreed with him, and he had many friends. When Constable Mahoney, Sergeant Mulduckie, or Private O'Brien met him they greeted him like a brother; they winked knowingly, dug him jocularly in the ribs, and insinuated that he was a sly dog. These zealous guardians of public property and morality had mastered the art which was necessary to every 'mimber av the foorce' who would have his bank-book and little terrace in the suburbs—the art of not seeing too much.

Beyond the little shop adorned with the pendant fowl, stretched to the right and left till the back premises of the houses in the block seemed to be absorbed, were numerous small rooms—cabins reeking with the nauseating odour of opium and pollution and Chinamen, and always clouded with smoke. There was no order, no design, in the building of these cribs; big rooms had been portioned off and holes cut in partitions recklessly. You groped through the place, and might find your way, to your great surprise, into two or three filthy lanes at the back, right or left. The curious European, on a voyage of discovery, saw in these rooms, through the clouds of choking, evil-smelling opium fumes, debilitated Chinamen, with animalized faces, floating to hell in the midst of visions of heaven; lank, skinny coolies, Indians, and other vile Asiatics; and, worst of all, European girls, corrupt below anything else in nature, excepting only the ghouls they consorted with. Girls of sixteen, decoyed in at the front door by the sheen of silk and the jingle of gold, percolating through that terrible den, to be finally cast out amongst the slime and rottenness of the lanes—abject wrecks, with nothing of humanity left within them, and hardly the semblance without.

Mrs Sin Fat was well and hearty; she had fine clothes galore, and no longer thought of deserting her dear lord—perhaps because she saw that he was not now so very anxious to prevent it. A great assistance in the business was the tall, dark woman, who could 'put on style;' she clung to her old love—the gin-bottle—and frequently worked up a small cyclone, an hysterical fit peculiarly her own, which militated against the prosperity of the house by suspending business for the time being. In these moments she called herself many vile and unladylike names, bit her arms, tore her hair, spat upon her lord, and spurned him with something heavy and hard, even going to the extent of hurling bottles and other dangerous projectiles at the shaven heads of the best customers. This was unpleasant, but Sin condescended to overlook it when she sallied forth in fine raiment, with a thick veil concealing half her face, to wander in the public parks and gardens, and enter into conversation with young girls who were airing babies, or reading romances in the shade. She talked with them so sweetly (one at a time always) about babies, birds, or flowers; but she was at her best when describing with poetic fervour gorgeous dresses, all bespangled and glittering, or dwelling upon hats that were dreams of loveliness. She was always making appointments with these girls, and gradually, deftly leading them by a golden thread, she drew them into the shop of Sin Fat the cook, and the sign over the door might well have read:—'Abandon all hope ye who enter here.' Mrs Fat was not always successful; but one success condoned for fifty failures. Sin Fat's trade was so extensive that he was enabled to give other women commissions in this line; none of them, however, succeeded so well as his wife.

Two years rolled by, and Sin Fat's business increased and multiplied in every branch. A polished fowl still hung in the little window, and the green and golden sign published the same old lie. Sin was even jollier and more rotund; he was looked up to as a Chow among Chows. His capital at interest had grown apace, and he fondly dreamed of selling out and returning home to the Flowery Land, there to buy a Celestial C.M.G.-ship, and lord it as a representative Australian. His wife by this time was source of grave uneasiness to him; her temper had intensified, she had grown hypochondriacal, and refused for months to tout for the business. Her bursts of passion were terrible to contemplate, and Sin Fat, Esq,. had now attained a station so exalted that to be seen evading the wrath of a tall female armed with a poker or a bottle compromised his dignity. He felt that it was time to assert his authority.

One day Sin, as head of the firm, was overjoyed at the advent of a new victim. The decoy in this case was a loudly dressed young woman who shortly before had developed marvellous ability in that line. The new girl was aged about seventeen, tall, dark, and thin, but handsome—the spoilt daughter of a weak parent. She had been caught with the golden cord, and the hook had been baited with her own vanity. A few hours after her advent he was seated with her in the one room of the place which had any pretensions to cleanliness and attractions. It was draped and hung about with all kinds of ridiculous, highly-coloured Chinese gew-gaws, and fairly furnished. This was the bower into which all novices were first introduced; when they left it they had received their initial lesson in the hard course of misery just entered upon. Sin was introducing this girl to her first pipe of opium—that devil's drug and Chinaman's greatest ally. The obese Confucian prattled to her in tender tones, like the jolly old gallant he was, and the girl, half-stretched upon a sort of settee, laughed and joked with the boldness of an old hand.

Suddenly the door opened and Mrs Sin Fat entered. She had come to inspect the strange girl for the first time. She looked wild and uncanny enough as she stepped over the threshold, but when her eyes encountered the face of the new-comer her countenance became horrifying.

'Great ——!' she whispered, supporting her shivering limbs against the door. The exclamation was not blasphemous—for a wonder—it was half a prayer, half the expression of strong inward agony. Then a fierce determination seemed to strengthen every muscle and sinew in her tall frame; she strode into the room, dashed the pipe from the girl's hands, and, seizing her by the arms with a force that made the bones crack, she said hoarsely:

'Who are you, my fine miss? Your name? What's your name? You need not scream, Jessie Hill. You see I know you. I have watched you from a distance for years. So your tender-hearted father has let you drift this way, as he did me. He is too kind for devils like us. You go out of this—back to your father! Do you hear me? You go now, and if you ever come here again I'll stab you to death! Remember, I swear I will watch for you, and if you come here again I will kill you on the spot! They told you you would have rich dresses, handsome admirers, pockets full of gold, didn't they? They have lied, as they lied to the miserable wretches who have gone before you. There is no finery here—nothing but filth and misery and degradation. Come here again, and I will throw your dead body into the gutter. Now, go!'

But the girl had fainted, and no wonder, for the woman gripped her like a vice, and her face was as frightful as a nightmare. Mrs Sin Fat ran out for water; when she returned her husband had locked the outer door and placed the key in his pocket. She rushed at him in a fury, but checked herself with her hands in the air.

'That girl has got to go!' she hissed.

'No savee,' muttered Sin, putting on a bolder front than ever he had dared to do before.

'I tell you she shall go; she is my daughter, my child!'

'No savee. Stay here all a same.' And he crossed into another room. Sin had paid his agent a big commission on this girl, and was determined not to lose her. Besides, he had taken a fancy to her himself; he would rather have lost the mother than the daughter. Mrs Sin Fat did not storm and rage, but turned away with a calmness that was unnatural, and presently followed Sin into the room, and came close to him, concealing one hand in the folds of her dress.

'That girl,' she said, calmly; 'is she to go?'

'No, no! Go yourself—'

These memorable words were the last ever spoken by the great, the prosperous Sin Fat. A knife flashed before his eyes, and was driven to the hilt in his side. He fell forward with only a groan, and the fall forced the heavy handle of the weapon still deeper between his ribs. Mrs Sin Fat, coolly removing the keys from his pocket, went out, followed by a little stream of bright blood, which ran along the floor under the closed door, as if to keep watch upon her, and entered the room where she had left the new girl— her own daughter, as the fates would have it. The new girl was sitting gazing about her, frightened and confused.

'Here, come with me,' said the woman, seizing her roughly by the arm; 'come with me, and see the delightful life you will have of it in this house!' She led the girl through the vile den, showed her all its abominations, and at last pushed her into one of the filthy alleys. 'Here,' she said, 'you would be thrown out in a few months time, a degraded wretch. A fine, gay life, eh? Now go, and be a good woman if you can. So help me Heaven, if you ever come back I will kill you. Remember that, night and day!' The girl hurried away, full of horror and fear, but saved, and her mother followed her at a distance.

Sin Fat was found, and duly inquested. A verdict of murder was returned, and a warrant issued for Mrs Sin Fat, but she was never caught. Only one man ever cast eyes on her again. A week after the murder a stoical old ferryman was working his lumbering craft across the river late one night, when something struck the prow, turned slowly round, and quietly drifted with the dark waters. It was a body. It turned over after the contact with the boat, and the man saw a white, bleached face in the moonlight, surrounded by a mass of black hair, which formed a sombre halo. The ferryman looked after it curiously for a time, then resumed his rowing, muttering: 'Only a body! Well, I don't want t' be mixed up in no inkwests.'

THE STORY
OF WILLS' LEAP

R. Spencer Browne

ABOUT ELEVEN YEARS AGO—and how those eleven years have rattled by—I found myself, after a long absence, in my native town in New South Wales. I had gone up from Sydney to have a look at the old place. The journey was by rail to Campbelltown and thence a ten-mile drive took me to dear old Oaklands, one of the most ancient of the homes in the mother colony. And such a drive it was! How little the old landmarks had changed. I remembered every spot along the road. There was Hurley's Hill just outside Campbelltown, the scene of the Fisher murder and the alleged appearance of the notorious Fisher's ghost. What a strange creepy feeling we youngsters used to experience as we passed the spot at night, and how indignantly we resented the scepticism of those who were not inclined to accept the ghost story as genuine. Away to Wrixon's Hill, where the old windmill stood of yore; past Bray's Hill, and down its slope at a breakneck pace; past Mount Gilead—where I had spent many happy days, climbing the hills and watching the lights changing on the fair blue range away beyond Menangle—thence through farms, the name of every one of which I knew, and concerning whose occupants I worried my companion—an old school-fellow—with questions which would have provoked to anger a less good tempered man.

Many of the old folk were there still; they farmed the land on which they were born, or their sons followed them in the work. Some had gone away out into the world, and had long since ceased to write to their friends; others had gone a longer journey—had crossed the great river and were at rest; but it was remarkable how few changes had occurred. In nearly every case where the father had died, a son had succeeded him and the old names sounded sweet to me, coming back after long years. In that district, poor and quiet though it may be, there are no rack-renting landlords, no lords of the soil whose rent means everything his tenant earns over and above what will barely keep body and soul together.

An hour's drive brought us to the gates at Oaklands. It was a summer's evening and all round the old place the English oaks planted there by my great grandfather, and now nearly eighty years old, were out in leaf. Fancy over a mile of these grand old trees in an unbroken line, grown to a greater size than they ever attain in colder climates and all fine, strong, and healthy. Through the gates we passed, and up the short drive to the house. The poor old home was a sad wreck, but the air was heavy with the odours of the loquat blossoms, and the great trees covered with their kindly shadows the decaying walls and roof.

Round we drove to the stables, built over half a century before of ironbark wood, and standing as firm as the day they were raised. There many a race-horse, famous in the early days of the Colony, had gone through his preparation before appearing at Homebush; and what names are more familiar to old antipodean sportsmen than Kauri Gum, and Old Jorrocks? On the old place we had the course, where the local races were held, and in another field, was the ground where the cricketers of Appin so often did battle for the local honour and glory. Gate money! Ah, we didn't think of gate money in those days. The grounds were thrown open whenever they were wanted.

And there I stood once more in the old square plot where I learnt my earliest lessons in this world. To me Oaklands is the sweetest spot on earth. I have seen some of the sights of the world: quaint eastern towns in India and China, quiet farming districts under English skies; great European Cities, the Galleries and Churches, where pictures with famous names upon them are worshipped by art lovers; have heard the sacred chants echoing through St Paul's, and have reverentially stood over the spot in Westminster where the greatest and brightest of England's dead sleep the long sleep; but never elsewhere have I experienced the same good and joyous feeling that grew over me as I walked once again the ground of my old home.

And then we walked out to the wattle paddock to see the sun drop down behind the Blue Mountains. The sky was flushed with red and gold; great streaks rose up from the hilltops to the heavens like rays of supernatural light; the valley of the Nepean River lay under a golden mist, and the purple hills that led down from the mountain range seemed like clouds, so covered were they with the changing glory. I lingered there until the shadows on the mountains darkened, and one after another, the gentle stars peeped out above me. Though the boys who had so often watched those sunsets with me, were scattered, and the good mother was far away, it was a 'coming home.'

We Australians love our land, sometimes I think, too well. We cannot bear to leave it for long, and for our old homes, we have a reverential regard. Why I even looked with delight on the old harness house, and hailed with genuine joy the memory of a flogging I had received there once from my father, for giving a draft horse a surreptitious spin without a saddle, and with a piece of twisted stringy bark as a bridle. That was at about the mature age of nine. I only hope that when I'm an old man, I'll have money enough to take me back there, and that my last days will be spent in the quiet of home.

Next morning I had to join a shooting party, and drive out to the Nepean River for a day with the wallabys. I don't want to say anything of the sport, because the story I have to tell has nothing to do with it; but I know that at luncheon time I was with a very old identity in Appin, a long way from the rest of the party, and we sat down about half a mile above the East Bargo Crossing, to eat our sandwiches, and drink from the pure mountain stream. How we had worked our way down there I cannot remember, but our halting place was at a spot known as Wills' Peak. We had munched our sandwiches and lighted our pipes, and lay back under the cool shade of a stream ti-tree, the red bloom from which was spreading a carpet on the rocks.

Presently I asked my companion, 'Why is that place called Wills' Peak?'

I had known it by the name always, but had never before imagined who or what Wills was, and why he should have been so distinguished, as to have a geographical honour done him.

Old Paddy didn't express wonder at my ignorance, and he proceeded to tell me the whole, 'why and wherefore,' as he put it. I cannot at this distance of time remember his words exactly, but the story he told was this.

Over forty years before, 'in the old masther's time'—as he expressed it—there lived at East Bargo, a settler named Ross, who, like many another 'true patriot' of his time, had left his country for his country's good. He had, by steady industry, grown fairly wealthy, and had married a free woman, who, after a couple of years of happy life died, leaving a baby, Evelyn. As Miss Ross grew up, she developed a wayward spirit, and exercised quite a despotic rule over the young fellows in the district. But she had no more devoted admirer than Felix O'Brien, a fine young Irishman, and the son of well-to-do parents at home. It was generally thought, that when Miss Evelyn made up her mind to take unto herself a husband, Felix would quite naturally be the happy man. But the advent of Godfrey Wills, a good-looking young Englishman, quite upset the little calculations. Wills had been sent out to New South Wales to his uncle's estate, to get Colonial experience. In the old country he had been a ne'er-do-well, and as a matter of fact, his friends has shipped him off to Australia to get him out of the way, and give him a chance of reforming in a land where his peculiarities were not known. He was a clever fellow, well educated, had had all the advantages of good society, could ride and shoot well, and soon became a popular man in the district. Evelyn Ross could not but compare his polished style, and his fashionable attainments, with the rather awkward manner, and not over brilliant intellect of Felix O'Brien, and it is needless to say the comparison was not to the advantage of her old admirer. She did not calculate upon a possible selfishness in the constitution of Wills, which would render him incapable of devotedness through weary years, when perhaps life would be no longer young or bright. Had she compared his inner manhood with that of O'Brien, she would have found the latter possessing qualities which, unhappily, her favourite lacked. But it was the old story, and before Wills had been three months in the district his engagement with Evelyn Ross was announced.

Felix O'Brien said nothing, but avoided both Evelyn and her lover, and went quietly on with his work.

What he felt he kept within his breast.

Soon the marriage time came, and Wills took his new-made bride to a small place old Ross had purchased for them. For a time all went happily, but Wills soon wearied of domestic life, and was frequently away from home. His wife fretted and upbraided him. This made matters worse, and the wayward girl was soon changed to a care-worn woman.

'Bye and bye,' she thought, 'when there is a baby, he will stay at home.'

When the little one came Wills did give more of his time to his wife's society, but it was not for long. He went to Sydney, and gambled and bet and lost more money than he could afford to pay, and was forced to give up the place Ross had bought for them, and go with his wife and child to the old man's house. Then it appeared that Wills would settle down, but in a few months he went away again. He drank heavily, and frequently ill-used his wife; but she bore his brutality without a murmur, and, as old Paddy put it, 'Sure she loved him the better for it.'

It is certain that her spirit was broken, but she was still passionately attached to the good-for-nothing whom she had taken 'for better or worse.'

There was in store for the poor girl a worse experience yet.

Wills forged Felix O'Brien's name for £200, and the forgery being discovered, but not its author, the matter was placed in the hands of the police, and the crime traced ultimately to the proper source.

The forger was arrested and placed upon his trial. The court was crowded, and, seated near the witness stand, and thickly veiled, was Evelyn Wills.

Her old lover, Felix O'Brien, was the principal witness.

The forged cheque was handed him, and the Chief Constable who conducted the prosecution, asked—

'Do you see that document, Mr. O'Brien?'

'I do,' said Felix, scarcely glancing at it.

'Examine the signature, if you please.'

The witness examined it.

'Now', said the officer, 'tell the Court is that your signature?'

There was a pause.

With a quick movement, Evelyn turned, and with her veil raised, gave one glance at Felix O'Brien.

It was a mute appeal for mercy.

God knows she need not have craved it of Felix O'Brien.

Her face was pale; she looked worn and ill. How unlike the bright, capricious girl he would have given his life to have spared one pang.

'Come Mr. O'Brien,' the officer repeated, 'is that your signature?'

'It is,' said the man who had sworn to tell the truth, and had called his God to witness.

There were no further questions asked, and Godfrey Wills was allowed to go free.

Felix left the court hurriedly.

Now-a-days there would be more questions asked, but at the time of which I write, Felix O'Brien was not a likely man to be badgered, if he wished to hush a matter up.

It would have been a good thing for Wills had he been convicted and sent to prison, for his escape made matters worse for those who should have been dear to him. He who had so degraded himself felt further degraded that an old lover of his wife should have given him his freedom. He went straight on a downward course, and at last was concerned in an attempt to rob a mail, in which affray the coach driver was shot dead.

The police went to Evelyn's old home to arrest her husband, who, well mounted, sought to escape. An exciting chase ensued, and shots were exchanged, though without effect. The police tried to work their man down to the river, where they expected to capture him. As he neared the precipice—which frowned three hundred feet above where we sat—Wills wheeled to the left, and was making down through the rough country, towards the road. The police were left behind, and the fugitive was gaining ground, when, suddenly, a woman on horseback appeared in the line of the chase.

It was Wills' wife.

She called to him to turn, that he was riding where other officers were waiting in ambush for him.

Where was he to go?

To ride on or to stop meant certain capture, trial, and execution. His wife called out to him in a clear steady voice—

'Ride for the cliff!'

She knew it was death. So did he.

'Aye Sir,' said old Paddy, 'I can see him now, jam his hat down over his eyes and send the black horse full tilt at the precipice. The poor brute tried to stop when it saw the danger; but it was too late. Over they went, and Evelyn rode round to the road, and was here, where we now sit, long before the police. She knew every inch of the ground. When we reached this place, she sat just where that lizard is sunning himself, and on her lap lay the mangled head of her husband; the man to whom she had given all her young life, and who was now dead and disgraced in her arms.'

Old Paddy wiped a tear away from his weather-beaten cheek, and said in a whisper,

'Whist, Sir! The poor girl was staring mad; looking with big frightened eyes at her dead man; by turns calling him by the dearest names, and calling down heaven's curses on us. It was a dreadful scene in this wild place.'

'What became of her and the child?' I asked.

'Sure she died in Tarban Creek (Gladesville Asylum), poor dear,' was the reply, 'and the child—well the child is the lady who lives with poor old Felix O'Brien, and he took her as an infant when old Ross died broken-hearted, and has watched over her ever since with more than a father's care.'

I knew now why Felix O'Brien had remained single, and why he seemed such a quiet fellow always in my recollection.

We rose and stretched ourselves, and as I looked up at the great wall of rock above, Paddy said—

'Sure it's a dirty place to ride over, Sir.'

It was.

CHINESE GINNIE

A. G. Hales

'SOMETHIN' 'LL HEV TER BE DONE, mates, or we'll get no luck in these diggin's. Look at 'em down there now!'

And the group of diggers did look, and they let their human feelings rise up and bubble over in sundry powerful expletives as they saw about forty calm-looking Chinamen carting wash-dirt down to the banks of the little stream that divided the two camps. The Celestials didn't seem to mind how much cursing was expended upon them by the band of European gold-fossickers, and they went jogging along in the twilight as if the blasphemy hurled at them was good for their health. Each man had a long cane on his shoulder, and at each end of this instrument there was a canvas bag attached, after the fashion of the Mongolian vegetable hawkers in and around the city of Sydney. They were a silent crowd, and all day from dawn until dark they pegged away and seldom spoke to one another; and when they did, it was in their own sweet tongue, which to English ears sounded like the clucking of a moulting duck in the bowels of a gunny-bag.

'Curse 'em.' growled the white diggers, 'I'd like ter get fourpence ha'penny a scalp for the whole gang. I'd make one good day's pay onyway.'

'Fourpence ha'penny! I'd give the Government my share of the year's clean up for the privilege of scalping the yellow crew for nothing.'

Judging by the tenor of these remarks a stranger entering the camp might have been justified in surmising that the white folks were considerably riled, and so they were. Seven months prior to that evening I had ridden from Melbourne to this rush, which was located in the very heart of the Mountains, and I had found the place full of contentment and go. Americans, Englishmen, Dutchmen, Germans, Frenchmen, Italians, and Australians were all there, and the greater number of them were getting good gold. The tents lined the mountain ridges, and the caravans, drinking and gambling shanties did a roaring business, and all seemed prosperous. One morning a long yellow line was seen advancing at a trot through the mouth of the gully, and a mob of Chinamen in Indian file came into view. They didn't meddle with anyone. They didn't speak unless spoken to, and then they smiled with the half-cracked expression which they know so well how to send cantering over their mahogany-coloured features, and seemed so hopelessly imbecile that the impression gained ground in our camp that the whole boiling lot of Celestials had recently escaped from a third-class lunatic asylum in the Flowery Land, and were quite harmless. But from that hour trouble overtook the field—first of all came fever, and the boys began to peg out, and were planted away in a shady spot amongst the trees; then litigation followed, and that just raised hell, for no man's ground was secure. As soon as a fellow bottomed on good pay dirt then his claim would be jumped, and a law suit and fights would follow, and at last the gold seemed to peter out. The only thing that kept steadily on was the Chinese element, and that never shifted or varied, week in or week out, until it began to be whispered about that the Mongolians had killed the luck of the camp, and slowly one by one the diggers dropped away from the place, for the genuine fossicker is as superstitious as a seaman, and once let him get an idea that a spot is unlucky, and all the gold in Australia wouldn't keep him hanging round. And now, on this Christmas Eve, the remnant of the once flourishing camp consisted of about five-and-twenty diggers, and they looked down on their luck, if ever a crowd did. After a spell, one of the boys began to build up the camp fire for the night and the rest followed suit, and soon billies were hissing on the logs, and bacon spluttered in the flames; and the moon came out and shed a soft light down on the wooded heights, and the evening breezes fluttered through the trees, and the stream rippled along and watered the plains at the foot of the ranges, and the men lay round the camp fires and smoked and told tales of other lands until the barking of a kangaroo hound told the approach of an outsider. I was sitting at our fireside reading to half-a-dozen fellows 'The Romance of Britomarte,' as Adam Gordon, the bushman poet, had written it, when the yelping of the hound caused me to arise to hurl a junk of quartz at the animal, when I suddenly saw a woman

advancing. I knew her in a moment. It was Chinese Ginnie, a poor
devil from the slums of Little Bourke-street who had herded in
with the Mongolians.

The boys began to curse her and order her off, but she beckoned
me aside, and throwing down my book I left the camp and went
with her into the shadow of the forest trees.

'What's up, Ginnie?'

'I've come to tell you something.'

'Well.'

'Ah Ling knocked me down again to-night, and Li Hung kicked
me all over.'

'Poor devil.'

'They are always thumping me and bashing me round.'

'Why don't you quit 'em?'

'Quit 'em! Where else can I go? I'm a woman of the Chinese
camps, and the lowest hell in all Melbourne wouldn't give me
room. No, I can't quit; besides they give me opium sometimes,
and I can't live without it now.'

'God help you.'

'They've turned me out to-night to starve, or rot, or die like a
dog!'

'Why?'

''Cause they've found rich gold, and don't want white folks to
know it.'

'Where is it?'

'Away up behind their camp on the slope of the hill, an' they
intend to go and peg out all along the line at daybreak.'

'Ah, you'd better camp with us to-night, Ginnie.'

'No, I'll go back, and after you have pegged out your rich claim
you won't forget me; I know that. Send me somewhere where I
can die in peace. I'm young yet, and you might get doctors that
could stop this craving that's on me. Good night.'

She slipped away in the bush.

Ten minutes later I was in the centre of a mob of quiet, but
desperately-determined men. I had told of the Chinaman's find,
and waited to hear what would follow.

Black Andy was the first to speak.

'Boys,' he said, and his voice was fearfully low and husky,
'Boys, we must save that unfortunate female.' And as he spoke he
knocked the head off his pick and spat on his hands, and began to
fondle the handle tenderly.

'That's fact,' echoed the rest, and in less than a quarter of an hour
five-and-twenty men were sneaking through the darkness towards
the Chinese camp. Each one gripped a bare pick-handle, and

walked on his toes. At the base of the hill, within a stone's throw of the Mongolian huts, Black Andy paused and drew the band up to him and sobbed:—

'Boys, we all on us had mothers once, recollect that an' foller me. We're goin' to rescue a poor lone woman, an' disperse a crowd of yaller devils wot never grew on this soil. Whoop, come on!' And they went. A wild half-hour followed, and at the expiration of that time there wasn't a Chinaman within five miles of the spot except two, who met with accidents as they attempted to leave in a hurry, and had to be planted later on in an old abandoned shaft. The poor woman was saved—and I might also remark that the line of rich country was pegged in peace at dawn, and no heathen son of Confucius ever troubled that locality again.

AN OLD-TIME EPISODE IN TASMANIA

'Tasma'

THE GIG WAS WAITING upon the narrow gravel drive in front of the fuchsia-wreathed porch of Cowa Cottage. Perched upon the seat, holding the whip in two small, plump, ungloved hands, sat Trucaninny, Mr. Paton's youngest daughter, whose straw-coloured, sun-steeped hair, and clear, sky-reflecting eyes, seemed to protest against the name of a black gin that some 'clay-brained cleric' had bestowed upon her irresponsible little person at the baptismal font some eight or nine years ago. The scene of this outrage was Old St. David's Cathedral, Hobart,—or, as it was then called, Hobart *Town*,—chief city of the Arcadian island of Tasmania; and just at this moment, eight o'clock on a November morning, the said cathedral tower, round and ungainly, coated with a surface of dingy white plaster, reflected back the purest, brightest light in the world. From Trucaninny's perch—she had taken the driver's seat—she could see, not only the cathedral, but a considerable portion of the town, which took the form of a capital S as it followed the windings of the coast. Beyond the wharves, against which a few whalers and fishing-boats were lying idle, the middle distance was represented by the broad waters of the Derwent, radiantly blue, and glittering with silver sparkles; while the far-off background showed a long stretch of yellow sand, and the hazy, undulating outline of low-lying purple hills. Behind her the aspect was different. Tiers of hills rose one above the other in grand confusion, until they culminated in the towering height of Mount Wellington, keeping guard in majestic silence over the lonely little city that encircled its base. This portion of the view, however, was hidden from Trucaninny's gaze by the weatherboard cottage in front of which the gig was standing,—though I doubt whether in any case she would have turned her head to look at it; the faculty of enjoying a beautiful landscape being an acquisition of later years than she had attained since the perpetration of the afore-mentioned outrage of her christening. Conversely, as Herbert Spencer says, the young man who was holding the horse's head until such time as the owner of the gig should emerge from the fuchsia-wreathed porch, fastened his eyes upon the beautiful scene before him with more than an artist's appeciation in their gaze. He was dressed in the rough clothes of a working gardener, and so much of his head as could be seen beneath the old felt wide-awake that covered it, bore ominous evidence of having been recently shaved. I use the word ominous advisedly, for a shaven head in connection with a working suit had nothing priestly in its suggestion, and could bear, indeed, only one interpretation in the wicked old times in Tasmania. The young man keeping watch over the gig had clearly come into that fair scene for his country's good; and the explanation of the absence of a prison suit was doubtless due to the fact he was out on a ticket-of-leave. What the landscape had to say to him under these circumstances was not precisely clear. Perhaps all his soul was going out towards the white-sailed wool-ship tacking down the Bay on the first stage of a journey of most uncertain length; or possibly the wondrous beauty of the scene, contrasted with the unspeakable horror of the one he had left, brought the vague impression that it was merely some exquisite vision. That a place so appalling as his old prison should exist in the heart of all this peace and loveliness, seemed too strange an anomaly. Either that was a nightmare and this was real, or this was a fantastic dream and that was the revolting truth; but then which was which, and how had he, Richard Cole, late No. 213, come to be mixed up with either?

As though to give a practical answer to his melancholy question, the sharp tingle of a whip's lash made itself felt at this instant across his cheek. In aiming the cumbersome driving-whip at the persistent flies exploring the mare's back, Trucaninny had brought it down in a direction she had not intended it to take. For a moment she stood aghast. Richard's face was white with passion. He turned fiercely round; his flaming eyes seemed literally to send out sparks of anger. 'Oh, please, I didn't mean it,' cried the child penitently. 'I wanted to hit the flies. I did indeed. I hope I didn't hurt you?'

The *amende honorable* brought about an immediate reaction. The change in the young man's face was wonderful to behold. As he smiled back full reassurance at the offender, it might be seen that his eyes could express the extremes of contrary feeling at the very shortest notice. For all answer, he raised his old felt wide-awake in a half-mocking though entirely courtly fashion, like some nine-teenth century Don César de Bazan, and made a graceful bow.

'Are *you* talking to the man, Truca?' cried a querulous voice at this moment from the porch, with a stress on the you that made the little girl lower her head, shame-faced. 'What do you mean by disobeying orders, miss?'

The lady who swept out upon the verandah at the close of this tirade was in entire accord with her voice. 'British matron' would have been the complete description of Miss Paton, if fate had not willed that she should be only a British spinster. The inflexibility that comes of finality of opinion regarding what is proper and what is the reverse,—a rule of conduct that is of universal application for the true British matron,—expressed itself in every line of her face and in every fold of her gown. That she was relentlessly respectable and unyielding might be read at the first glance; that she had been handsome, in the same hard way, a great many years before Truca was maltreated at the baptismal font, might also have been guessed at from present indications. But that she should be the 'own sister' of the good-looking, military-moustached, debonair man (I use the word debonair here in the French sense) who now followed her out of the porch, was less easy to divine. The character of the features as well as of the expression spoke of two widely differing temperaments. Indeed, save for a curious dent between the eyebrows, and a something in the nostrils that seemed to say he was not to be trifled with, Mr. Paton might have sat for the portrait of one of those jolly good fellows who reiterate so tunefully that they 'won't go home till morning,' and who are as good as their word afterwards.

Yet 'jolly good fellow' as he showed himself in card-rooms and among so-called boon companions, he could reveal himself in a very different light to the convicts who fell under his rule. Forming part of a system for the crushing down of the unhappy prisoners, in accordance with the principle of 'Woe be to him through whom the offence cometh,' he could return with a light heart to his break-fast or his dinner, after seeing some score of his fellow-men abjectly writhing under the lash, or pinioned in a ghastly row upon the hideous gallows. 'Use,' says Shakespeare, 'can almost change the stamp of Nature.' In Mr. Paton's case it had warped as well as changed it. Like the people who live in the atmosphere of Courts, and come to regard all outsiders as another and inferior race, he had come to look upon humanity as divisible into two classes—namely, those who were convicts, and those who were not. For the latter, he had still some ready drops of the milk of human kind-ness at his disposal. For the former, he had no more feeling than we have for snakes or sharks, as the typical and popular embodiments of evil.

Miss Paton had speedily adopted her brother's views in this respect. Summoned from England to keep house for him at the death of Trucaninny's mother, she showed an aptitude for introducing prison discipline into her domestic rule. From constant association with the severe *régime* that she was accustomed to see exercised upon the convicts, she had ended by regarding disobedience to orders, whether in children or in servants, as the unpardonable sin. One of her laws, as of the Medes and Persians, was that the young people in the Paton household should never exchange a word with the convict servants in their father's employ. It was hard to observe the letter of the law in the case of the indoor servants, above all for Truca, who was by nature a garrulous little girl. Being a truthful little girl as well, she was often obliged to confess to having had a talk with the latest importation from the gaol,—an avowal which signified, as she well knew, the immediate forfeiture of all her week's pocket-money.

On the present occasion her apologies to the gardener were the latest infringement of the rule.

She looked timidly towards her aunt as the latter advanced austerely in the direction of the gig, but, to her relief, Miss Paton hardly seemed to notice her.

'I suppose you will bring the creature back with you, Wilfrid?' she said, half-questioningly, half-authoritatively, as her brother mounted into the gig and took the reins from Truca's chubby hands. 'Last time we had a drunkard *and* a thief. The time before, a thief, and—and a—really I don't know which was worse. It is frightful to be reduced to such a choice of evils, but I would almost suggest your looking among the—you know—the—*in-fan-ti-cide* cases this time.'

She mouthed the word in separate syllables at her brother, fearful of pronouncing it openly before Truca and the convict gardener.

Mr. Paton nodded. It was not the first time he had been sent upon the delicate mission of choosing a maid for his sister from the female prison, politely called the Factory, at the foot of Mount Wellington. For some reason it would be difficult to explain, his selections were generally rather more successful than hers. Besides which, it was a satisfaction to have some one upon whom to throw the responsibility of the inevitable catastrophe that terminated the career of every successive ticket-of-leave in turn.

The morning, as we have seen, was beautiful. The gig bowled smoothly over the macadamized length of Macquarrie Street. Truca was allowed to drive; and so deftly did her little fingers guide the mare that her father lighted his cigar, and allowed himself to ruminate upon a thousand things that it would have been better perhaps to leave alone. In certain moods he was apt to deplore the fate that had landed—or stranded—him in this God-forsaken corner of the world. Talk of prisoners, indeed! What was he himself but a prisoner, since the day when he had madly passed sentence of transportation on himself and his family, because the pay of a Government clerk in England did not increase in the same ratio as the income-tax. As a matter of fact, he did not wear a canary-coloured livery, and his prison was as near an approach, people said, to an earthly Paradise as could well be conceived. With its encircling chains of mountains, folded one around the other, it was like a mighty rose, tossed from the Creator's hand into the desolate Southern Ocean. Here to his right towered purple Mount Wellington, with rugged cliffs gleaming forth from a purple background. To his left the wide Derwent shone and sparkled in blue robe and silver spangles, like the Bay of Naples, he had been told. Well, he had never seen the Bay of Naples, but there were times when he would have given all the beauty here, and as much more to spare, for a strip of London pavement in front of his old club. Mr. Paton's world, indeed, was out of joint. Perhaps twelve years of unthinking acquiescence in the flogging and hanging of convicts had distorted his mental focus. As for the joys of home-life, he told himself that those which had fallen to his share brought him but cold comfort. His sister was a Puritan, and she was making his children hypocrites, with the exception, perhaps, of Truca. Another disagreeable subject of reflection was the one that his groom Richard was about to leave him. In a month's time, Richard, like his royal namesake, would be himself again. For the past five years he had been only No. 213, expiating in that capacity a righteous blow aimed at a cowardly ruffian who had sworn to marry his sister—by fair means or by foul. The blow had been only too well aimed. Richard was convicted of manslaughter, and sentenced to seven years' transportation beyond the seas. His sister, who had sought to screen him, was tried and condemned for perjury. Of the latter, nothing was known. Of the former, Mr. Paton only knew that he would be extremely loth to part with so good a servant. Silent as the Slave of the Lamp, exact as any machine, performing the least of his duties with the same intelligent scrupulousness, his very presence in the household was a safeguard and a reassurance. It was like his luck, Mr. Paton reflected in his present pessimistic mood, to have chanced upon such a fellow, just as by his d—d good conduct he had managed to obtain a curtailment of his sentence. If Richard had been justly dealt with, he would have had two good years left to devote to the service of his employer. As to keeping him after he was a free man, that was not to be hoped for. Besides which, Mr. Paton was not sure that he should feel at all at his ease in dealing with a free man. The slave-making instinct, which is always inherent in the human race whatever civilization may have done to repress it, had become his sole rule of conduct in his relations with those who served him.

There was one means perhaps of keeping the young man in bondage, but it was a means that even Mr. Paton himself hesitated to employ. By an almost superhuman adherence to impossible rules, Richard had escaped hitherto the humiliation of the lash; but if a flogging could be laid to his charge, his time of probation would be of necessity prolonged, and he might continue to groom the mare and tend the garden for an indefinite space of time, with the ever intelligent thoroughness that distinguished him. A slip of paper in a sealed envelope, which the victim would carry himself to the nearest justice of the peace, would effect the desired object. The etiquette of the proceeding did not require that any explanation should be given.

Richard would be fastened to the triangles, and any subsequent revolt on his part could only involve him more deeply than before. Mr. Paton had no wish to hurt him; but he was after all an invaluable servant, and perhaps he would be intelligent enough to understand that the disagreeable formality to which he was subjected was in reality only a striking mark of his master's esteem for him.

Truca's father had arrived thus far in his meditations when the gig pulled up before the Factory gate. It was a large bare building, with white unshaded walls, but the landscape which framed it gave it a magnificent setting. The little girl was allowed to accompany her father indoors, while a man in a grey prison suit, under the immediate surveillance of an armed warder, stood at the mare's head.

Mr. Paton's mission was a delicate one. To gently scan his brother man, and still gentler sister woman, did not apply to his treatment of convicts. He brought his sternest official expression to bear upon the aspirants who defiled past him at the matron's bidding, in their disfiguring prison livery. One or two, who thought they detected a likely looking man behind the Government official, threw him equivocal glances as they went by. Of these he took no notice. His choice seemed to lie in the end between a sullen-looking elderly woman, whom the superintendent qualified as a 'sour jade,' and a half-imbecile girl, when his attention was suddenly attracted to a new arrival, who stood out in such marked contrast with the rest, that she looked like a dove in the midst of a flock of vultures.

'Who is that?' he asked the matron in a peremptory aside.

'That, sir,'—the woman's lips assumed a tight expression as she spoke,—'she's No. 27—Amelia Clare—she came out with the last batch.'

'Call her up, will you?' was the short rejoinder, and the matron reluctantly obeyed.

In his early days Truca's father had been a great lover of Italian opera. There was hardly an air of Bellini's or Donizetti's that he did not know by heart. As No. 27 came slowly towards him, something in her manner of walking, coupled with the half-abstracted, half-fixed expression in her beautiful grey eyes, reminded him of Amina in the *Sonnambula*. So strong, indeed, was the impression, that he would hardly have been surprised to see No. 27 take off her unbecoming prison cap and jacket, and disclose two round white arms to match her face, or to hear her sing '*Ah! non giunge*' in soft dreamy tones. He could have hummed or whistled a tuneful second himself at a moment's notice, for the matter of that. However, save in the market scene in *Martha*, there is no precedent for warbling a duet with the young person you are about to engage as a domestic servant. Mr. Paton remembered this in time, and confined himself to what the French call *le stricte nécessaire*. He inquired of Amelia whether she could do fine sewing, and whether she could clear-starch. His sister had impressed these questions upon him, and he was pleased with himself for remembering them.

Amelia, or Amina (she was really very like Amina), did not reply at once. She had to bring her mind back from the far-away sphere to which it had wandered, or, in other words, to pull herself together first. When the reply did come, it was uttered in just the low, melodious tones one might have expected. She expressed her willingness to attempt whatever was required of her, but seemed very diffident as regarded her power of execution. 'I have forgotten so many things,' she concluded, with a profound sigh.

'*Sir*, you impertinent minx,' corrected the matron.

Amelia did not seem to hear, and her new employer hastened to interpose.

'We will give you a trial,' he said, in a curiously modified tone, 'and I hope you won't give me any occasion to regret it.'

The necessary formalities were hurried through. Mr. Paton disregarded the deferential disclaimers of the matron, but experienced, nevertheless, something of a shock when he saw Amelia divested of her prison garb. She had a thorough-bred air that discomfited him. Worse still, she was undeniably pretty. The scissors that had clipped her fair locks had left a number of short rings that clung like tendrils round her shapely little head. She wore a black stuff jacket of extreme simplicity and faultless cut, and a little black bonnet that might have been worn by a Nursing Sister or a '*grande dame*' with equal appropriateness. Thus attired, her appearance was so effective, that Mr. Paton asked himself whether he was not doing an unpardonably rash thing in driving No. 27 down Macquarrie Street in his gig, and introducing her into his household afterwards.

It was not Truca, for she had 'driven and lived' that morning, whose *mauvais quart-d'heure* was now to come. It was her father's turn to fall under its influence, as he sat, stern and rigid, on the driver's seat, with his little girl nestling up to him as close as she was able, and that strange, fair, mysterious presence on the other side, towards which he had the annoyance of seeing all the heads of the passers-by turn as he drove on towards home.

Arrived at Cowa Cottage, the young gardener ran forward to open the gate; and here an unexpected incident occurred. As Richard's eyes rested upon the new arrival, he uttered an exclamation that caused her to look round. Their eyes met, a flash of instant recognition was visible in both. Then, like the night that follows a sudden discharge of electricity, the gloom that was habitual to both faces settled down upon them once more. Richard shut the gate with his accustomed machine-like precision. Amelia looked at the intangible something in the clouds that had power to fix her gaze upon itself. Yet the emotion she had betrayed was not lost upon her employer. Who could say? As No. 213 and No. 27, these two might have crossed each other's paths before, That the convicts had wonderful and incomprehensible means of communicating with each other, was well known to Mr. Paton. That young men and young women have an equal facility for understanding each other, was also a fact he did not ignore. But which of these two explanations might account for the signs of mutual recognition and sympathy he had just witnessed? Curiously enough, he felt, as he pondered over the mystery later in the day, that he should prefer the former solution. An offensive and defensive alliance was well known to exist among the convicts, and he told himself that he could meet and deal with the difficulties arising from such a cause as he had met and dealt with them before. That was a matter which came within his province, but the taking into account of any sentimental kind of rubbish did *not* come within his province. For some unaccountable reason, the thought of having Richard flogged presented itself anew at this juncture to his mind.

He put it away, as he had done before, angered with himself for having harboured it. But it returned at intervals during the succeeding week, and was never stronger than one afternoon, when his little girl ran out to him as he sat smoking in the verandah, with an illustrated volume of *Grimm's Tales* in her hands.

'Oh, papa, look! I've found some one just like Amelia in my book of Grimm. It's the picture of Snow-White. Only look, papa! Isn't it the very living image of Amelia?'

'Nonsense!' said her father; but he looked at the page nevertheless. Truca was right. The snowmaiden in the woodcut had the very eyes and mouth of Amelia Clare—frozen through some mysterious influence into beautiful, unyielding rigidity. Mr. Paton wished sometimes he had never brought the girl into his house. Not that there was any kind of fault to be found with her. Even his sister, who might have passed for 'She-who-must-be-obeyed,' if Rider Haggard's books had existed at that time, could not complain of want of docile obedience to orders on the part of the new maid. Nevertheless, her presence was oppressive to the master of the house. Two lines of Byron's haunted him constantly in connection with her—

So coldly sweet, so deadly fair,
We start—for life is wanting there.

If Richard worked like an automaton, then she worked like a spirit; and when she moved noiselessly about the room where he happened to be sitting, he could not help following her uneasily with his eyes.

The days wore on, succeeding each other and resembling each other, as the French proverb has it, with desperate monotony. Christmas, replete with roses and strawberries, had come and gone. Mr. Paton was alternately swayed by two demons, one of which whispered in his ear, 'Richard Cole is in love with No. 27. The time for him to regain his freedom is at hand. The first use he will make of it will be to leave you, and the next to marry Amelia Clare. You will thus be deprived of everything at one blow. You will lose the best man-servant you have ever known, and your sister, the best maid. And more than this, you will lose an interest in life that gives it a stimulating flavour it has not had for many a long year. Whatever may be the impulse that prompts you to wonder what that ice-bound face and form hide, it is an impulse that makes your heart beat and your blood course warmly through your veins. When this fair, uncanny presence is removed from your home, your life will become stagnant as it was before'. To this demon Mr. Paton would reply energetically, 'I won't give the fellow the chance of marrying No. 27. As soon as he has his freedom, I will give him the sack, and forbid him the premises. As for Amelia, she is my prisoner, and I would send her back to gaol to-morrow if I thought there were any nonsense up between her and him.'

At this point demon No. 2 would intervene: 'There is a better way of arranging matters. You have it in your power to degrade the fellow in his own eyes and in those of the girl he is after. There is more covert insolence in that impenetrable exterior of his than you have yet found out. Only give him proper provocation, and you will have ample justification for bringing him down. A good flogging would put everything upon its proper footing,—you would keep your servant, and you would put a stop to the nonsense that is very probably going on. But don't lose too much time; for if you wait until the last moment, you will betray your hand. The fellow is useful to him, they will say of Richard, but it is rather rough upon him to be made aware of it in such a way as that.'

One evening in January, Mr. Paton was supposed to be at his club. In reality he was seated upon a bench in a bushy part of the garden, known as the shrubbery—in parley with the demons. The night had come down upon him almost without his being aware of it—a night heavy with heat and blackness, and noisy with the cracking and whirring of the locusts entombed in the dry soil. All at once he heard a slight rustling in the branches behind him. There was a light pressure of hands on his shoulders, and a face that felt like velvet to the touch was laid against his cheeks. Two firm, warm feminine lips pressed themselves upon his, and a voice that he recognized as Amelia's said in caressing tones, 'Dearest Dick, have I kept you waiting?'

Had it been proposed to our hero some time ago that he should change places with No. 213, he would have declared that he would rather die first. But at this instant the convict's identity seemed so preferable to his own, that he hardly ventured to breathe lest he should betray the fact that he was only his own forlorn self. His silence disconcerted the intruder.

'Why don't you answer, Dick?' she asked impatiently.

'Answer? What am I to say?' responded her master. 'I am not in the secret.'

Amelia did not give him time to say more. With a cry of terror she turned and fled, disappearing as swiftly and mysteriously as she had come. The words 'Dearest Dick' continued to ring in Mr. Paton's ears long after she had gone; and the more persistently the refrain was repeated, the more he felt tempted to give Richard a taste of his quality. He had tried to provoke him to some act of

overt insolence in vain. He had worried and harried and insulted
him all he could. The convict's constancy had never once deserted
him. That his employer should have no pretext whereby he might
have him degraded and imprisoned, he had acted upon the scrip-
tural precept of turning his left cheek when he was smitten on the
right. There were times when his master felt something of a
persecutor's impotent rage against him. But now at least he felt he
had entire justification for making an example of him. He would
teach the fellow to play Romeo and Juliet with a fellow-convict
behind his back. So thoroughly did the demon indoctrinate Mr.
Paton with these ideas, that he felt next morning as though he were
doing the most righteous action in the world, when he called
Richard to him after breakfast, and said in a tone which he tried
to render as careless as of custom, 'Here, you! just take this note
over to Mr. Merton with my compliments, and *wait for the answer.*'

There was nothing in this command to cause the person who
received it to grow suddenly livid. Richard had received such an
order at least a score of times before, and had carried messages to
and fro between his master and the justice of the peace with no
more emotion than the occasion was worth. But on this particular
morning, as he took the fatal note into his hands, he turned deadly
pale. Instead of retreating with it in his customary automatic
fashion, he fixed his eyes upon his employer's face, and something
in their expression actually constrained Mr. Paton to lower his
own.

'May I speak a word with you, sir?' he said, in low, uncertain
tones.

It was the first time such a thing had happened, and it seemed
to Richard's master that the best way of meeting it would be to
'damn' the man and send him about his business.

But Richard did not go. He stood for an instant with his head
thrown back, and the desperate look of an animal at bay in his eyes.
At this critical moment a woman's form suddenly interposed itself
between Mr. Paton and his victim. Amelia was there, looking like
Amina after she had awoken from her trance. She came close to
her master,—she had never addressed him before,—and raised her
liquid eyes to his.

'You will not be hard on—my brother, sir, for the mistake I
made last night?'

'Who said I was going to be hard on him?' retorted Mr. Paton,
too much taken back to find any more dignified form of rejoinder.
'And if he is your brother, why do you wait until it is dark to
indulge in your family effusions?'

The question was accompanied by a through and through look, before which Amelia did not quail.

'Have I your permission to speak to him in the day-time, sir?' she said submissively.

'I will institute an inquiry,' interrupted her master. 'Here, go about your business,' he added, turning to Richard; 'fetch out the mare, and hand me back that note. I'll ride over with it myself.'

Three weeks later Richard Cole was a free man, and within four months from the date upon which Mr. Paton had driven Amelia Clare down Macquarrie Street in his gig, she came to take respectful leave of him, dressed in the identical close-fitting jacket and demure little bonnet he remembered. Thenceforth she was nobody's bondswoman. He had a small heap of coin in readiness to hand over to her, with the payment of which, and a few gratuitous words of counsel on his part, the leave-taking would have been definitely decorously accomplished. To tell her that he was more loth than ever to part with her, did not enter into the official programme. She was her own mistress now, as much or more so than the Queen of England herself, and it was hardly to be wondered at if the first use she made of her freedom was to shake the dust of Cowa Cottage off her feet. Still, if she had only known—if she had only known. It seemed too hard to let her go with the certainty that she never did or could know. Was it not for her sake that he had been swayed by all the conflicting impulses that had made him a changed man of late? For her that he had so narrowly escaped being a criminal awhile ago, and for her that he was appearing in the novel *rôle* of a reformer of the convict system now? He never doubted that she would have understood him if she *had* known. But to explain was out of the question. He must avow either all or nothing, and the all meant more than he dared to admit even to himself.

This was the reason why Amelia Clare departed sphinx-like as she had come. A fortnight after she had gone, as Mr. Paton was gloomily smoking by his library fire in the early dark of a wintry August evening, a letter bearing the N. S. Wales postmark was handed to him. The handwriting, very small and fine, had something familiar in its aspect. He broke open the seal,—letters were still habitually sealed in those days,—and read as follows:—

'SIR,—I am prompted to make you a confession—why, I cannot say, for I shall probably never cross your path again. I was married last week to Richard Cole, who was not my brother, as I led you to suppose, but my affianced husband, in whose behalf I would willingly suffer again to be unjustly condemned and transported.

I have the warrant of Scripture for having assumed, like Sarah, the *rôle* of sister in preference to that of wife; besides which, it is hard to divest myself of an instinctive belief that the deceit was useful to Richard on one occasion. I trust you will pardon me.—Yours respectfully, 'AMELIA COLE.'

The kindly phase Mr. Paton had passed through with regard to his convict victims came to an abrupt termination. The reaction was terrible. His name is inscribed among those 'who foremost shall be damn'd to Fame' in Tasmania.

MISS JACKSON

Francis Adams

HE STOPPED SUDDENLY and stared in front of him. Then he turned to me and said: 'Do you see that girl?'

We were in King Street, Sydney; it was about four o'clock on a lovely autumn afternoon, and Murdoch and I were taking a stroll. Murdoch is a very old friend of mine. We were at Marlborough together, and again at University College, London, when he was a student of medicine and I a student of all things in general and nothing in particular. I had just lit on him in Sydney, lately married, and a flourishing young suburban medico, and we were full of reminiscence and narrative. We had lunch at Compagnoni's, and were sauntering along when, turning round one of the corners of Pitt and King Streets, he stopped suddenly, stared in front of him, turned to me and said:

'Do you see that girl?'

I glanced in the direction indicated by his eyes and the wave of the hand holding his cigar, and saw a lady standing in front of a jeweller's window looking carelessly in, rather with the air of a person who was whiling away the moments of an expected rendez-vous than of a passer-by attracted by the wares exposed. I knew her at once. It was Mrs. Medwin. Mrs. Medwin is the wife—the young second wife—of one of our best-known Victorian squatters and politicians. Perhaps she was here on the return from her honeymoon. It was only six or seven months ago that Medwin married her, and the two went off at once for a trip to England, purposing to return by New York and San Francisco.

We were now directly opposite her, and, as she was still looking in at the window, it seemed improbable that she would see us. A

small group of pedestrians, coming from the opposite direction
upon us, compelled me to step ahead of Murdoch. At that very
moment I saw, by the glance I cast over my left shoulder as I
advanced, that she turned rather suddenly. She almost ran into him.
By the time I had wheeled round it was all over. Their eyes had
met; an extraordinary expression had flashed over her beautiful
face; he had raised his hat, she had bowed her head slightly, and
then he was with me and we were walking on together again and
away from her. That impression of her face as their eyes met is as
vivid to me at this moment as it was then.

I behold her before me as I write. She never had much colour,
but you could not call her pale. I have seen Italian women at Naples
with just her warm, moulded features, like olive-hued marble. Her
eyes had a singular look that reminded me of the jewelled,
enamelled eyes in certain statues. Whenever I saw her the prevalent
colour of her dress was always something metallic—golden or
silver or bronze. Probably she did it on purpose. She knew it suited
her peculiar style of beauty. I saw her married, and the orange and
glistering white of her toilet were like solid bronze and silver. I
never thought her cold. She gave me the impression of passion in
a calm and deep slumber, but I confess that that sudden glimpse
of her face as she saw Murdoch, and the subtle heightening of its
colour—not a blush or even a flush, it was so faint and evenly
distributed—made her, for the first time, strike me as not only a
beautiful statue, but a lovely woman.

He did not repeat his question, and I did not answer it for quite
a minute. We walked on side by side. Then I said:

'Girl? You would scarcely call her a girl. She is every inch of her
a woman. She is Mrs. Medwin.'

'Mrs. Medwin? Mrs. Medwin?' he repeated, vaguely. 'I know
the name somehow.'

'Medwin is one of the richest men in Victoria or Australia. His
first wife was, perhaps, the best-known personage in Melbourne
"society." She ruled it like an empress. Imagine the luck of that
great, hulking brute to have found such a woman as that as her
successor! Did you know her in England?' I asked mildly, after
having eased him off with this.

But he still refused to be communicative.

I tried a second flight.

'It seems amazing,' I said, 'to light on a face or form like hers
here. She is the sort of feminine type one meets in the drawing-
rooms of old superb civilisations, one of the ladies of Imperial
Rome, or mediæval Florence or Venice, at the court of Henri
Quatre, or, perchance, at some Viennese embassy. What has fecund

splendour like this to do with the "ghastly, thin-cheeked" aperies of this tenth-rate pseudo-civilisation of ours here in Australia? The music to which such a woman walks is that of a Galuppi or a Chopin; and, lo, Australian social life thrills to the vulgar temerity of barbarous iron-framed pianos, usually bought on the time-payment system! She seemed quite unconscious of us all, thank Heaven! Everyone was looking at her, and she paid about as much heed to them as Faustina did when she sat with poor, dear Marcus Aurelius in the Imperial box at the amphitheatre, and the Roman mob united with Roman "society" in canvassing her character.'

'That is beastly high-flown,' he said, a little irritably, 'I should have thought five years of Australia would have toned down your exuberant fancy a bit more, old man.'

We went on right up King Street, and, following some imperceptible impulse, passed over into Hyde Park. We entered a shady alley and paced on side by side, smoking in silence.

'How she is changed,' he said reflectively, 'and yet not changed. She is just the same—exactly the same. It is only that she is richer, riper. She has finer clothes now, and has been living well. She was inclined to be even a bit skinny then. I came out in the same ship with that girl,' he added, to me more particularly. 'Her name was Jackson, Miss Jackson.'

'It was,' I said.

'I was doctor on the ship—a sailer, one of the old Blackwall liners. We came by the Cape, of course. There were thirteen of us in the saloon, and the skipper and first and second mates. Miss Jackson was one. She came out alone in the skipper's charge, or his wife's, or both, and she had a cabin to herself. The ship had many cabins but few passengers.'

He paused for a moment. He was speaking in rather a dreamy way now, looking in front of him as if at the rising shapes of his memories. Then he suddenly seemed to decide to sit down on an empty bench under a dense-leaved Moreton Bay fig, and I took my place beside him.

'I will tell you about her,' he said, 'what I know. It isn't much. We were rather above the average collection of people on board— for a sailer. There were only five women; the rest men. There was the skipper's wife, a stout, rather showy, but at bottom motherly old soul; the wife of one of the passengers, also stout and showy, and addicted to divers liquors; an old maid of a long and lean but rather nice type, reading nice books and playing nice music; her cabin-companion, the grown-up daughter of another of the passengers, an old colonist who had made his pile; and, lastly, Miss Jackson. Among the men there were two sets, both of which, however, were on very good terms with each other. There was the sporting set, the fellows who played "nap" perpetually; got up deck games; fished for sharks or albatrosses, and the rest. And there was another set that was quieter, read the better class of novels, played chess, and talked rather "intelektooal." The women had a tendency to keep to themselves. There was one fellow who understood the whole lot, and in his quiet way got on with the whole lot. His name was Allenson.'

He paused again. Then, turning and looking at me, said:

'Allenson was just a devil. He was rather like you.'

I laughed.

'Thank you,' I said.

'Not like what you are *now*,' he proceeded, 'but like what you were at Marlborough, and even a bit at the College. He was what you call a thorough gentlemen. He was always quite at his ease, calm, courteous, with lots of tact. He never showed you he despised you, or, rather, did not consider you of the very least importance—in fact, thought himself almost of another flesh and blood to you; but that was what in his heart he must have felt. He never said so, but I am quite certain he was of some swell family. I have no idea what was bringing him out in a Blackwall liner to Australia. Perhaps he had been overdoing things in town, and had made up his mind to a health-voyage and some quiet travel at the other end. I'll admit that he was the best-looking man I ever saw. He was a bit "intelektooal" too. When he came on board he looked pale and rather worn, but this soon passed and presently he was magnificent. He dressed finely—in the very best taste, and he was the only perfectly made man I ever met. I can't tell you how I hated him!'

He looked at me again.

'If you could have been like him,' he said, 'you would have been happy. He was your ideal—your ideal in the old school and college days. And this Allenson turned his eyes on Miss Jackson.'

He threw away the end of his cigar, frowned, and drove his hands into his pockets.

'You know her?' he said. 'You met her, perhaps, before she married Medwin?'

'I met her once or twice,' I said, 'but it was nothing.'

'Well,' he proceeded, 'I think she was even nicer then than she is now. She wasn't so beautiful. She has bloomed out since. She was rather thin, and did not seem robust. She was poor, going out, an orphan, to a new land, to a strange home, with a distant relation who had agreed to take her. The skipper knew the man—a half-uncle or something. He lived up near Sandhurst, and was manager of a mine. Her outlook was far from bright. I myself,' he said, with a sudden rapidity, 'had no notion of what might be in store for me, for I wasn't such a fool as to think fortunes were to be got for the mere seeking in Australia nowadays—but—but—Well, what am I talking about?'

'You were talking about Miss Jackson,' I said, incidentally wondering to myself what sort of 'girl' was the 'girl' who presided over the domestic arrangements in that medical suburban home where I was to partake of dinner that evening.

'Allenson,' he proceeded again, 'was a terribly dangerous sort of man for women. No woman can ever get over the fact of a genuinely good-looking man. Even if he's a fool and a stick, they can't get over it—and what can they do, what *do* they do, when he is the very reverse of a fool and a stick? I watched the devil drop his meshes round that girl day by day, and could effect nothing. I couldn't even quarrel with him. The man witched me as he did everybody. Even the stupid brewer lot—there were three of them—swore by him. They said he was very "affable!" It was sickening!'

He drew his hands out of his pockets in a quick, nervous manner; leant his elbows on his knees, and bent forward.

'She got a way, presently,' he said, 'of looking up with a curious expression whenever he came to her or spoke to her. I knew what that meant. And yet she was as proud as Lucifer. Anyone could see that. It came out over and over again. I never for a moment imagined he intended marrying her. Men like that don't marry till they begin to get bald and take an infatuation, a *grande passion*— (you know)—or else they wait till they've got heads as bare as billiard-balls and make fools of themselves. Perhaps he wasn't rich enough. He might have sought the earth through to get a girl to equal her, anyway! I thought he was amusing himself with her— creating an "interest" on the voyage. Not that he seemed bored, but he had a way of sitting in his deck-chair, motionless like a statue, looking in front of him, and I know he must have found us dreadful poor company. Then one night in the tropics I got a shock.'

Once more he paused.

'It was a dark warm evening;' he said, 'no moon and the stars not very bright. It wasn't oppressively hot. There was a steady breeze aft, sending us along at five or six knots an hour—the tail-end of the trades. Most of the passengers were down in the saloon, playing cards, singing or reading. There was nobody on the poop but the man at the wheel and the officer of the watch. I came up for a breath of air and walked down one side of the poop and round by the helm and up the other. I had on indiarubber-soled deck-shoes, and it was so dark, outside of the glare coming from the sides of the saloon sky-lights, that I was upon them before I was aware of it. They were standing below the boat, leaning together, their elbows on the taffrail, and his hand holding hers. I passed on immediately and went below.'

He sat up.

'That was all,' he said 'all I saw of their love-making. I don't know how it went. I could only guess, but that guessing process used to drive me wild. For about a fortnight she looked a different girl, like a rose-bud that had bloomed out into a rose. Then came another change. I could see her day by day suffering torture. And I could say nothing—do nothing. I tried once. It was merely the vaguest expression of sympathy, of kindly feeling. She would not look at me for a week. I suffered torture too. I can't describe it. Especially at nights.'

He paused.

'And so,' he said with a sigh, 'day followed day, and week week, and things went from bad to worse. I saw he was getting tired of her. I used to long to smash his face in. Not that he behaved brutally or rudely to her: I should have done it if he had. No, he was just the same, calm and courteous, only to her it was a little cold and distant, and, so to say, oblivious. We were round the Cape now, and into the roaring forties. Some days we made great runs—280 or even 300 miles. We had the wind right behind us, bowling us along to Australia at full speed. Then we had a taste of storm for two days with heavy rain.'

He paused once more, and longer than before, sitting looking in front of him at the asphalt of the walk.

'It was the second evening after the storm,' he went on slowly. 'The ship was close-hauled, and heeled over very considerably to leeward. The rain had drawn off a little towards sunset, and three or four of them—the skipper, his wife and the old maid, with one or two of the men—were walking up and down the weather-side of the poop, getting up an appetite for dinner. It grew so dark that you couldn't see more than a few yards clearly in front of you. Every now and then a shower of spray broke over the poop, and this ended in driving the ladies below, but the skipper, one of the young brewers and myself still kept up our walk. At last I had had enough for the nonce, and turned off between the sky-lights and was passing down to the lee-side of the deck when I almost lurched up against Miss Jackson. She was standing with her back to me in just the position as that other time. I did not dare to speak to her, and went on to the ladder. Allenson was coming up it. I drew back without a word, and he mounted and passed me. I went down onto the main deck and hung about, talking with one of the mates. The first bell for dinner hadn't gone yet; so having nothing to do, I went up again by the other ladder on the poop to the skipper and the young brewer, who were still tramping up and down, and fell in with them. We staggered along on the oblique deck and discussed the construction of iron ships, and the future of sail as against steam. About a minute later, as we were all turning by the ladder, we saw the form of a woman come out from round the first sky-light. It was so dark that it was possible only to guess even so much as that. She came along steadily to us, and was with us as we made our first few steps forward together. I knew who it was of course, at once. It was Miss Jackson. She addressed the skipper.

'Captain,' she said in a quiet voice, 'I heard a cry, I think. Is every one on board?'

The skipper was incredulous.

'Where did you hear it?' he asked, in a light tone.

'Along by the helmsman,' she said. 'Someone passed a moment ago, and sat on the rail.'

We left her and went aft to the helmsman.

'If it's any one,' said the skipper, 'it's Mr. Allenson. I warned him only yesterday about sitting on the taffrail.'

'The helmsman said that four or five minutes ago someone had come and sat on the taffrail behind him, and then went forward a bit, but it was dark and he'd such a lot to do to keep her head up to the wind that he didn't notice who it was. That was all. No one ever saw any more of Allenson.'

He stopped suddenly and showed no sign of continuing.

'What do you mean?' I asked. 'How did he fall overboard?'

'I don't know. No one ever knew. No one was ever sure, even, that he fell overboard that evening at that time, or when. The last time he was seen (unless the helmsman saw him) was up on the fo'c'sle half-an-hour or so before. Several people saw him there.'

'But how can that be,' I asked, 'since you yourself said you saw him come up the ladder onto the lee side of the poop by Miss Jackson?'

'Did I say so? I never said so at the investigation we held.'

He got up.

'Let's go on,' he said.

We walked away together.

'But, look here,' I said, 'I don't understand. Do you mean to imply that it was an accident, or that he went down behind the helmsman and sat on the taffrail again, talking to her, and she shoved him over?'

He had taken out another cigar.

'What do I know about it anyway?' he said, biting off the end and spitting it out. 'Can you give us a light?'

'LONG FORSTER'

Francis Adams

THE FIRST TIME I saw Tony, generally called 'Long,' Forster he was slouching along Ruthven Street, Toowoomba. Tony wasn't the sort of man you could easily miss. In the first place, he stood six feet eight inches in his stockings; but, anyway, he had a face and a general sort of look about him that made you turn your head and have a stare when he'd passed. On one occasion I remember hearing a shopman ask a customer, a new chum, if he'd seen Long Forster down the street? The new chum replied: 'I don't know. What's he like?' Whereto the shopman: 'A sort of hand-me-down-a-star chap, rolling around the pavement, half asleep, and with his eye in the gutter.' The new chum recognised the description at once. I also recognised it that day when I first saw Tony in Ruthven Street, Toowoomba. I was walking with my friend Johnson. Johnson knew him well. In many a shed had they sheared together; once they had been chums up in the Gulf. Anywhere from the Gulf to the New South Wales Riverina they had knocked against one another, and the man with the money had held out his purse to the man without, in the good old up-country style. I said:

'Why, there's Long Forster!'

'You've hit it,' said Johnson. 'There wasn't much room to miss.'

We stood and watched the giant rolling lackadaisically along, hands deep in the pockets of his stupendous trousers, parasol-like hat slouched over his eyes. A small child of two or three years old was playing on the pavement a few yards in front of him. Suddenly looking up and seeing this huge moving tower coming down upon her, the little maid seemed to think it was high time to be getting out of it. Rising onto her feet and extending her tiny arms as if to feel her way, she lowered her head and advanced courageously, with her eyes shut. At this moment Tony became aware of the diminutive figure at his base, and stopped. The little maid, continuing to advance, reached his legs and, still feeling her way, passed right through them and out at the other side, when she opened her eyes, and with a big and very audible sigh of relief trotted off. Tony, mildly astonished at the whole proceeding, had wheeled round and was solemnly watching her as she went. Johnson burst into a fit of laughing, and so did I.

'You know,' said Johnson, 'that chap's about the softest-hearted cuss ever lived. He wouldn't hurt a fly. He won't go on till he's sure he hasn't put one of his floppers onto that little kid just by mistake. Let's go over.'

We went over.

'Well, Tony,' said Johnson, 'you came near killing her that time. By Jingo, you did!'

'Did I?' said Tony. '*Go on!*'

Johnson appealed to me.

I laughed and admitted that it was a close shave.

Johnson introduced us to one another.

'This is my particular friend, Acheson,' he said. 'He's *white!*'

'I'm glad to make your acquaintance,' said Tony, drawing out and enveloping my hand in the broadest palm I ever felt or saw on mortal man.

We proceeded down Ruthven Street, Tony in the middle.

'And what brings you in, old man?' asked Johnson.

'A bit of business,' said Tony.

'Where're yer stopping?'

'At Billy White's.'

'Not on the bust?'

Tony shook his head.

'No,' he said. 'Will you come up? Got anything to do?'

'Nothing particler.'

'Friend come too?'

I accepted, and we turned off up Herries Street towards White's Hotel.

Johnson and Tony had plenty of questions and answers to give and take. It was long since they had met, and, now that Johnson had taken up a bit of a selection by Helidon and hadn't gone round shearing these last two years, he had lots of bush news to learn. My part in the talk was largely that of silent member, till we had got up to White's and were seated in the dark little 'private room' behind the bar, with liquor before us and pipes on the smoke. I took the chance to examine Tony more closely. His name is a name of might from one end of the Queensland interior to the other, He never was more than a passable shearer; his great height prevented that. The wonder was that he could stand the work at all, bent double in the stifling atmosphere of the abominable holes the philanthropic squatter provides for his shearers. Tony, indeed, had determined at last definitely to give it up. He had determined to give it up years and years ago, but these were only samples of the proverbial good intentions which serve the devil for road metal, and must long since have glutted him too. Latterly, however, Tony had not been feeling quite himself, and his heart, he said, was 'getting sorter way of leppin' up into the bottom of his throat, and wouldn't hunk out of it for no end of a time,' which was a disconcerting habit on the part of the cardiac action of any man. The long and the short of it was, that Tony was going to retire, and was even now 'in town' (Toowoomba with its single street, post-office, school of arts, and assembly rooms, is 'town' to the Darling Downs and back-block shearer) on business connected with a permanent billet. All this Tony related in his slow, quiet way, supplying the commas, semi-colons, and full stops of conversation with puffs of his pipe, though it is to be admitted that his sense of punctuation was not very highly developed. I watched his face. A curious face it was. The brow was broad and well shaped, the eyes of a mild blue, and there were moments when they seemed languid and even expressionless. Ineffable good humour radiated from every feature. There was something comical in the long nose that ended in a brown fleshy bunch tilted a little on one side and a little up. The dark-brown beard with lighter tints of yellowy gold, thick and clipped square at the base of the throat, seemed the visible manifestation of a mind at peace with all men. The red-lipped, insouciant mouth spoke of this, and made the commonplace bushman's oaths quite rich and genial. Tall as he was, he was not the least misshapen. The proportion of parts was well preserved. The fine head was set by a splendid throat on magnificent shoulders and chest. Giants of this sort spring up everywhere, and generally leave the memory behind them of having been henpecked husbands. It made me laugh as I sat there and looked at Tony, to think of him being 'run' by some decided little piece of femininity who recognised that this was his inevitable destiny as well as he did himself. To tell you the truth, I thought there was something of that sort in the air now. Perchance, undeterred by squattorial rulings (in some cases the shearers actually themselves sign their acquiescence in them and take the chance of dismissal), Tony had wandered up 'in the gloaming,' after the shed had knocked off work, and, philandering with the cook and the maids, had lost his heart to some bush Delilah. There was a mild bashfulness and hesitancy about the particulars of that 'billet' which made me see more in it than met the eye. 'Long Forster' in love was a delicious contingency.

It was about this point that the conversation began to flag, and, happening to catch Johnson's right eye, I found him slightly closing it at me as a sign of something in the wind.

'Look here, old man,' he said to Tony, as if struck by a thought, 'When we was up at Hamilton, Acheson and me, we heard a most jammed-up yarn about you and thirteen niggers in a cave there.'

Tony looked at his friend with mild astonishment.

'Why, old man,' he said, 'I remember telling you that yarn up on the Barcoo three years ago.'

'Did yer?' said Johnson. 'Well, anyway, I forget the particulars of it, and I s'pose you might as well sling it us along again. For Acheson told me he'd very much like to hear it from you.'

I reasserted the fact.

Tony seemed to consider it, turning his eyes onto the tablecloth between his two elbows. After a pause he relieved himself of his superfluous saliva onto the floor to the left of him and began slowly but straight away.

'Well,' he said, 'I've no objecshun to tellin' you that thing, no particular objecshun, considerin' that it's *you* that wants it. But, you know, old man, I'm not *fond* of tellin' it. It sorter harrers a man's feelin's, as you may say, to think of his mate bein' wiped out by them —— niggers, and all unprepared-like, and never a bit of anything to show for it, but just gone, there, right off. In the midst of life,' added Tony musingly, 'we are in death, and that's the everlastin' truth that the Book says.'

Johnson and I acquiesced.

'Well,' said Tony, 'it happened suthing in this way. You never saw Jimmy Jackson, neither of you, I know it. He died before your time, old man, before you and your governor bust out at one another, and you came out on the Mitchell shearin', and we struck company. But Jimmy Jackson was about as white a sort of man as they make 'em, here or anny-weer else, or all over the inhabited airth! He nursed me through the Gulf fever when I was clean off my chump and howlin' round about watercourses and the old brook at home and had to be tied up to a —— tree and—I *know!* We worked together and ate together and chummed it right from the Murray to Carpentaria, and—and I loved him. I didn't make any more bones about it. I knew that chap better than I did myself, and he was right on good, through and through him, and I loved him.'

Tony paused to regain his complete composure, looking at the tablecloth as before and pulling at his pipe. The accumulation of saliva having once more been disposed of as before, he proceeded.

'Well, as I was saying,' he said, 'Jimmy Jackson and me sort of knocked about together all over this bloomin' kolny, and the adjacent kolnies, too—anyway, New South Wales and a bit of South Australia. There was nothing mean or dirty about him. He came out here a boy for his health (his lungs was bad), and he picked up amazin', and I knew him from the first. Well, it happened quite sudden and unexpected, and in this way. It was July—the 21st July, as I know right well—and we was both of us pretty dried up and hungry for a sight of the shears again, and all the boys bending to it, and one chap maybe spinning a song to keep our hearts straight. Them was his own words, Jimmy's words, that very mornin' when he lef' the water-hole. I hear him now. He was always fond of a song, Jimmy.'

Another pause.

'Well, it was pleasant humping that time. Pretty cold at nights, of course, and the wind would get through you if you got out from behind your lorg and give it a chance. But it was as dry as a bone, and warm by ten, and clear and invigoratin', as they say. We were skirting rouned the desert that time. Johnson, you know the desert well, but maybe Mr. Acheson doesn't. You know it isn't a desert all sand like. It's quite green, and there's lots of water, and it's the best wooded land in the country, but that there green is all —— spinifex, and if you walk over it you'll bleed yourself to a shadder, and it's death on horses. Well, we was skirtin' round that—sort of making up for Tarradilla, where they allays begin shearin's six weeks afore any one else. That's Tommy Twidle's way, and he's a bit of a crank, but he's the best luck for fine weather in shearin' time of any man in Queensland. The niggers were pretty bad up there that time. I mind once or twice Jimmy and me thought they was after us, and we played up on 'em with the fires.'

Tony turned to me to explain.

'You see, the niggers come tumblin' along when they see smoke, and if you got droppin' off to sleep you may reckon to be a deadly goner in no time, as they say in Kanady. So what you do is this: You camp at meal time and does your damper and then leaves the fire burning, and camps for the night further on. And the —— fools go wanderin' round about that fire lookin' for you, and can't make out where the —— you've got to!'

We all laughed.

'Well,' Tony proceeded, 'that was the way we done that night, and in the mornin' we kem back to the waterhole where the fire'd

bin, and filled up all we could, inside and out, for it was an infernil·
long stage ahead. And then it was Jimmy said that about bein'
hungry for a sight of the shears again, and the boys bending to it,
and one on 'em in the shed givin' us a warble to keep our hearts
straight. I reckon that was about suthin' after six or so, and we set
off right away. We kep on at it for several hours without sayin'
much, for Jimmy wasn't much of a talker when he had to stump
it, and no more was I. You see, Jimmy's weak point was allays his
wind, and I've known him to go up a hill—a straight-up, perpen-
dikler hill—in zigzags, like a artful old hoss with a load on.'

Tony paused for a moment, his eyes and face melting with
tenderness over this picture of his old mate in the character of an
'artful old hoss with a load on.'

'Well,' he continued, 'after a bit we got into loose, sandy soil—
heavy walkin'—and sorter quite unconscious, as they say, I got on
a bit ahead of Jimmy. You see,' said Tony explanatively, 'my legs
is a bit long, and if I don't keep a heye on them they takes me
where I'm not allays prepared for.'

We intimated that we understood.

'Onst,' he said, 'I mind turnin' back and hollarin' out some chaff
at him, and he hollared back, and he couldn't have been more'n
thirty or forty yards behind, and I turned and kep on agin. I was
carryin' more'n Jimmy, and I had the tommyhawk. We'd only one
tommyhawk, and Jimmy had a knife. My knife was broke. But
we didn't trouble about that. I never yet carried a revolver for the
sake of them niggers, and I never shall; they ain't worth it.'

'No,' said Johnson, 'they ain't worth it.'

'Well,' proceeded Tony, 'it was 'bout 'leven, or half past, as I
reckon, and I was beginnin' to get a bit like havin' a camp and feed,
but I was still keepin' on, goin' along over the sand through the
bushes, and thinkin' of nothin' particular, when I began to feel
somehow as if I wanted fer to turn round and see Jimmy. I can't
tell yer how 't was, but that was the way. So presently round I
turns and looks for him, but couldn't seen him, 'count of the
bushes. I mind all this as if 'twas yesterday. There wasn't a cloud
in the blue, and a cool fresh breeze blowing all the bushes one way.
So I stood and looked for him comin' along, and waited and
waited, and still he didn't come. So, thinks I to myself, I'll give
him a call, and I did. But he didn't answer, and that struck me
curous, because the wind was blowin' from me to him. So I called
again and let it roll, a regular cooee. But nary a sound out of him.
'That's curous,' thinks I to myself, 'very curous,' and I begins goin'
back, sorter irresolute, as they say, wondrin' why he didn't
answer.'

Tony put down his hand with his pipe in it onto the table-cloth, his eyes having a fixed look into the air just in front of him, as if he was looking at what he was describing.

'Well,' he said, 'I went on back and back, maybe forty yards or maybe fifty, and no show of him anywhire, and then all at onst, as I came round the lee of a big bush, what did I see through a break right ahead of me? Gord. I thought I was dreamin'! There was Jimmy down on the sand with the spears all stickin' out of him, and a mob of infernal niggers, like a swarm of ants, pullin' his swag to pieces and riflin' his incensit corpus. It made me blood run cold and I just stood a minute like a blausted pelikin, gapin' at 'em. Then I reconised it all, and I puts down my swag on the sand there, lookin' at 'em all the while, and I takes out the tommyhawk, holdin' it well for runnin', and I comes on right straight for 'em like a cat on her belly after a mouse. I reckon they was fifty or sixty yards off, but I'd not got ten afore one of the devils spotted me, and he shouts out 'How, how, how!' and all the others stopped and took to lookin' at me. That got me clean wild, that did, and I just give a sorter whoop, and swung up the tommyhawk and rushed at 'em.'

Tony was transfigured—his huge trunk, erect and swelling, supported his great strained throat, and made him, as it seemed to me, something like a gigantic python. His eyes glared, his lips drew back from his bristling teeth.

'There was thirteen of 'em,' he said, 'men and gins, and I wanted the whole lot. I wasn't goin' to stop till I had 'um. Strike me dead, but every —— fiend of that push had to die for it. I knew it! And, by Gord, so did they! The whole lot just slewed round and took off, jabbering like mad, into the scrub. If I'd gone right for 'um, they'd 've split up and some of 'um 'd got away. I didn't run my hardest. I kep' on after 'um, driving 'um all afore me, every now and then givin' 'm a whoop to tell 'um they was to go on. It was like drivin' wild hosses into a snare. They'd got the fear o' Gord in 'um. I knew they'd keep together right on, and they did. They went for their waterhole.'

He paused a moment.

'I never saw that waterhole afore; I never knew of it. When all at onst I couldn't hear 'em on ahead o' me, and broke out into a bit of a dry gully, I knew I'd never seen it afore. But I knew I had 'um all there; I knew it as well's could be. There was a cave. The waterhole was right in the rock—worn out, a pocket, just off where the stream went—a sorter back-water. Then a ledge. Along the ledge a bit of a pad. And then a black hole, and that was the cave. I couldn't stop to go along the ledge. I took a run and came smash in, doubled up, into the cave, onto the very top of the whole pile. None of 'em made a sound, except a low sorter whimperin' like blind pups. I caught hold of one by the neck with my hand and lugged him out and smashed his skull in with a blow of the tommyhawk. Then I reached in and got hold of another. It was a gin, and I gripped her by the leg and pulled her out, and 'bout broke her head off with a crack on the back of the neck. Then I laid hold on another one and smashed his skull in like the first one. And all the while I was reachin' in and pullin' 'em out they never made a sound, but kept up that sorter whimperin' like pups when the mother's gone. I killed the whole lot. There was thirteen of 'um. I counted.'

There was a pause, a long and complete pause.

'Well,' said Tony, suddenly softening, his eyes getting an extraordinary wild, sad look, 'and then I went back to Jimmy. They'd done him. They'd finished him right off. He'd never speak to me again any more. He'd not said good-bye to me—nary a word at all, nary a hand-shake—but gone right away from me for ever and ever and ever, wiped out by them damned niggers— Jimmy Jackson, my mate—Jimmy!'

Slowly the tears welled up to his eyes and overflowed, streaming down his face. He bent his head down into his arms on the table, and his great body shook to his sobs. And there we sat in the dark little 'private room' behind the hotel bar, silently looking at him.

HOW MUSTER-MASTER STONEMAN EARNED HIS BREAKFAST

Price Warung

I

AN UNPRETENTIOUS BUILDING of rough-hewn stone standing in the middle of a small, stockaded enclosure. A doorway in the wall of the building facing the entrance-gate to the yard. To the left of the doorway, a glazed window of the ordinary size. To its right a paneless aperture, so low and narrow that were the four upright and two transverse bars which grate it doubled in thickness no interstice would be left for the admission of light or air to the interior. Behind the bars—a face.

Sixteen hours hence that face will look its last upon the world which has stricken it countless cruel blows. In a corner of the enclosure the executioner's hand is even now busy stitching into a shapeless cap, a square of grey serge. To-morrow the same hand will use the cap to hood the face, as one of the few simple preliminaries to swinging the carcase to which the face is attached from the rude platform now in course of erection against the stockade fence and barely 20 yards in front of the stone building.

The building is the gaol—locally known as the 'cage'—of Oatlands, a small township in the midlands of Van Diemen's Land, which has gradually grown up round a convict 'muster-station,' established by Governor Davey. The time is five o'clock on a September evening, 55 years ago. At nine o'clock on the following morning, Convict Glancy, No. 17,927, transportee *ex* ship Pestonjee Bomanjee (second trip), originally under sentence for seven years for the theft of a silk handkerchief from a London 'swell,' will suffer the extreme penalty of the law for having, in an intemperate moment, objected to the mild discipline with which a genial and loving motherland had sought to correct his criminal tendencies. In other words, Convict Glancy, metaphorically goaded by the wordy insults and literally by the bayonet-tip of one of his motherland's reformatory agents—to wit, Road-gang Overseer James Jones—had scattered J.J.'s brains over a good six square yards of metalled roadway. The deed has been rapturously applauded by Glancy's fellow-gangers, all of whom had the inclination, but lacked the courage, to wield the crowbar that has been the means of erasing this particular tyrant's name from the pay-sheets of His Britannic Majesty's Colonial Penal Establishment. Nevertheless and notwithstanding such tribute of appreciation. H.B.M.'s Colonial representatives, police, judicial and gubernatorial, have thought it rather one to be censured and have, accordingly, left Convict Glancy for execution.

This decision of the duly-constituted authorities Convict Glancy has somewhat irrelevantly (as it will seem to us at this enlightened day) acknowledged by a fervent 'Thank God!'—an ejaculation rendered the more remarkable by the fact that never before in his convict history had he linked the name of the Deity with any expression of gratitude for the many blessings enjoyed by him in that state of penal servitude to which it had pleased the same Deity to call him. On the contrary, he had constantly indulged in maledictions on his fate and on his Maker. He had resolutely cursed the benignant forces with which the System and the King's Regulations had surrounded him, and he had failed to reverence as he ought the triangles, the gang-chains, the hominy, the prodding bayonet, and the other things which would have conduced to his reformation had be but manifested a more humble and obedient spirit. No wonder, therefore, as Chaplain Ford said, that it has come about that he has qualified for the capital doom.

Upon this doom, in so far as it could be represented by the gallows. Convict Glancy was now gazing with an unflinching eye. On this September evening he stands at his cell-window looking on half-a-dozen brown-clothed figures handling saw, and square, and hammer, as they fix in the earth two sturdy uprights, and to those a projecting cross-beam; as they bind the two with a solid tie-piece of knotless hardwood; as they build a narrow platform of planks around the gallows-tree; as they fasten a rope to the notched end of the cross-beam; and as they slope to the edge of the planks, ten feet from the ground, a rude ladder. All the drowsy afternoon he had watched the working party, though Chaplain Ford had stood by his side droning of the grace which had been withheld from him in life, but might still be his in death. He had felt interested, had Convict Glancy, in these preparations for the event in which he was to act such a prominent part on the morrow. He had even laughed at the grim humour of one of the brown-garbed workers who, when the warder's eye was off him, had gone through the pantomime of noosing the rope-end round his own neck—a little joke which contributed much to the (necessarily noiseless) delight of the rest of the gang.

Altogether, Convict Glancy reflected as dusk fell, and the working party gathered up their tools, and the setting sun tipped the bayonets of the guard with a diamond iridescence, that he had spent many a duller afternoon. If the Chaplain had only held his tongue, the time would have passed with real pleasantness. He said as much to the good man as the latter remarked to the warder on duty in the cell that he would look in again after supper.

'You may save yourself the trouble, sir,' quoth, respectfully enough, Convict Glancy. 'You have spoilt my last afternoon. Don't spoil my last night!'

Chaplain Ford winced at the words. He was still comparatively new to the work of spiritually superintending a hundred or so monsters who looked upon the orthodox hell as a place where residence would be pleasantly recreative after Port Arthur Settlement and Norfolk Island; and the time lay still in the future when, being completely embruted, he would come to regard it as a very curious circumstance indeed that Christ had omitted eulogistic reference to the System from the Sermon on the Mount. Consequently he winced and sighed, not so much—to do him justice—at the utter depravity of Convict Glancy as at his own inability to reach the reprobate's heart. But he took the hint; he mournfully said he would not return that evening, but would be with the prisoner by half-past 5 o'clock in the morning.

II

When Chaplain Ford entered the enclosure immediately before the hour he had named, he at once understood, from the excitement manifested by a group assembled in front of the 'cage,' that something was amiss. Voices were uttering fearful words, impetuously, almost shriekingly, and hands swung lanterns—the grey dawn had not yet driven the darkness from the stockade—and brandished muskets furiously. A very brief space of time served to inform the reverend functionary what had gone wrong.

Convict Glancy had made his escape, having previously murdered, with the victim's own bayonet, the warder who had been told-off to watch him during the night. This latter circumstance was, of course, unfortunate, but alone it would not have created the excitement, for the murder of prison-official was a common enough occurrence. It was the other thing that galled the gesticulating and blaspheming group. That a prisoner, fettered with ten-pound irons, should have broken out of gaol on the very eve of his execution—why, it was calculated to shake the confidence of the Comptroller-General himself in the infallibility and perfect righteousness of the System. And, popular and authoritative belief in the System once shattered, where would they be?

The murdered man had gone on duty at 10 o'clock, and very shortly afterwards he must have met with his fate. How Glancy had obtained possession of the bayonet could only be conjectured. As was the custom during the day or two preceding a convict's execution, he had been left unmanacled, and ironed with double leg-chains only. Thus his hands were free to perpetrate the deed once he grasped the weapon. Glancy, on his escape, had taken the instrument with him, but there was no doubt that he had inflicted death with it, the wound in the dead man's breast being obviously caused by the regulation bayonet. Possibly the sentinel had nodded, and then a violent wrench of the prisoner's wrist and a sudden stab had extended his momentary slumber into an eternal sleep. The bayonet had also been used by Glancy to prise up a flooring-flag, and to scoop out an aperture under the wall, the base-stones of which, following the slipshod architecture of the time, rested on the surface and were not sunk into the ground.

The work of excavation must have taken the convict several hours, and must have been conducted as noiselessly as the manner of committing the crime itself. A solitary warder occupied the outer guard-room, but he asserted that he had heard no sound except the exchange of whistle-signals between the dormitory guard at the convict-barracks (a quarter-of-mile away at the rear of the gaol-stockade) and the military patrol. The night routine of the 'cage' did not insist upon the whistle-signal between the men on duty, but they passed a simple 'All's well' every hour. And this the guardroom-warder maintained he had done with the officer inside the condemned cell, the response being given in a low tone, from consideration, so the former thought, for the sleeping convict so soon to die. Of course, if this man was to be believed, Glancy must have uttered the words. It was not the first time the signal which should have been given by a prison officer had been made by his convict murderer.

The murder was discovered on the arrival of the relief watch at five o'clock. The last 'All's well' was exchanged at four. Consequently the escapee had less than an hour's start. The scaling of the stockade would not be difficult even for a man in irons, and once in the bush an experienced hand would soon find a method of fracturing the links.

It must be admitted that this contumacious proceeding of Convict Glancy was most vexatious. Under-Sheriff Ropewell, now soundly reposing at the township inn, would be forthcoming at 9 o'clock with his Excellency's warrant in his hand to demand from Muster-Master Stoneman the body of one James Glancy, and Muster-Master Stoneman would have to apologise for his inability to produce the said body. The difficulty was quite unprecedented, and Stoneman, as he stood in the midst of his minions, groaned audibly at the prospect of having to do the thing most abhorrent to the official mind—establish a precedent.

'Such a thing was never heard of!' he cried. 'A man to bolt just when he was to be turned off? And the d——d hypocrite tried to make his Honor and all of us think that he was only too happy to be scragged. It's too d——d bad!'

It certainly did seem peculiar that Glancy, who had apparently much rejoiced at the contemplation of his early decease, should give leg-bail just when he was to realise his wishes. He had told the judge that 'he was —— glad they were going to kill him right off instead of by inches,' and yet he had voluntarily thrown off the noose when it was virtually round his neck. Was it the mere contrariness of the convict nature that prompted the escape? Or, was it the innate love of life that becomes stronger as the benefits of living become fewer and fewer? Had the craving for existence and for freedom surged over his despair and recklessness at the eleventh hour?

Such were the enquiries which Chaplain Ford put to himself as, horrified, he took in the particulars of No. 17,927's crowning enormities from the hubbub of the group.

'Damn it!' said the Muster-Master at last, 'we are losing time. The devil can't have gone far with those ten-pounders on him. We'll have to put the regulars on the track as well as our own men. Warder Briggs, report to Captain White at the barracks, and—'

Muster-Master Stoneman stopped short. Through the foggy air there came the familiar sound as of a convict dragging his irons. What could it be? No prisoners had been as yet loosed from the dormitory? Whence could the noise proceed?

Clink—clank—s-sh—dr-g-g—clink—clank—dr-g-g. The sound drew nearer, and Convict Glancy turned in at the enclosure gateway—unescorted. He had severed the leg-chain at the link which connected with the basil of the left anklet but had not taken the trouble to remove the other part of the chain. Thus, while he could take his natural pace with his left foot, he dragged the fetters behind his right leg.

A moment of hushed surprise, and then three or four men rushed towards him. The first who touched him he felled with a blow.

'Not yet,' said he, grimly. 'I give myself up, Mr. Stoneman— you don't take me! I give myself up—you ain't going to get ten quid* for taking me.' And then Convict Glancy laughed, and held out his hands for the handcuffs. He laughed more heartily as the subordinate hirelings of the System threw themselves upon him like hounds on their prey.

'No need to turn out the sodgers now, Muster-Master—not till nine o'clock.' Once more his hideous laugh rang through the yards. 'You had an easier job than you expected, hadn't you, Stoneman, old cove?'

Muster-Master Stoneman had been surprised into silence and into an unusual abstinence from blasphemy by the re-appearance—quite unprecedented under the circumstances!—of the doomed wretch. But the desperado's jeering tones whipped him into speech.

'Curse you!' he yelled. 'I'll teach you to laugh on the other side of your mouth presently. You'd better have kept away.' He liter-ally foamed in his mad anger.

'Do you think I couldn't have stopped away if I'd wanted to, having got clear?' A lofty scorn rang out in the words. 'But do you think I was going to run away when I was so near Freedom as that?' And the wretch jerked his manacled hands in the direction of the gallows. 'You d——d fool!'

No one spoke for a full half-minute. Then: 'Why did you break gaol then?' asked the Muster-Master.

'*Because I wanted to spit on Jones' grave!*' was the reply.

III

Muster-Master Stoneman was as good as his word. Death couldn't drive the smile from Glancy's face. That could only be done by one thing—the lash.

When next the Muster-Master spoke it was to order the prisoner a double ration of cocoa and bread. And, 'Briggs,' he continued, 'while he is getting it, see that the triangles are rigged.'

'The triangles, sir!' exclaimed Officer Briggs and Convict Glancy together.

'I said the triangles, and I mean the triangles. No. 17,927 has broken gaol, and as Muster-Master of this station, and governor

---

* 'Ten quid.'—The reward of ten pounds paid by Government on the re-capture of an escaped prisoner.

of this gaol, and as a magistrate of the territory, I can give him 750 lashes for escaping. But as he has to go through another little ceremony this morning I'll let him off with a "canary"'— (a hundred lashes.)*

'You surely cannot mean it, sir!' exclaimed Parson Ford.

'Mean it, sir! By G——, I'll show you I mean it,' replied the M. M., whose blaspheming no presence restrained save that of his official superiors. 'Give him the cocoa. Warder Tuff, give the doctor my compliments, and tell him his attendance is required here. Tell him he'd better bring his smelling-salts—they may be wanted,' he sneered in conclusion.

'You devil!' cried Glancy. The reckless grin passed away, and his face faded to the pallor of the death he was so soon to die.

As Muster-Master Stoneman turned on his heel to prepare the warrant for the flogging, he looked at his watch. It was half-past six.

At seven o'clock the first lash from the cat-o'-nine-tails fell upon Convict Glancy's back.

At 7.30 his groaning and bleeding body, which had received the full hundred of flaying stripes, lay on the pallet of the cell where he had murdered the night-guard but a few hours before.

At eight o'clock Executioner Johnson entered the cell. 'I've brought yer sumthink to 'arden yer, Glancy, ol' man. I'll rub it in, an' it'll help yer to keep up.' So tender a sympathy inspired Mr. Johnson's words that anyone not knowing him would have thought he was the bearer of some priceless balsam. But Convict Glancy knew him; and, maddened by pain though he was, had still sensibility enough left to make a shuddering resistance to the hangman as he proceeded to rub into the gashed flesh a handful of coarse salt. 'By the Muster-Master's orders, sonny,' soothingly remarked Johnson. 'To 'arden yer.'

At 8.45 Under-Sheriff Ropewell, who had been apprised while at breakfast of the murder and escape, appeared on the scene escorted by his javelin-men. This gentleman, too, had been greatly perplexed by Convict Glancy's proceedings. 'Really it was most inconsiderate of the man,' he said to the Muster-Master. 'I do not know whether I ought to proceed to execution, pending his trial for this second murder.'

'Oh,' said the latter functionary—flicking with his handkerchief

---

* Muster-Master Stoneman had doubtless in his mind's eye when he made this remark the decision of a Sydney Court which has legalised the infliction, by an official holding a plurality of offices of a sentence passed by him in each capacity, but for the one offence.

from his coat-sleeve as he spoke a drop of Convict Glancy's blood that had fallen there from a reflex swirl of the lash, 'I think your duty is clear. You must hang him at nine o'clock, and try him afterwards for the last crime.'

And as Convict Glancy, per Pestonjee Bomanjee (second), No. 17,927, was punctually hanged at 9.5, it is to be presumed that the Under-Sheriff had accepted this solution of the difficulty.

At 10.15 a mass of carrion having been huddled into a shell, and certain formalities, which in the estimation of the System served as efficiently as a coroner's inquest, having been duly attended to, Muster-Master Stoneman bethought himself that he had not breakfasted.

'I'll see you later, Mr. Ropewell,' he said, as the latter was endorsing the Governor's warrant with the sham verdict; 'I'm going to breakfast. I think I've earned it this morning.'

THE LUCKIEST MAN IN THE COLONY

E. W. Hornung

THAT IS NEVER a nice moment when your horse knocks up under you, and you know quite well that he has done so, and that to ride him another inch would be a cruelty—another mile a sheer impossibility. But when it happens in the bush, the moment becomes more than negatively disagreeable; for you may be miles from the nearest habitation, and an unpremeditated bivouac, with neither food nor blankets, demands a philosophic temperament as well as the quality of endurance. This once befell the manager of Dandong, in the back-blocks of New South Wales, just on the right side of the Dandong boundary fence, which is fourteen miles from the homestead. Fortunately Deverell, of Dandong, was a young man, well used, from his boyhood, to the casual hardships of station life, and well fitted by physique to endure them. Also he had the personal advantage of possessing the philosophic temperament large-sized. He dismounted the moment he knew for certain what was the matter. A ridge of pines—a sandy ridge, where camping properly equipped would have been perfect luxury—rose against the stars a few hundred yards ahead. But Deverell took off the saddle on the spot, and carried it himself as far as that ridge, where he took off the bridle also, hobbled the done-up beast with a stirrup-leather, and turned him adrift.

Deverell, of Dandong, was a good master to his horses and his dogs, and not a bad one to his men. Always the master first, and the man afterwards, he was a little selfish, as becomes your masterful man. On the other hand, he was a singularly frank young fellow. He would freely own, for instance, that he was the luckiest man in the back-blocks. This, to be sure, was no more than the truth. But Deverell never lost sight of his luck, nor was he ever ashamed to recognise it: wherein he differed from the average lucky man, who says that luck had nothing to do with it. Deverell could gloat over his luck, and do nothing else—when he had nothing else to do. And in this way he faced contentedly even this lonely, hungry night, his back to a pine at the north side of the ridge, and a short briar pipe in full blast.

He was the new manager of Dandong, to begin with. That was one of the best managerships in the colony, and Deverell had got it young—in his twenties, at all events, if not by much. The salary was seven hundred a year, and the homestead was charming. Furthermore, Deverell was within a month of his marriage; and the coming Mrs Deverell was a girl of some social distinction down in Melbourne, and a belle into the bargain, to say nothing of another element, which was entirely satisfactory, without being so ample as to imperil a man's independence. The homestead would be charming indeed in a few weeks, in time for Christmas. Meanwhile, the 'clip' had been a capital one, and the rains abundant; the paddocks were in a prosperous state, the tanks overflowing, everything going smoothly in its right groove (as things do not always go on a big station), and the proprietors perfectly delighted with their new manager. Well, the new manager was somewhat delighted with himself. He was lucky in his work and lucky in his love—and what can the gods do more for you? Considering that he had rather worse than no antecedents at all—antecedents with so dark a stain upon them that, anywhere but in a colony, the man would have been a ruined man from his infancy—he was really incredibly lucky in his love affair. But whatever his parents had been or had done, he had now no relatives at all of his own: and this is a great thing when you are about to make new ones in an inner circle: so that here, once more, Deverell was in his usual luck.

It does one good to see a man thoroughly appreciating his good luck. The thing is so seldom done. Deverell not only did this, but did it with complete sincerity. Even to-night, though personally most uncomfortable, and tightening his belt after every pipe, he could gaze at the stars with grateful eyes, obscure them with clouds of smoke, watch the clouds disperse and the stars shine bright again, and call himself again and again, and yet again, the very luckiest man in the Colony.

While Deverell sat thus, returning thanks on an empty stomach, at the northern edge of the ridge, a man tramped into the pines from the south. The heavy sand muffled his steps; but he stopped long before he came near Deverell, and threw down his swag with an emancipated air. The man was old, but he held himself more erect than does the inveterate swagman. The march through life with a cylinder of blankets on one's shoulders, with all one's worldly goods packed in that cylinder, causes a certain stoop of a very palpable kind; and this the old man, apparently, had never contracted. Other points slightly distinguished him from the ordinary run of swagmen. His garments were orthodox, but the felt wide-awake was stiff and new, and so were the moleskins, which, indeed, would have stood upright without any legs in them at all. The old man's cheeks, chin, and upper lip were covered with short gray bristles, like spikes of steel; his face was lean, eager, and deeply lined.

He rested a little on his swag. 'So this is Dandong,' he muttered, with his eyes upon the Dandong sand between his feet. 'Well, now that I am within his boundary-fence at last, I am content to rest. Here I camp. Tomorrow I shall see him!'

Deverell, at the other side of the ridge, dimming the stars with his smoke, for the pleasure of seeing them shine bright again, heard presently a sound which was sudden music to his ears. The sound was a crackle. Deverell stopped smoking, but did not move; it was difficult to believe his ears. But the crackle grew louder; Deverell jumped up and saw the swagman's fire within a hundred yards of him; and the difficult thing to believe in *then* was his own unparalleled good luck.

'There is no end to it,' he chuckled, taking his saddle over one arm and snatching up the waterbag and bridle. 'Here's a swaggie stopped to camp, with flour for a damper and a handful of tea for the quart-pot, as safe as the bank! Perhaps a bit of blanket for me too! But I *am* the luckiest beggar alive; this wouldn't have happened to any one else!'

He went over to the fire, and the swagman, who was crouching at the other side of it, peered at him from under a floury palm. He was making the damper already. His welcome to Deverell took a substantial shape; he doubled the flour for the damper. Otherwise the old tramp did not gush.

Deverell did the talking. Lying at full length on the blankets, which had been unrolled, his face to the flames, and his strong jaws cupped in his hands, he discoursed very freely of his luck.

'You're saving my life,' said he gaily. 'I should have starved. I didn't think it at the time, but now I know I should. I thought I could hold out, between belt and 'baccy; but I couldn't now, anyhow. If I hold out till the damper's baked, it's all I can do now. It's like my luck! I never saw anything look quite so good before. There now, bake up. Got any tea?'

'Yes.'

'Meat?'

'No.'

'Well, we could have done with meat, but it can't be helped. I'm lucky enough to get anything. It's my luck all over. I'm the luckiest man in this Colony, let me tell you. But we could have done with chops. Gad, but I'd have some yet, if I saw a sheep! They're all wethers in this paddock, but they don't draw down towards the gate much.'

He turned his head, and knitted his brows, but it was difficult to distinguish things beyond the immediate circle of firelit sand, and he saw no sheep. To be sure, he would not have touched one; he had said what he did not mean; but something in his way of saying it made the old man stare at him hard.

'Then you're one of the gentlemen from Dandong Station, sir?'

'I am,' said Deverell. 'My horse is fresh off the grass, and a bit green. He's knocked up, but he'll be all right in the morning; the crab-holes are full of water, and there's plenty of feed about. Indeed, it's the best season we've had for years—my luck again, you see!'

The tramp did not seem to hear all he said. He had turned his back, and was kneeling over the fire, deeply engrossed with the water-bag and the quart-pot, which he was filling. It was with much apparent preoccupation that he asked:

'Is Mr. Deverell the boss there now?'

'He is.' Deverell spoke drily, and thought a minute. After all, there was no object in talking about himself in the third person to a man who would come applying to him for work the next day. Realising this, he added, with a touch of dignity, 'I'm he.'

The tramp's arm jerked, a small fountain played out of the bottle neck of the water-bag and fell with a hiss upon the fire. The tramp still knelt with his back to Deverell. The blood had left his face, his eyes were raised to the pale, bright stars, his lips moved. By a great effort he knelt as he had been kneeling before Deverell spoke; until Deverell spoke again.

'You were on your way to see me, eh?'

'I was on my way to Dandong.'

'Wanting work? Well, you shall have it,' said Deverell, with decision. 'I don't want hands, but I'll take *you* on; you've saved my life, my good fellow; or you're going to, in a brace of shakes! How goes the damper?'

'Well,' said the old man, answering Deverell's last question shortly, but ignoring his first altogether. 'Shall I sweeten the tea or not?'

'Sweeten it.'

The old man got ready a handful of tea and another of sugar to throw into the quart-pot the moment the water boiled. He had not yet turned round. Still kneeling, with the soles of his boots under Deverell's nose, he moved the damper from time to time, and made the tea. His hands shook.

Deverell made himself remarkably happy during the next half-hour. He ate the hot damper, he drank the strong tea, in a way that indicated unbounded confidence in his digestive powers. A dyspeptic must have wept for envy. Towards the end of the meal Deverell discovered that the swagman, who sat remote from the fire, and seemed to be regarding him with extreme interest, had scarcely broken his bread.

'Aren't you hungry?' asked Deverell, with his mouth full.

'No.'

But Deverell was, and that, after all, was the main thing. If the old man had no appetite, there was no earthly reason for him to eat; his abstinence could not hurt him under the circumstances, and naturally it did not worry Deverell. If, on the other hand, the old man preferred to feed off Deverell—with his eyes—why, there was no accounting for preferences, and that did not worry Deverell either. Indeed, by the time his pipe was once more in blast, he felt most kindly disposed towards this taciturn tramp. He would give him a billet. He would take him on as a rabbiter, and rig him out with a tent, camp fixings, traps, and perhaps even a dog or two. He would thus repay in princely fashion to-night's good turn—but now, confound the thing! He had been sitting the whole evening on the old fool's blankets, and the old fool had been sitting on the ground!

'I say! Why on earth don't you come and sit on your own blankets?' The young man spoke a little roughly; for to catch oneself in a grossly thoughtless act is always irritating.

'I am all right here, thank you,' returned the swagman mildly. 'The sand is as soft as the blankets.'

'Well, I don't want to monopolise your blankets, you know,' said Deverell, without moving. 'Take a fill from my pouch, will you?'

He tossed over his pouch of tobacco. The swagman handed it back; he did not smoke; had got out of the way of it, he said. Deverell was disappointed. He had a genuine desire at all times to repay in kind anything resembling a good turn. He could not help being a little selfish; it was constitutional.

'I'll tell you what,' said he, learning backward on one elbow, and again clouding the stars with wreaths of blue smoke. 'I've got a little berth that ought to suit you down to the ground. It's rabbiting. Done any rabbiting before? No. Well, it's easy enough;

what's more, you're your own boss. Catch as many as you can or care to, bring in the skins, and get sixpence each for 'em. Now the berth I mean is a box-clump, close to a tank, where there's been a camp before, and the last man did very well there; still you'll find he has left plenty of rabbits behind him. It's the very spot for you; and look here. I'll start you with rations, tent, camp-oven, traps, and all the rest of it!' wound up Deverell generously. He had spoken out of the fulness of his soul and body. He had seldom spoken so decently to a pound-a-week hand—never to a swagman.

Yet the swagman did not jump at the offer.

'Mr. Deverell,' said he, rolling the name on his tongue in a curious way. 'I was not coming exactly for work. I was coming to see you. I knew your father!'

'The deuce you did!' said Deverell.

The old man was watching him keenly. In an instant Deverell had flushed up from his collar to his wideawake. He was manifestly uncomfortable. 'Where did you know him?' he asked doggedly.

The tramp bared his head; the short gray hair stood crisply on end all over it. He tapped his head significantly, and ran the palm of his hand over the strong bristles of his beard.

'So,' said Deverell, drawing his breath hard. 'Now I see; you are a brother convict!'

The tramp nodded.

'And you know all about him—the whole story?'

The tramp nodded again.

'By God!' cried Deverell, 'if you've come here to trade on what you know, you've chosen the wrong place and the wrong man!'

The tramp smiled. 'I have not come to trade upon what I know,' said he quietly, repeating the other's expression with simple sarcasm. 'Now that I've seen you, I can go back the way I came; no need to go on to Dandong now. I came because my old mate asked me to find you out and wish you well from him: that was all.'

'He went in for life,' said Deverell, reflecting bitterly. 'I have the vaguest memories of him; it happened when I was so very young. Is he well?'

'He was.'

'And you have been in gaol together! And you know what brought him there, the whole story!' Curiosity crept into the young man's tone, and made it less bitter. He filled a pipe. 'For my part,' he said sadly, 'I never had the rights of that story.'

'There were no rights,' said the convict. 'It was all wrong together. Your father robbed the bank of which he himself was manager. He had lost money in mining speculations. He took to the bush, and fought desperately for his life.'

'I'm glad he did that!' exclaimed Deverell.

The other's eyes kindled, but he only said, 'It was what any one would have done in his place.'

'Is it?' answered Deverell scornfully. 'Did *you*, for instance?'

The old man shrugged his shoulders. Deverell laughed aloud. His father might have been a villain, but he had not been a coward. That was one consolation.

A silence fell between the two men. There were no more flames from the fire, but only the glow of red-hot embers. This reddened the face of Deverell, but it did not reach that of the old man. He was thus free to stare at Deverell as hard and as long as he liked, and his eyes never left the young man's face. It was a sufficiently handsome face, with eyes as dark as those of the old man, only lightened and brightened by an expression altogether different. Deverell's pipe had soothed him. He seemed as serene now as he had been before he knew that his companion had been also the companion of his father—in prison. After all, he had grown up with the knowledge that his father was a convicted felon; to be reminded of it casually, but also privately, was not to receive a new wound; and the old one was too old to smart severely at a touch. The tramp, staring at him with a fierce yearning in his eyes, which the young man could not see, seemed to divine this, but said:

'It cannot be pleasant for you to see me. I wouldn't have come, only I promised to see you; I promised to let him hear about you. It would have been worse, you know, had he got out on ticket-of-leave, and come himself!'

'It would so!' cried Deverell sincerely.

In the dark, the old man grinned like one in torment.

'It would so,' Deverell repeated, unable to repress a grim chuckle. 'It would be the most awkward thing that could possibly happen to me—especially if it happened now. At present I call myself the luckiest man in the Colony; but if my poor father were to turn up——'

Deverell was not interrupted: he stopped himself.

'You are pretty safe,' said his companion, in a somewhat singular tone—which, however, he quickly changed. 'As your father's mate, I am glad you are so lucky; it is good hearing.'

Deverell explained how he was so lucky. He felt that the sentiments he had expressed concerning his father's possible appearance on the scene required some explanation, if not excuse. This feeling, growing upon him as he spoke, led him into explanations that were very full indeed, under the circumstances. He explained the position he had attained as manager of Dandong; and the position he was about to attain through his marriage was quite as clearly (though unintentionally) indicated. It was made plain to the meanest perception how very awkward it would be for the young man, from every point of view, if the young man's father did turn up and ostentatiously reveal himself. While Deverell was speaking the swagman broke branches from the nearest pines and made up the fire; when he finished the faces of both were once more illumined; and that of the old man was stern with resolve.

'And yet,' said he, 'suppose the impossible, or at any rate the unlikely: say that he does come back! I know him well; he wouldn't be a drag or a burden to you. He'd only just like to see you. All he would ask would be to see his son sometimes! That would be enough for him. I was his chum, mind you, so I know. And if he was to come up here, as I have come, you could take him on, couldn't you, as you offer to take me?' He leant forward with sudden eagerness—his voice vibrated. 'You could give him work, as you say you'll give me, couldn't you? No one'd know it was your father! No one would ever guess!'

'No!' said Deverell decidedly. 'I'll give *you* work, but my father I couldn't. I don't do thing by halves: I'd treat my father *as* my father, and damn the odds! He had pluck. I like to think how he was taken fighting! Whatever he did, he had grit, and I should be unworthy of him—no matter what he did—if I played the coward. It would be worse than cowardly to disown your father, whatever he had done, and I wouldn't disown mine—I'd sooner shoot myself! No, I'd take him in, and be a son to him for the rest of his days, that's what I'd do—that's what I *will* do, If ever he gets out on ticket-of-leave, and comes to me!'

The young man spoke with a feeling and intensity of which he had exhibited no signs before, leaning forward with his pipe between his fingers. The old man held his breath.

'But it would be devilish awkward!' exclaimed Deverell frankly. 'People would remember what they've been good enough to forget; and everybody would know what now next to none know. In this country, thank God, the man is taken for what the man is worth; his father neither helps nor hinders him, when once he's gone. So I've managed to take my own part, and to get on well, thanks to my own luck. Yes, it would be devilish awkward. But I'd stand by him, before Heaven I would!'

The old man breathed hard.

'I don't know how I've come to say so much to you, though you did know my father,' added Deverell, with a sudden change of tone. 'It isn't my way at all. I needn't tell you that from to-morrow forward you're the same as any other man to me. And if you ever go to see my father, you must not tell him all I have said to you about what, as you say, is never likely to happen. But you may tell him—you may tell him I am glad he was taken fighting!'

The old man was once more quite calm. 'I shall never see your father again. No more will you,' he said slowly and solemnly; 'for your father is dead! I promised him to find you out when my time was up, and to tell you. I have taken my own way of breaking the news to you. Forgive me, but I couldn't resist just seeing, first of all, if it would cut you up very badly!'

Deverell did not notice the quiet bitterness of the last words. He smoked his pipe out in silence. Then he said: 'God rest him! Perhaps it's for the best. As for you, you've a billet at Dandong for the rest of your days, if you like to take and keep it. Let us turn in.'

The worn moon rose very late, and skimmed behind the pines, but never rose clear of them, and was down before dawn. It shone faintly upon the two men lying side by side, packed up each in a blanket—Deverell in the better one. From the other blanket a hand would steal out from time to time, grope tremulously over Deverell's back, lie a minute, and then be gently withdrawn. Long before dawn, however, the old man noiselessly arose and rolled up his swag. He packed up everything that he had brought—everything except the better blanket. Over that he smiled, as though it was an intense pleasure to him to leave it behind, lapped round the unconscious form of Deverell. Just before going, when the swag was on his back, he stooped down once and put his face very close to that of Deverell. The worn moon glimmered through the pines upon them both. The faces were strangely alike; only Deverell's was smiling in his dreams, while the old man's lips moved tremulously, and he seemed much older than before: for the eager look had gone for ever.

A few minutes later the gate in the Dandong boundary-fence closed behind the gaol-bird tramp. And Deverell's father was dead indeed—to Deverell. Lucky for Deverell, of course. But then he was the luckiest man in the whole Colony. Didn't he say so himself?

'SOJUR JIM'

J. A. Barry

BRIGHTLY BLAZED the watch-fires into the still night air, brightly
from within the circle formed by them gleamed thousands of
sparkling eyes, and fell on the ear a low, continuous sound, like
the soft distant murmur of some summer sea on a shingly beach,
as twelve thousand sheep peacefully chewed their cuds after the
long day's travel.

The weather was close and sultry. So, feeling indisposed to sleep,
I had left my hot tent and was walking round the whitish, indistinct
mass of recumbent figures, when I nearly stumbled against the
watchman, who, as one of the fires flared up, I saw was the eccentric individual known in the camp by the nickname of 'Sojur Jim';
and, in pursuance of an idea I had long borne in mind, first assuring
myself that all was right with my fleecy charges, I lit my pipe,
stretched myself out on the short, thick grass and sand, and said,
whilst looking at my watch,—

'Now, Jim, spin us a yarn that will help to pass away the time.'

But my companion is well-deserving of a more particular
description. 'Sojur Jim' was the only name by which he was called,
and this he had gained by an extraordinary mania he possessed for
destroying those small terrors of the Australian bush, familiar to
all dwellers therein as 'Soldier' or 'Bull-dog' ants; insects fierce,
intractable and venomous. These, then, seemed objects of especial
aversion to Jim; and many a time, whilst travelling along, would
one of the men sing out, 'Jim, Jim, sojurs!' The effect was electrical;
Jim, leaving his flock, would bound away towards the nest, and,
dexterously using the long stick, flattened at both ends in rude
shovel shape, which was his constant companion, he would
furiously, regardless of innumerable stings, uproot and turn over

the 'sojurs' stronghold, and, having exposed its inmost recesses, complete the work of destruction by lighting a great fire upon it, and all this he would do with a set stern expression on his grim face, as of one who avenges never-to-be-forgiven or forgotten injuries.

He was indeed a remarkable looking man, strong and athletic, and, in spite of his snow-white hair, probably not more than fifty years of age. Part of his nose, the lobes and cartilages of his ears, and one eye were wanting, whilst the rest of his face was scarred and seamed as if at one time a cross-cut saw had been roughly drawn to and fro over it. And as I watched him sitting there on a fallen log, the flickering blaze playing fitfully on the white hair and corrugated, mutilated features, I felt more than ever sure that the man had a story well worth the hearing could he but be induced to tell it.

Amongst his fellows in the camp he was taciturn and morose, never smiling, speaking rarely, apparently always lost in his own gloomy reflections. My request, therefore, was made with but faint hopes of success; but, to my surprise, after a few minutes silence, he replied,—

'Very well, I'll tell you a story. I don't often tell it; but I will to-night. If at times you feel disinclined to believe it you have only to look at my face. I'm going now to tell you how I got all these pretty lumps and scars and ridges, and how I partly paid the men who made me what I am. "Sojur Jim" they call me, and think I am mad. God knows, I fancy so myself some times. Well,' he went on, in language at times rude and unpolished, at others showing signs of more than average education, 'Did you ever hear of Captain Jakes?'

'Of course,' I answered, for the notoriously cruel bushranger had, after his own fashion, helped to make minor Australian history.

'Yes,' muttered Jim abstractedly, 'he's accounted for. So is his mate—the one who laughed the loudest of any. But there were three of them, and there's still another left somewhere. Not dead yet!' he suddenly exclaimed in a loud voice. 'Surely not! My God, no! After all these years of ceaseless search! That would be too hard?' And here he stood up and gazed excitedly into the outer darkness.

'But the story, Jim,' I ventured to remark, after a long pause.

'Right you are,' he replied, as he again sat down, and calmly resumed. 'Well, it was the year of the big rush, the first one, to the Ovens. I was a strapping young fellow then, with all my life hopeful and bright before me, as I left the old mother and the girl

I loved to try my luck on the diggings. Three years went by before I thought of returning to the little Victorian township on the Avoca, where we had long been settled; but then I struck it pretty rich, and made up my mind to go back and marry, and settle down alongside the old farm; for a pair of loving hearts were, I knew, growing weary of waiting for the return of the wanderer.

'Like a fool, however, instead of sending down my last lot of gold by the escort, I all of a sudden got impatient, and, packing it in my saddle-bags, along with a tidy parcel of notes and sovereigns, I set off alone. The third night out I camped on a good-sized creek, hobbled my horses, and after planting my saddle-bags in a hollow log, I started to boil the billy for supper. Presently, up rides three chaps, and, before I could get to my swag, I was covered by as many revolvers; while one of the men says, 'Come along, now, hand over the metal. We know you've got it, and if you don't give it quiet, why, we'll take it rough.'

'"You've got hold of the wrong party, this time, mates," says I, as cool as I could. "I'm on the wallaby, looking for shearing, and, worse luck, hav'n't got no gold."

'"Gammon," says the first speaker. "Turn his swag over, mates."

'Well, they found nothing, of course. Then they searched all over the bush round about, and one fellow actually puts his hand up the hollow of the log in which lay hid my treasure; and I thought it was all up with it, when he lets a yell out of him and starts cutting all sorts of capers, with half-a-dozen big sojurs hanging to his fingers.

'Jakes (for he was the leader of the gang) now got real savage, and putting a pistol to my head, swore that he would blow my brains out unless I told where the gold was. Well, I wouldn't let on, for I thought they were trying to bounce me, and that if I held out I might get clear off, so I still stuck to it that they'd mistaken their man.

'Seeing I was pretty firm, they drew off for a while, and, after a short talk, they began to laugh like madmen; and one, taking a tomahawk, cut down a couple of saplings, whilst another gets ready some stout cord; and Jakes himself goes poking about in the saltbush as if looking for something he'd lost. Before this they had tied my arms and legs together with saddle-straps and greenhide thongs; and there I lay, quite helpless, wondering greatly what they were up to.

'Presently the three came up, and tying me tightly to the saplings—one along my back, and one crossways—they carried me away a short distance to where I had noticed Jakes searching around, and then laid me down face uppermost, partly stripping me at the same time. I lay there quietly enough, puzzling my brains to try and guess what it was all about, and those three devils standing laughing fit to split their sides.

'"Tell us now, will you," said they, "where that gold's planted? How does your bed feel? Are you warm enough?" and such like chaff, till I began to think they must have gone suddenly cranky, for I felt nothing at all. Perceiving that was the case, one of them took a stick and thrust it under me into the ground; and then—oh, God! it was awful!'

Here Sojur Jim paused suddenly, and a baleful light gleamed from that solitary bright eye of his, whilst a spasm shook his whole frame, and his scarred features were contorted as of once more undergoing the agonies of that terrible torture.

The wind sighed with an eerie sound through the tall forest trees around us; the cry of some night-bird came mournfully through the darkness, whilst black clouds flitted across the young moon, filling the sombre Australian glade with weird shadows—making the scene, all at once, dismally in unison with the story, as with a shiver I stirred the fire, and patiently waited for its narrator to go on.

'Yes,' he continued at length, 'I dropped down to it quickly enough then. I was tied on to a sojur-ants' nest, and they swarmed about me in thousands—into my nose, ears, eyes, mouth, everywhere—sting, sting, sting, and tear, tear, tear, till I shrieked and and yelled for mercy.'

'"Tell us where the gold is planted," said one of the laughing fiends—I heard him laugh again years afterward over the same story—"and we'll let you go."

'"Yes!" I screamed, "I'll tell you. But for God Almighty's sake take me out of this!" "Not much," replied he. "Tell us first, and then you can jump into the creek and give your little friends a drink." "Look in the big log," I groaned at last. Then, one of them, remembering the sojurs, gets a stick and fossicks about till he felt the bags, when he shoves his arm up and drags them out.

'"A square thing, by G—d!" says Jakes, and turning to me, he said, "Mate, you've given us a lot of trouble, and as you look as if you were comfortably turned in for the night, it would be a pity to disturb you. So long, and pleasant dreams!" And, with that, away the three of them rode, laughing loudly at my screams for mercy. As you may think,' went on Jim, 'I was by this time nearly raving mad with pain. Thousands of those devil-ants were eating into my flesh, and me lying there like a log. Hell! hell will never be as bad as that was!

'Six months afterward I came to my senses again. It was a

sunshiny spring morning, and I heard the magpies whistling outside the old humpy on the Ovens, as I tried to get up and go down to the claim, thinking that I'd had the nightmare terrible bad. But when I got off my bunk I fainted clean away on the floor, and there my mates found me when they came home to dinner. Good lads they were, true men, who had nursed me and tended me through all the long months of fever and madness that had passed since the Escort, for which I should have waited, had by the merest chance come across me and sent me back again to die, as everyone thought.

'But,' and here, for the first time, Jim's voice faltered and shook, 'there was another and a gentler nurse who—God bless her—helped me back to life; the little girl who loved me came up—my mother was dead—and would have kept her word to me, too, and taken my half-eaten carcase into her keeping wholly, had I been mean enough to let her do it. But that was more than I could stand the thought of. So one morning I slipped quietly away to begin my man-hunting; for I had vowed a merciless retribution upon my undoers if I had to track them the wide world over. That's close on fifteen years ago. I can account for two, and live on in hopes of yet meeting with the third.

'You've heard how Jakes pegged out?' asked Jim abruptly.

'Yes,' I answered, 'Sergeant O'Brien shot him in the Long Swamp.'

'So most people think,' was his reply. 'But I know who was first in at the end; and when, crouching up to his neck in the mud and long reeds, with my fingers grasping his throat, I think, as he turned his bloodshot and protruding eyes on mine, I think, I say, that he knew me again, all changed as I was. He never spoke, though, and I let him die slowly, for I was sure that the sergeant was a long way behind. I held him there, I tell you, and watched him as he tried to blow the bubbles of blood and froth from out his pale lips, and at last I told him who I was, and how I had tracked him down, and was now about to send his vile soul to perdition. Then, as I heard the galloping tramp of the trooper's horse, I smothered him in the stagnant ooze of that foul swamp. Truly a dog's death, but one too good for him! O'Brien, coming up soon afterward, found the body, put a couple of pistol bullets into it, and received the Government reward and promotion, whilst I set off in search of the others.

'One I came across four years afterwards on the Adelaide side. I had taken a job of shepherding up Port Augusta way, when, one night, who should come to the hut but Number Two, the one who laughed the longest and loudest of the three, as I lay in agony on the sojurs' nest. I knew him in a minute and heartily welcomed him to stop that night. "Just put those sheep in the yard, matey," I says, "while I make some bread for our supper."

'Well, I makes two smallish johnnycakes, and we had our tea. Then we starts smoking and yarning, and at length I turned the talk on to ants, saying I couldn't keep nothing there because of them. With that he falls to laughing, and, says he, "My word, mate, I could tell you a yarn if I liked 'bout ants—sojurs—that'd make you laugh for a week, only you see it ain't always safe, even in the bush, to talk among strangers."

'All of a sudden he turned as white as a sheet, and drops off the stool, and twists and groans. Then he sings out, "I'm going to die."

'You see,' remarked Jim, with the cold impassiveness which had, almost throughout, characterised his manner, 'the strychnine in the johnnycake that had fallen to his share was beginning to work him, and as I laughingly reminded him of old times, and asked him to go on with his story about the sojur ants, he also knew me, and shrieked and prayed for the mercy that I had once so unavailingly implored at his hands. He was very soon, however, too far gone to say much. A few more struggles and it was all over, and then I dragged the dead carrion out of my hut and buried it eight feet deep under the sheep-dung in the yard, where, likely enough, it is yet. So much for Number Two!' exclaimed Jim, as I sat looking rather doubtfully at him. Not that I questioned the truthfulness of his story—that was stamped on every word he uttered—but that I began to think him rather a dangerous kind of monomaniac to have in a drover's camp. 'And now, sir,' he went on presently, 'you've had the story you asked me for, and if ever we meet again after this trip, maybe I'll have something to tell you about Number Three; that business it is that brought me down about these parts, for I heard he was working at some of the stations on the river. And as God made me!' he exclaimed, with a subdued sort of gloomy ferocity in his voice, 'when we do meet, he shall feel the vengeance of the man whose life and love and fortune he helped to ruin so utterly. I could pick him out of a thousand, with his great nose all of a skew, and his one leg shorter than the other.'

The watch-fires were glimmering dimly. The cool air which heralds the Australian dawn was blowing, and the sheep were moving silently out of their camp in long strings as I rose to my feet. In the white tents all was silence. Thanks to Sojur Jim, their occupants had passed an undisturbed night. Absorbed in his gruesome story—that dark tale of torture and retribution, with just that one little trait of woman's constancy and devotion shining out like some bright star from a murky sky—the time had slipped away unheeded. Sending him to call the cook, I put the sheep together, wondering mightily to myself, as the man, with his bent-down head and slouching gait, moved away, whether he really could be the same creature who through the silent watches of the night had unfolded to my view such a concentrated, tireless, and as yet unsatiated thirst for revenge, such a fixed and relentless purpose of retaliation, unweakened through the years, but burning freshly and fiercely to-day, as, when with the scarcely healed scars still smarting, disfigured, ruined, hopeless, forsaking all, he went forth alone into the world to hunt down his persecutors.

A few days after Sojur Jim had related to me the story told above, one evening, at dusk, a swagman entered the camp and asked the cook for a piece of meat and some bread. Instead of eating it at once with the accompanying offered drink of tea, he turned away, and, a few minutes later, we saw his fire burning brightly a little further along the lagoon, the banks of which formed our resting-place for the night. Evidently, as the men remarked amongst themselves, our visitor was a 'hatter.'

Next morning, when Sojur Jim was called out to take his flock, he was missing. His blankets and few belongings still lay as he had arranged them in the tent the night before, ready for turning in; and I at once ordered a search to be made.

It was of very short duration. Just in front of the swagman's fire, in the shallow water of the lagoon, we found the two bodies. The stranger's throat was grasped by Jim's fingers in a vice-like clutch, that, even in death, we long strove in vain to sunder. When parted at last, and we had washed the slimy mud from the features of the dead traveller, a truly villainous countenance was disclosed to view; the huge mouth, low, retreating forehead, and heavy, thick-set jaws, all betokened their owner to have belonged to the very lowest order of humanity. But what struck me at once was that the nose, which was of great size, had, at one time, been knocked completely over to the left side of the face, and as we straightened the body out, it could plainly be seen that one leg was much shorter than its fellow.

Was this, then, indeed 'Number Three,' and had Sojur Jim's vengeful quest, his vow of bitter retaliation, ended at last? I believed so. But, as I gazed down upon the poor, scarred dead clay of a wasted and ruined life lying there, now so calm and still, all its fierce desires and useless repinings, all its feverish passions and longings for dread retribution at rest, forcibly came to my mind the words of the sacred and solemn injunction—'Vengeance is Mine, saith the Lord; I will repay.'

MALCHOOK'S DOOM: A NICHOLSON RIVER STORY

Ernest Favenc

IT WAS MALCHOOK who told the beginning of this story, and Malchook was supposed to be the biggest liar on the Gulf of Carpentaria. However, it was on record that he told the truth sometimes, when he was in a blue funk, for instance, and on this occasion his state of funk was a dazzling purple—blue was no name for it.

We were camped on the Nicholson for the wet season. The cattle had been turned out and we had hard work to keep them together, for, after the rain set in and the country became boggy, the niggers commenced playing up and we had to keep going. It was raining cats and dogs that night, and we were all huddled together round the fire under a bit of a bark lean-to which we had put up. Malchook was not there—his horses were absent that morning and he had been away all day after them. It was about eight o'clock when we heard him coming; he had found his horses and was driving them right up to the camp. Then, instead of hobbling them, he got a bridle and a halter, caught his steeds and tied them to a tree.

Some of the fellows sang out to him to know what he was doing, but he took no notice, and, after turning out the horse he had been riding, came up to the fire and told Reeve (the boss) that he wanted a word with him. Reeve got up, and the two walked over to his tent. Presently Malchook emerged, went to where his belongings were under the tarpaulin that had been rigged up over the rations, and commenced to roll them up. Reeve came back to the fire.

'What's up?' asked Thomas, Reeve's cousin.

'Only that fellow wants to leave to-night straight off, so I gave him his cheque and told him to slide as soon as he liked; he's no great loss, anyway.'

'What does he want to leave for?'

'Says the camp is doomed, and he is going to put as many miles as possible between himself and us before our fate overtakes us.'

There was a general laugh, and just then Malchook came out with his swag and commenced to saddle up in the pouring rain. There was a good moon, nearly full, although, of course, it was not visible.

The fellows commenced chaffing him, for he was not a favourite; too reckless a liar. He stood it without a word until he was ready to mount; then he got on his horse, and, turning round, said— 'Laugh away, this time tomorrow I'll have the laugh of you; this camp is doomed!' He dug his heels into his horse and disappeared— swish, swish, swish, through the bog down the bank of the river, and we heard him swearing at his pack-horse as he crossed the sand.

There was much laughter and wonderment at what had sent Malchook 'off his chump,' but eccentricity was common in those days, from various causes, and presently we all turned in.

I was sleeping under the tarpaulin where the rations were stored, and about two o'clock in the morning I suddenly awoke. It was brilliant moonlight, the wind had changed, the rain had ceased, and the moon, by reason of the scud which flitted across the sky, seemed to travel at express rate through an archipelago of cloudlets. Some impulse made me leave the shelter of the mosquito-net, go to the opening at the end of the tarpaulin and look out.

Everything was still and quiet; all the horses were camped, for not a bell could be heard, and I stood some time aimlessly listening and looking at the glistening pools of water upon the flat between our camp and the bank, when suddenly I distinctly heard a human voice in the bed of the river. I waited for a moment to make sure, then I got my Martini and a couple of cartridges and sneaked towards the bank. Last full-moon the niggers had nearly clubbed the cook in his mosquito-net when he was sleeping outside the tent one night; this time, I thought, it would be a case of biters bitten.

About a hundred yards from the camp I stopped and listened. The voice was now much nearer. It was a white man's, it was Malchook's, and he was kicking his knocked up horse along and dragging the pack-horse after him. I waited behind a tree until be came up, and then I stepped out. I was only in my shirt, with the carbine in my hand.

'Great God!' he cried, with a kind of choke, 'he's here again!'

'What the deuce is up with you?' I said; 'why didn't you stop away when you went? Got bushed, I suppose, and the horses brought you back?'

He sat on his horse and panted for a few minutes without speaking. Then he said: 'That infernal old nigger won't let me go. He hunted me back. I've got to share your fate, so let's get it over.'

He jabbed his heels in his horse's ribs, but I stopped him. 'Don't wake the camp up,' I said. 'What nigger do you mean?'

'The nigger that Jacky the Span and I roasted in the spinifex. He's headed me back every road I've tried, and I give it up. Let me turn the horses out, and get a wink of sleep.'

Jacky the Span was an old blackguard of a Mexican who had been knocked on the head about six months previously. Everybody said he richly deserved it, and everybody was right.

'When were you up here with Jacky Span?' I asked.

'About two years ago, the time Bratten was killed; but let me turn out the horses and I'll tell you all about it.'

We went quietly back to camp, and let the tired horses go, and then Malchook sat down on his blankets beside me. The tarpaulin was rigged some distance from the other tents. and the boys were done up and sleeping soundly, so nobody awoke. This is what Malchook told me.

Two years before, he and the old Mexican had come up to join Bratten in mustering some horses that had got away from the lower part of the river and were supposed to be knocking about below the first gorge. Like most half-breeds, Jacky the Span (short for Spaniard) was a most inhuman brute towards the natives whenever he got a chance, and Malchook, being a blowhard and a bully, was of the same cowardly disposition—most liars are. One day they spotted an old man and a young gin at the foot of a spinifex ridge that runs in on the Upper Nicholson. I knew the place—real old man spinifex that would go through a leather legging. They rounded the old black up on the top of the ridge, but missed the gin, and Jacky Span said he would make the man find her or he should suffer, and Malchook, in order to keep up his reputation as a flash man and a real old Gulf-hand, aided and abetted him.

I suppose the poor devil was too frightened to understand what they really wanted, but, anyhow, all the half-caste devilry, which is the worst devilry in the world, was aroused in the Mexican, and Malchook followed suit.

They selected a bank of spinifex, and rolled the naked nigger in it 'for sport.' Now, spinifex is beastly poisonous stuff; get your shins well pricked, and it is worse than any number of mosquito-bites for irritating you and making you itch. Horses will not face it after a day or two in really bad country, and if you run your hand down their shins you will soon see the reason why. Every little prick festers, and their legs are covered with tiny boils and ulcers. The blacks always burn it ahead of them before they travel through it. Out in the 'Never-Never' they have regular tracks which they keep burnt down.

By the time they had rolled this nigger in the spinifex for some minutes, he must have been in a raging hell of torment; and he knew no more what they wanted with him than at the start. Then, according to Malchook, Jacky rolled him into a big bank of dry stuff—they had tied his feet together—and set fire to it. Spinifex is rare stuff to blaze; being full of turpentine, it burns with a fierce heat and a black smoke, so the old nigger was well roasted, and when it burnt out they rolled him into another bank and set that alight. A gust of wind sprang up and started the whole ridge ablaze, and the gin, who had been hidden close by, watching it all, rushed out and ran; Jacky Span picked up the old man's club and took after her. He was away about half-an-hour; meanwhile the old fellow died, groaning awfully, and Malchook began to feel as if things had been better left alone.

Presently, Jacky Span came back with the club in his hand—big two-handed clubs they use on the Nicholson—and showed Malchook some blood and hair on it, and laughed like a devil. No need to repeat here all he said.

Now, if Malchook had there and then blown a Government road through the brute, there might have been some chance of repentance left for him, but he didn't. He sniggered and let Jacky Span tell him all about it, and camped with him for weeks afterwards. Jacky Span was killed, as I said before, and Malchook assured me, in a sweating blue funk when he spoke, that just at dark he had met his horses coming back, with the old roasted nigger behind driving them. He went on to say that this thing had followed him right up to the river, and shrieked at him that he would die in the camp. Then he went on to tell that when he tried to get away from the camp that night the old nigger had met him at every point of the compass, so that at last he gave it up and returned.

Now, I knew that there had been an importation of brandy lately into the Gulf country, generally known as the 'possum brand,' each bottle of which was calculated to make a man see more devils than six bottles of any other brand. It was very popular, for it would eat holes in a saddle-cloth, so I concluded that Malchook had got some of it, for one of the fellows had returned from Burketown that day. This would account for the ghost of the blackfellow, but the rest of the yarn about Jacky Span I felt to be true, so I told Malchook to clear out and sleep somewhere else—I wouldn't have him under the same tarpaulin with me. He begged and prayed to be allowed to remain, but I told him I would wake the camp and tell everything if he didn't go, so he went, sobbing bitterly. I explained to him that the best thing he could do was to shoot himself, that a man who could follow the lead of a miserable half-caste out of pure flashness was too contemptible to live; but he didn't appreciate my kindness, and slouched off to a bit of a sand-hump, about 150 yards from the camp, and I saw him throw his blankets down and then lie down on them. I got into my bunk again and went fast asleep in two minutes.

Reeve woke me up. It was broad daylight. 'The niggers were here last night,' he said. 'Did you hear anything?'

'No,' I replied; 'but Malchook came back; I saw him.'

'Yes. They knocked him on the head—bashed his skull in. He was sleeping out under that tree—I suppose he was ashamed to wake us up.'

'Nobody heard anything?' I asked.

'Not a sound. There are the traces of about six niggers coming out of the river towards the camp, and they must have stumbled right on top of Malchook. Poor devil! Polished him off and cleared out. The camp *was* doomed for him, after all.'

I concluded to tell nothing, beyond having seen Malchook come back and speaking to him. Sometimes I wonder whether I was not responsible for his death by hunting him away from the camp, but I always console myself with the reflection that he only got what he deserved.

NOTES ON THE AUTHORS

FRANCIS ADAMS (1862–93) was born in Malta, educated in England, travelled on the continent, came to Australia in 1884, and remained for five years; he was one of the two most brilliant journalists (with Marcus Clarke) in Australia last century. He lived and wrote in Melbourne, Sydney, and Brisbane, but returned to England in 1889, suffering from consumption. Died by suicide. 'Miss Jackson' and 'Long Forster' both come from *Australian Life* (1892).

J. A. BARRY (1850–1911) was born in England, went to sea and obtained a mate's certificate. He came to Australia in his twenties and followed a variety of outback occupations, including writing for newspapers and magazines. Barry, who died in Sydney, was the author of eight volumes, most of them collections of short stories. 'Sojur Jim' comes from *Steve Brown's Bunyip* (1893).

JAMES SKIPP BORLASE (1839–?) was born at Truro in Cornwall, son of James John and Frances Catharine Borlase. He emigrated to Australia. He is said to have been a lawyer in Victoria (his father was an attorney) and a trooper in Victoria and possibly in other States. Some of his stories may be based on his own experiences. 'Mystery and Murder' comes from *Daring Deeds* (1868).

ELLEN CLACY (Mrs Charles Clacy), daughter of a clergyman, came out with her brother to Melbourne in 1852, lived for a short time on the diggings, and returned to England early in 1853. She wrote her impressions on the spot, so that the account of her adventures was about complete when she reached England, and was published in that year. She was married in Melbourne near the end of 1852, just before departing for England. 'Retribution' comes from *Lights and Shadows of Australian Bush Life* (1854).

MARCUS CLARKE (1846–81) was born in London, and came to Melbourne at the age of seventeen where he worked in a bank, before taking a job on a property near Glenorchy. Then he returned to Melbourne, where he became a journalist and wrote a great number of varied literary works, and was for some years Sub-Librarian in the Public Library. 'The Romance of Lively Creek' comes from *Four Stories High* (1877); 'Human Repetends' from *The Mystery of Major Molineaux and Human Repetends* (1881).

EDWARD DYSON (1865–1931) was born at Ballarat, where his father was a mining engineer. He worked at a variety of occupations and was also a freelance writer. About half of his dozen volumes are collections of comic short stories set in the city. 'Mr and Mrs Sin Fat' comes from *A Golden Shanty* (1890), compiled by J. F.

Archibald to indicate the contribution of *Bulletin* writers in its first ten years.

ERNEST FAVENC (1845–1908) was born in England and educated partly in England, partly in Germany. He came to Australia at the age of eighteen. Favenc was a bushman and explorer in northern Australia for over twenty years, and wrote accounts of exploration, geographical studies, fiction, and poetry. His last years were spent in Sydney, where he died. 'Malchook's Doom' comes from *The Last of Six* (1893).

A. G. HALES (1860–1936) was born in Adelaide, and undertook varied work—as journalist, prospector, boxer, war correspondent. His first volume, *Wanderings of a Simple Child*, was extremely successful. Hales went to London in 1895 and reported on the Boer War. His McGlusky novels, with their Scottish-Australian hero, made his fortune. 'Chinese Ginnie' comes from *Wanderings of a Simple Child* (1890).

E. W. HORNUNG (1866–1921) was born in England, came to New South Wales in 1884, but stayed only about two to three years before returning to England. He wrote fiction about Australia while here, and continued to do so after his departure. About twenty of his volumes contain some Australian settings or references. 'The Luckiest Man in the Colony' comes from *Under Two Skies* (1892).

JOHN LANG (1816–64) was born at Parramatta, educated at Sydney College and then at Cambridge (for a few weeks) and the Middle Temple. After practising as a lawyer in Sydney, he went to India, where he was very successful and where he died. Lang was the first Australian-born novelist. Both 'The Master and His Man' and 'Music a Terror' come from *Botany Bay* (1859).

ROSA PRAED (1851–1935), née Murray-Prior, for about twenty-five years lived on stations in southern Queensland, and on an island with her husband Campbell Praed, whom she married in 1872. The pair moved to London in 1876. She became devoted to the occult, and some of her three dozen novels deal with its manifestations. 'Miss Pallavant' comes from *Oak-Bough and Wattle-Blossom*, edited by Mrs A. P. Martin (1888).

R. SPENCER BROWNE (1856–1943) was born at Appin, New South Wales and served in the Boer War and in World War I. He was an active journalist and traveller in New South Wales and Queensland, and for a time was associate-editor of the *Courier* in Brisbane. His reminiscences, *A Journalist's Memories* (1927), contain accounts of many of his contemporaries. 'The Story of Wills' Leap' comes from *Romances of Gold Field and Bush* (1890).

'TASMA' (1848–97), in real life Jessie Couvreur (née Jessie Huybers), was born in London. In 1852 the family emigrated to Tasmania, where Jessie married Charles Fraser in 1867. In 1873 she, her mother and other members of the Huybers family went to Europe for two years. She divorced Fraser in 1883. Returning to London, she married Auguste Couvreur in 1885. Of her seven volumes of fiction, only one contains short stories. 'An Old-Time Episode in Tasmania' comes from *Coo-ee*, edited by Mrs Patchett Martin (1891).

MARY VIDAL (1815–69), née Johnson, wife of the Rev. Francis Vidal, came to Australia with her husband and children in 1840. After about five years in New South Wales they returned to England. Some of her fiction uses the scenes she saw when she accompanied her husband on his pastoral tours. 'The Convict Laundress' comes from the fourth (expanded) edition (1852) of her *Tales for the Bush* (1845).

PRICE WARUNG (1855–1911) was the pen-name of William Astley, who was born in England, and came to Australia as a child with his parents. After leaving school became a journalist, and worked on behalf of the Labour Party and the Federation movement. He began to write his stories of convictism for the *Bulletin* in 1890. His five volumes do not contain all his short stories. 'How Muster-Master Stoneman Earned His Breakfast' comes from *Tales of the Convict System* (1892).

BIBLIOGRAPHY

Primary sources

1830   Howison, J. *Tales of the Colonies.*
1842   Burn, David *Our First Lieutenant and Fugitive Pieces in Prose.*
1843   Rowcroft, Charles *Tales of the Colonies.*
1845   McCombie, Thomas *Arabin.*
        Vidal, Mrs F. *Tales for the Bush.*
1848   Cozens, Charles *Adventures of a Guardsman.*
        Nathan, Isaac (ed.) *The Southern Euphrsyne.*
185–   *The Black Troopers.*
1851   *The Australian Souvenir.*
1854   Clacy, Mrs Charles *Lights and Shadows of Australian Bush Life.*
        Howitt, William *A Boy's Adventures in the Wilds of Australia.*
1856   Capper, John *The Emigrant's Guide to Australia.*
1857   Cooper, Fredric *Wild Adventures in Australia and New South Wales.*
        Journal of Australasia.
        Turner, H. G. *Tales of the Colony.*
        Wright, George *Wattle Blossoms.*
1858   Dexter, Caroline (ed.) *The Ladies' Almanac.*
        The Literary Chateleine.
        Rowe, Richard *Peter Possum's Portfolio.*
1859   Lang, John *Botany Bay.*
        The Australian Souvenir.
186–   *New Year's Day on the Mountain.*
1861   Earle, Horace *Ups and Downs.*

McCombie, Thomas *Australian Sketches*
Pendragon, A. (Isaacs, G.?) (ed.) *Number One.*
1862 *The Children's Magazine.*
1863 Graham, J. *Laurence Struilby.*
1864 Winstanley, E. *Twenty Straws.*
1865 Wild, E. *Long Bay.*
1867 Borlase, James Skipp *The Night Fossickers.*
Houlding, J. R. *Christopher Cockle's Colonial Experiences*
Timmins, O. F. *Station Dangerous.*
Walch, Garnet *The Fireflash.*
1868 Arcanum Scribendo (ed.) *Squibs and Crackers.*
Borlase, James Skipp *Daring Deeds.*
Old Boomerang (Houlding, J. R.) *Australian Tales and Sketches from Real Life.*
1869 Isaacs, George *Not for Sale.*
Williams, W. H. (ed.) *A Holiday Medley.*
—— *Illustrated Australian Annual.*
1870 Mooney, E. M. *The Two Powers.*
Wattle Blossoms.
1871 Clarke, Marcus *Old Tales of a Young Country.*
W. W. (Waif Wander? Mrs Fortune?) *The Detective's Album.*
1872 Conroy, J. M. *False, and Other Tales.*
Foott, Mrs James *Sketches of Life in the Bush.*
Johnson, J. C. F. *On the Wallaby.*
Punch Staff Papers.
Stephen, H. W. & Bunster, G. *Our Christmas Budget.*
Whitworth, R. P. *Australian Stories Round the Camp Fire.*
—— *Beneath the Wattles.*
—— *Spangles and Sawdust.*
—— *Under the Dray.*
1873 Clarke, Marcus *Holiday Peak and Other Tales.*
Hobgoblins.
Johnson, J. C. F. *Christmas on Carringa.*
Kuz (Dunn, F.) *The Trial Four.*
1874 Farjeon, B. L. *Christmas Stories.*
Walch, Garnet *Head over Heels.*
1875 Swan, N. W. *Tales of Australian Life.*
Thatcher, Richmond (ed.) *Something to His Advantage.*
Whitworth, R. P. *Cobb's Box.*
1876 *A Christmas Bush.*
Apple Blossoms.
Geary, J. (ed.) *Mrs Sloper's Bundle.*
Sketches of Australian Life and Scenery (1876?)

1877   Clarke, Marcus *Four Stories High.*
        Thomas, J. (ed.) *The Vagabond Annual.*
        Tony the Pieman *Night Scenes of Melbourne.*
        Walch, Garnet *Hash.*
1878   Clarke, Marcus *The Man with the Oblong Box.*
        Hopkins, F. R. C. (ed.) *The Australian Ladies' Annual.*
        Stephen, H. W. H. *Fizz* (1878?).
        ——*Our Exhibition Annual.*
        Walch, Garnet *Australasia.*
1879   Martin, Mrs A. P. (ed.) *An Easter Omelette.*
        Mayne, D. *Westerly Busters.*
        Spence, C. (ed.) *Silver Wattle.*
        We 5. (1879?)
        Whitworth, R. P. (ed.) *The Australian Christmas Box* (1879?).
        Evans, G. C. *Stories Told Around the Camp Fire.*
        Pyke, W. T. *Australian Heroes and Adventurers.*
1880   Fenton, F. W. (ed.) *This Side Up.*
        Olio.
        Sutherland, G. *Tales of the Goldfields.*
1881   Clarke, Marcus *The Conscientious Stranger.*
        —— *The Mystery of Major Molineux and Human Repetends.*
        Crawford, Reginald *Echoes from Bushland.*
        Per Se (Sinnett, Percy) *Wattle Blossom.*
        The South Australian Christmas Annual.
        Thatcher, Richmond (ed.) *Thatcher's Holiday Book.*
1882   *Australian Stories.*
        Chads, Ellen Augusta *Tried as Pure Gold.*
        Faucett, Francis *A Bushman's Story.*
        Franc, Maud(e) Jean(ne) *Christmas Bells.*
        Garnet Walch's Annual.
1883   Boomerang (ed.) *Comicalities.*
1884   *Authors on the Wallaby—Bush Yarns.*
        The Marcus Clarke Memorial Volume.
1885   *The Savage Club Annual.*
1886   Hogan, J. F. *An Australian Christmas Collection.*
        Sensational Tales.
        Whitworth, R. P. *Velvet and Rags.*
1887   Butler, Alfred *Stray Sketches.*
        Loyau, G. E. (ed.) *The South Australian Annual.*
        McKellar, Campbell *The Premier's Secret and Other Tales.*
        Suttor, W. H. *Australian Stories Retold.*
        Walch, Garnet (ed.) *The Victorian Jubilee Book.*

1888   Blitz, Mrs A.   *Digger Dick's Darling.*
       Chads, Mrs E. A.   *The Snowdrop's Message.*
       Donohue, F. J.   *A Sheaf of Stories.*
       Hull, A. F. B.   *A Strange Experience.*
       Johnson, J. C. F.   *An Austral Christmas.*
       M(artin) A. P. (ed.)   *Oak-Bough and Wattle-Blossom.*
       'Overlander'   *Australian Sketches.*
       Pyke, W. T. (ed.)   *Bush Tales.*
       Tranmar, Ellie & Blackett, Evelyn   *The Chinese Interpreter.*
1889   *Australian Stories.*
       Barnet, N. J. (ed.)   *Mixed.*
       Cates, Frank (ed.)   *Gags.*
       Kennedy, E. B.   *Blacks and Bushrangers.*
       The Knightsbridge Papers.
       Martin, Mrs A. P. (ed.)   *Over the Sea.*
       Mennell, Philip (ed.)   *In Australian Wilds.*
1890   *A Golden Shanty.*
       Hales, A. G.   *The Wanderings of a Simple Child.*
       Martin, Mrs A. P. (ed.)   *Under the Gum Tree.*
       Pyke, W. T. (ed.)   *True Tales of the Early Days.*
       Spencer Browne, R.   *Romances of Gold Field and Bush.*
       'Tasma' (Couvreur, Jessie Catherine)   *A Sydney Sovereign.*
       Vogan, A. J.   *The Black Police.*
1891   Chads, Mrs E. A.   *Tracked by the Bushrangers.*
       Chambers,   C.   Haddon   *Thumb-Nail Sketches   of
         Australian Life.*
       Dunderdale, G.   *Prairie and Bush.*
       FitzGerald, M. A.   *King Bungaree's Pyalla.*
       Martin, Mrs A. P.   *Coo-ee.*
       Robertson,   Andrew   *The   Kidnapped   Squatter,   and
         Other Australian Tales.*
       Volcanic Gold.
       Walker, Thomas   *Felonry of New South Wales.*
1892   Adams, Francis   *Australian Life.*
       Browne, W. C.   *Encora.*
       Hornung, E. W.   *Under Two Skies.*
       Roberts, Morley   *King Billy of Ballarat.*
       Warung, Price (Astley, William)   *Tales of the
         Convict System.*
1893   Barlee, C. H.   *Humorous Tales and Sketches of
         Colonial Life.*
       Barry, J. A.   *Steve Brown's Bunyip.*
       Favenc, Ernest   *The Last of Six.*

Jeffrey, Mark (Burke, James Lester)   *A Burglar's Life.*
Nisbet, Hume   *The Haunted Station* (1893–94).
(1896   Clarke, Marcus   *Australian Tales*)

Selected secondary references

Mrs Chas Meredith, *Notes and Sketches of New South Wales* (London, 1844).

G. B. Barton, *Literature in New South Wales* (Sydney, 1866).

George Dunderdale, *The Book of the Bush* (London, 1870?)

The Austral Review (Melbourne, 1877).

A. J. Boyd; *Old Colonials* (London, 1882).

R. E. N. Twopeny, *Town Life in Australia* (London, 1883).

The Australasian Critic (Melbourne, 1 December 1890).

E. Morris Miller, *Australian Literature*, 2 vols (Melbourne, 1940) (essential for a worker in the period).

J. Hine, An Evaluation of the Australian Short Story Before 1880 (unpublished thesis, University of Sydney, 1945).

K. Levis, 'The Role of the *Bulletin* in Indigenous Short-Story Writing During the Eighties and Nineties', *Southerly* 4, 1950.

C. Roderick, *Australian Round-Up* (Sydney, 1953).

G. Nadel, *Australia's Colonial Culture* (London, 1957).

R. Ward, *The Australian Legend* (London, 1958).

L. James, *Fiction for the Working Man* (London, 1963).

Brian Matthews, *The Receding Wave* (Melbourne, 1972).

H. Heseltine (ed.), *The Penguin Book of Australian Short Stories* (Melbourne, 1976).

Brian Fletcher, *Colonial Australia before 1850* (Melbourne, 1976).

V. E. Neuburg, *Popular Literature* (London, 1977).

Richard White, *Inventing Australia* (Sydney, 1981).

J. B. Hirst, *Convict Society and Its Enemies* (Sydney, 1983).

M. Sturma, *Vice in a Vicious Society* (Brisbane, 1983).

Ross Gibson, *The Diminishing Paradise* (Sydney, 1984).

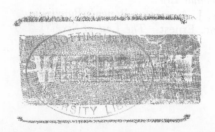